DIMENSIONS BEHIND
The TWILIGHT ZONE

DIMENSIONS BEHIND

The TwiLiGHT ZONE

A Backstage Tribute to Television's Groundbreaking Series

STEWART T. STANYARD

ECW Press

Published by ECW PRESS
2120 Queen Street East, Suite 200, Toronto, Ontario, Canada M4E 1E2

LIBRARY AND ARCHIVES CANADA CATALOGUING IN PUBLICATION
Stanyard, Stewart T.
Dimensions behind the Twilight zone : a backstage tribute to
television's groundbreaking series / Stewart T. Stanyard.

ISBN-13: 978-1-55022-744-4
ISBN-10: 1-55022-744-0

1. Twilight Zone (Television program : 1959).   I. Title.

PN1992.77.T87S73 2006   791.45'72   C2006-904107-5

Editor: Jennifer Hale
Cover and text design: Tania Craan
Typesetting: Tania Craan

Printed by Transcontinental

All photos courtesy of the author, except the following:
Tony Albarella: 13, 22 (#2), 23, 24, 26 (#1, 2), 29 (#4), 30, 32, 35 (#2), 37, 43 (#2), 45 (#1), 47 (#2), 58, 59 (#1), 86, 87, 88, 89, 101, 102, 117 (#2), 121, 126, 131 (#2), 140, 141, 142, 144, 159, 160, 161, 166, 167 (#2), 168, 174, 212, 213, 215, 216, 218, 228 (#2), 241 (#2), 251; Roger Anker: 18, 20; Paul Comi: page 190; Dwight Deskins: 34, 46 (#1), 49 (#1), 50 (#1), 53 (#1, 3), 64 (#3), 77, 85, 114, 116, 122, 123, 125, 170, 186 (#1), 200, 201, 203, 204, 205, 206, 228 (#1), 239, 247 (#2), 280; Dana Gould: page 66; Earl Holliman: pages 76, 78 (#1); Richard Kiel: page 51 (#3); Richard Matheson: page 22 (#1); Marc Moser: pages 10, 25 (#1); Carol Serling: pages 5, 39 (#1), 46 (#2), 48 (#3), 53 (#2), 61 (#1), 193, 231; Jim Hegedus: pages 69, 70

The Twilight Zone ™ is a registered trademark of CBS, Inc.

DISTRIBUTION

CANADA: Jaguar Book Group, 100 Armstrong Avenue, Georgetown, ON, L7G 5S4
UNITED STATES: Independent Publishers Group, 814 North Franklin Street, Chicago, Illinois 60610

PRINTED AND BOUND IN CANADA

ECW PRESS
ecwpress.com

To Rod Serling

With personal dedication
to the memories of my dear sister Christina Lynn (Tina)

Appreciation Essays

Acknowledgments

Big thanks to everyone at ECW Press for having made this wild trip come true! To my goddess of an editor, Jen Hale (Madam Cleaver), for steering this long awaited book into a reality, I will always be grateful. To Stuart Ross, for his superb copy editing, Tania Craan, for her wonderful design work, Kulsum Merchant, for getting the ball rolling and passing it over to Jen (it was a perfect play), Simon Ware, for public relations, and a gracious hats off to publisher Jack David for signing with me.

Thanks to those friends, associates, and alumni who helped pull together extra materials from their own personal collections; Tony Albarella, Dwight Deskins, Marc Moser, and Roger Anker. Also, Paul Comi, Dana Gould, Earl Holliman, Richard Kiel, Richard Matheson, and Carol Serling. Thanks to Bud Robertson for his diligent work in contacting a number of essay contributors, and, along with Richard Ballo at Goal Productions, for making available a portion of our *Twilight Zone Archives* interviews. Thanks to Jeanna Beasley for transcribing some of the later interviews, Tom Elkins for the comments of Beverly Garland and Evans Evans, and Bill Koeb for having a light bulb go on above his head that one day while mixing the title around.

Gracious thanks to Carol Serling for all of her support and for allowing me to give something back with this book, and to author Robert Serling, for his interview and the experience of getting to know him. Thanks to my friends at the Rod Serling Memorial Foundation (rodserling.com), Robert Keller, Andrew Polak, and Stephen Schlich, and to fond memories of Helen Foley.

Special thanks to *Twilight Zone* writer George Clayton Johnson, for his ongoing support and friendship. Thanks for having invited me into your life and for all the philosophical and heartfelt discussions we've shared. It's truly been an honor.

To those *Twilight Zone* alumni who granted interviews and offered interest and support: Richard Bare, James Best, Shelley Berman, Lloyd Bochner, Jean Carson, Paul Comi, Ivan Dixon, Richard Donner, Anne Francis, Bert Granet, Kevin Hagen, Earl Hamner Jr., Earl Holliman, George Clayton Johnson, Lamont

Johnson, Wright King, Ruta Lee, Joanne Linville, Nan Martin, Richard Matheson, Barry Morris, Bill Mumy (billmumy.com), Phillip Pine, Ted Post, Del Reisman, William Reynolds, Cliff Robertson, Joseph Ruskin, Jacqueline Scott, James Sheldon, Elliot Silverstein, Robert Sorrells, Warren Stevens, Dennis Weaver, Fritz Weaver, William Windom, and the comments of Robert Redford. Also, to the two directors I had the honor to visit, Don Medford and Jack Smight.

To those who contributed wonderful appreciation essays: Roger Anker, Christopher Beaumont, Michael Bonvillain, Pen Densham, Dana Gould, Dean Haglund, Jim Houghton, Kevin Hudson, George Clayton Johnson, John Ottman, Neil Peart, and Robert Hewitt Wolfe.

To those who endorsed the book: Neil Gaiman for his most excellent foreword, Carol Serling, George Clayton Johnson, Cliff Robertson, Bill Mumy, J.J. Abrams, William Shatner, and Marc Scott Zicree.

Personal thanks to all of my friends and family: especially my parents Gloria and Paul, for allowing me a childhood of growing up watching scary movies, and my brother Jonathan Kim, for holding me down at the early age of five or six and forcing my eyes open to watch *Hush, Hush, Sweet Charlotte*. Ah, good times.

We find what we need.

Sometimes we don't understand it, or don't take advantage of it. Sometimes it destroys us when we find it, and sometimes it becomes our salvation. Rod Serling knew.

(I'm writing this on a plane. I'm not worried. I'm barely scared of flying at all . . .)

I was fourteen when I first encountered *The Twilight Zone*. In geological time, even in human being time, this was not long ago. Still, it was in the days when the only way to watch something made for TV was to see it when it was broadcast. You had to be there. If no one was showing it, you didn't see it. If it was broadcast when you were a small child, if it wasn't shown in your country, you were a long way out of luck. When I was twelve, my parents added to the difficulty by deciding, when we moved, not to have a television.

Still, I found *The Twilight Zone*. It was what I needed. I was in conversation with a friend of my father's, an American Greek named Andy, and we were talking about television shows we'd enjoyed over the years (in a house without television, we could at least *talk* about television) and he mentioned *The Twilight Zone*. He hummed the theme tune. No, I said. I've never heard of it. Tell me more. Over the next few weeks, I forced him to tell me the plots of all the episodes he could remember, over and over, soaking them up. I might never see this thing, but I still wanted to know all about it. I made the episodes in my head, expanding on the themes: deadly dolls and twist endings and aliens and Death. . . .

A year or so later I was in Dark They Were and Golden-Eyed, a science fiction and comics shop in London, and I found a couple of *Twilight Zone* paperbacks — adaptations of *Twilight Zone* episodes into short story form (or possibly collections of the original stories that the episodes were based on. It was a long time ago, and the books have long since been lent out and never returned). I bought them, read them avidly. (Where were the DVDs you ask? Why didn't I watch the episodes on YouTube? Like I said, it was a long time ago. We didn't have the leisure to invent DVDs, back then, given the constant peril of dinosaur attacks and the marauding hordes of Genghis Khan, okay? We had three TV channels in the UK, and they all went off by midnight.) I was excited about the involvement of writers like Richard Matheson and Charles Beaumont, writers whose short stories and novels I had loved. I didn't know if I'd ever actually get to see any episodes of the show. I took what I could get.

And then, in the early eighties, when I was in my early twenties, possibly because the upcoming *Twilight Zone* movie had raised its profile and brought it back into the consciousness of the broadcasters, *The Twilight Zone* was shown on British television, and I stayed in that night, or I'd tape it, hoping that the video recorder would work, or that my landlady wouldn't change the channel, and, finally I got to see the episodes I'd been making in my head for all those years. I saw *The Twilight Zone* movie (a *meh* film, but I enjoyed the framing sequence). I bought Marc Zicree's *Twilight Zone Companion*, read it avidly. So, all through the eighties, on English TV, I finally watched *The Twilight Zone*.

It was better than I had ever hoped. Better than I had dreamed. It did not disappoint. It was beautifully filmed, excellently acted, and, above all, it was intelligent. I was watching half hour long journeys into the imagination, in which people found themselves saved or damned or human, unable to outrun their destiny, able to change only themselves. *The Twilight Zone* was a point of view, a way of talking about things. It was easy to imitate badly — just as it's easy to do a poor impersonation of Rod Serling's clipped delivery — but inimitable. Easily parodied, unable to be imitated. In the years since the original *Twilight Zone*, one thing we have learned from the attempts to imitate it, to revive it, to remake it, under the *Twilight Zone* name or another, is how astonishingly difficult it is to make something like that work, and it throws back into focus something it's easy to overlook — that *The Twilight Zone* was simply one of the high water marks of television.

Time passed. Every now and again I'd find myself talking to television executives about television shows, and I would hear them explain why an anthology series was impossible, and I would find myself impressed again by Rod Serling's achievement in getting *The Twilight Zone* onto the television at all, let alone that of not doing the same thing week after week, of creating a mood that was light or dark, creepy or exhilarating as the story demanded.

This book is a remarkable tribute to Rod Serling's creation — an analysis, a photographic record, and most of all, a journey backstage. (I say Rod Serling's creation, but one thing that this book delivers in spades, if there was any doubt about it, is what a remarkable team Serling assembled, and how very much they did.) There were many journeys backstage in the *Twilight Zone* — literal and metaphorical. If there was a favorite *Twilight Zone* plot, it was the one in which our protagonist discovers that what he or she or they believe to be the real world is something else, something other. There's a backstage. Someone can call "Cut" on your life, and you'll find that you're just a creature of fiction, a moment of slippage.

And now, in this age of DVD boxed sets, when everything is available, when things we thought were stories have been discovered to be content, it's appropriate that the best way backstage into *The Twilight Zone* is through words and pictures, through archival documents and interviews and commentary. If you want to know how it was done, if you want to marvel at how it was done, if you think that, possibly, one day, you'll be the one to bring back anthology television, then I commend this book to you.

We find what we need, after all.

(The cabin staff just announced that we'll be landing soon. I think I caught sight of something on the wing. . . .)

Let's go backstage.

Neil Gaiman
February 20, 2007

Above all other projects I've worked on, this book had a craving to see the light of day and needed to become a reality. The path of putting it together has been long and somewhat arduous — I could fill a pool with the coffee and aspirin I've consumed during its creation — but I can honestly and humbly say it's been one hell of an adventurous ride, and one I wouldn't change for anything. Interestingly enough, even though I've spent the last six years working on this book, its course began years before and it took much time for this moment to fully take form.

It all started back in 1979, when a collection of original production photos from a number of CBS television series was purchased at a memorabilia auction held in Hollywood. The Literary Department of M/D Management Limited stated that "all of these contact sheets were from Viacom and the sets included *I Love Lucy*, *Judy Garland Show*, *The Untouchables*, *Our Miss Brooks*, and, of course, *The Twilight Zone*. Various photographers working for the network or studio rendered these and then they became part of the syndication file for use by Viacom to help publicize the series. Just how they were secured from Viacom, before they were auctioned off, is not known."

As it ends up, the *Twilight Zone* portion of this original collection consisted of about 7,200 images shot during the filming of 75 episodes from the first three seasons. The episode sets were then individually offered for sale through a 1982 magazine ad, and 30 were sold and sadly scattered to the winds. The remaining sets were kept in an archive.

Ten years later, I came into the picture. I had become friends with Jim Benson, a Hollywood collector and eventual co-author of the book *Rod Serling's Night Gallery: An After Hours Tour*. We were both sure that little would remain of the photos, but my interest had been piqued. He furnished me with the old P.O. box from the ad, I wrote a letter, and eventually my query made it to the archivist. He replied with photocopies of one episode set and a list of the remaining collection — 45 episodes still remained, consisting of 4,395 images. The archivist made me an offer I couldn't refuse, and I instantly purchased the remaining lot. Yes, Franklin, I had won the jackpot!

From the list of available episode sets, it was clear that the more popular ones like "To Serve Man," "The Invaders," and "Time Enough at Last" had been sold, but a majority of this historical collection remained intact. And many great episodes were there, such as "The Obsolete Man," "Shadow Play," "Death's-Head Revisited," as well as incredible behind-the-scenes stills of Serling with cast and crew, discussing lines, cracking up, figuring out marks for his onscreen narrations and posing for candid shots. It was a lost visual step back in time.

I knew I had to share this collection, so in January 1999, I registered online as *The Twilight Zone Archives* (twilightzone.org), and began to build a site that would feature some of these shots. The site grew, my interest grew, and I found myself stepping behind the curtain. I met my now close friend and associate Tony Albarella, later editor of the book series, *As Timeless As Infinity: The Twilight Zone Scripts of Rod Serling*, where we were invited to tour Rod Serling's hometown of Binghamton with historian Robert Keller, and had dinner with Helen Foley, Rod's teacher and founder of the Rod Serling Memorial Foundation. It was like we had entered *The Twilight Zone*.

Little did I know that these beginnings would lead to writing a book, and during the course of working on it, I would have the opportunities to interview people like Richard Matheson, Richard Donner, and Cliff Robertson. That I would be having luncheon meetings with Carol Serling, having lengthy philosophical discussions with George Clayton Johnson, meeting Earl Hamner Jr. for lunch, and having a lengthy conversation with Rod's brother, Robert Serling. I was granted an opportunity to give something back to all of those who worked on *The Twilight Zone*. I can't help but ponder: Would Rod have liked this book? Would he have looked at it and smiled? I'd like to think so.

All I can hope for is that this book will be enjoyed by some, and appreciated by others. I hope you like *Dimensions Behind The Twilight Zone* as much as I have enjoyed working on it. It's simply one man's need to say thank you to Rod Serling. I hope I did your legacy proud, Rod.

Stewart T. Stanyard
December 2006

CHAPTER ONE

The Realm of Rod Serling

Submitted for your approval: a man known as Rod Serling, writer, master storyteller, dramatist, and founding member of the Golden Age of Television. A charismatic and creative person who had a way with words and soon found he had a talent for turning morality plays and tales of terror into a television series — a series so special, it would spark the minds of viewers for generations. Rod Serling, a man wanting only to be remembered as a writer, became an icon, as creator of the deepest dimension of imagination, known as . . . The Twilight Zone.

Hailed as grand master of all dimensions, Rod Serling will eternally be known as the American writer who created the classic black-and-white anthology television series *The Twilight Zone*. In the form of modern parables, morality plays, and short film-noir-like pictures set deep in shadow and substance, Rod Serling's creation opened our eyes and expanded our minds beyond the boundaries of our own imaginations to dimensions of limitless possibilities.

Most of Hollywood considered *The Twilight Zone* a groundbreaking television show. Running on CBS from 1959 to 1964, it surely exceeded the medium's standards of excellence and then some. Rod Serling not only

Rodman Edward Serling: December 25, 1924 – June 28, 1975

**Rod Serling performing his
on-camera narration for
"Shadow Play."**

wrote 92 of the 156 episodes, he was also the executive producer and host, both on- and off-camera. His narration style is forever synonymous with the series. Simply put, Rod Serling is *The Twilight Zone*.

It's easy to recognize that the success of the series began with a vision from Serling, for he knew well the craft of writing and producing quality dramatic television. As *Twilight Zone* producer Buck Houghton has stated, "The operative word is that basically nobody understood what made *The Twilight Zone* work except Rod." Although, looking at the full spectrum of what made the show work so well, aside from Serling's involvement, history must also credit the balance of Houghton's talented mind for production, and the artistic vision of cinematographer George T. Clemens.

Along with this primary trio of Serling, Houghton, and Clemens, it was at Hollywood's mighty MGM Studios that teams of filmmakers, directors, artists, and craftspeople took advantage of an incredible back lot of sets and properties used for hundreds of great films of the past. Christening a level of literature rarely seen in the new medium of television, these filmmakers created a timeless piece of modern art — a filmed series that went beyond what the network and sponsors expected or even understood, and, although it earned only moderate ratings during its original airing, has played worldwide in syndication ever since. The series continues to entertain and illuminate generations of viewing audiences with its captivating stories.

With MGM Studios' endless palette of expertise, and a superb award-winning writing team consisting primarily of Serling, Charles Beaumont, and Richard Matheson, *The Twilight Zone* proved to be filmmaking for television. Even though most of those who had worked in film looked down on the medium of television, some of these same filmmakers eventually brought their craft into this show, acknowledging *The Twilight Zone* as something more than the average television series.

Through the series, Rod Serling philosophized about the human condition much as he had done in his earlier Golden Age work. This time, however, he avoided network and sponsor interference by masking the social and political subject matter under a sci-fi guise of Martians, Venusians, and robots, oh my. The network executives, who thought they were purchasing a simple fantasy sci-fi series, misunderstood the deeper insights *The Twilight Zone* had to offer.

In *The Twilight Zone*'s themes that entertain and uplift the audience's imagi-

nation, we can observe the strong social understanding that was Serling's trademark. Audiences felt *The Twilight Zone*'s magic right away, guiding them into a realm of fantasy and science fiction unlike anything seen on television before. *The Twilight Zone* offered viewers poignancy and suspense, in a surreal style of storytelling that traveled between reality and unreality. These wonderful stories presented ordinary people in ordinary situations, then suddenly shocked that reality with a classic twist ending, shifting the perspective of realism into a surrealistic framework. Since the series was an anthology, and able to go beyond the linear cast of an average drama, western, or situation comedy of the time, the types of characters and situations the writers could create were unlimited.

Among these wondrous flights into the unknown, audiences meet some of the most memorable, lifelike characters to have emerged from television's dimension. We come to know these classic characters inside and out within the first few minutes of an episode. The well-written dialogue flowed naturally, offering an actor the opportunity to inhabit the spirit of a character and make

"Death's-Head Revisited" stars Oscar Beregi as Captain Lutze and Joseph Schildkraut as Becker. In this shot, we see the crew and actor Schildkraut at work during exterior shots on the back lot at MGM. It was said the buildings resembled Dachau.

it his own. And if an actor was having trouble with any of the lines, Serling was known to go offstage for a few minutes, then reappear with rewrites on the spot. Actors took comfort knowing that Serling was in their corner, creating camaraderie and a positive workspace, helping their creative process of bringing life to the characters.

The Twilight Zone's most beloved Serling episode, "Time Enough at Last," features Burgess Meredith as Henry Bemis. Bemis, a bookworm bank teller who wears thick glasses and longs to be left alone to read, becomes the sole survivor of a nuclear war one day while reading in the bank vault. Alone and afraid, he walks the city of rubble, not sure what to do with his time, when suddenly he comes across the remains of a public library. Dusty books are scattered everywhere, signaling a perfect chance for Bemis to at last pursue a lifetime of uninterrupted reading. But the surprise twist at the end punishes Bemis for his antisocial behavior, and his greatest desire is forever thwarted.

And then there's William Shatner's memorable performance in Richard Matheson's chilling story, "Nightmare at 20,000 Feet." Bob Wilson, traveling with his wife on a flight home after his recovery from a nervous breakdown, is the only passenger able to see a gremlin tampering with the wing of the plane. He tries desperately to warn his wife and convince the crew, but the gremlin flies away whenever anyone else looks. Is Wilson crazy, or is the gremlin real? The end of the episode reveals a truth that only we viewers can see, putting us in the same situation as Wilson.

However popular these two classic episodes may be to the masses, they represent only a fraction of *The Twilight Zone* universe and its hundreds of inhabitants. Most every episode carries its own weight by providing a great story, interesting characters, and a surprise ending to warp viewer perception. Since the series was an anthology, it utilized a plethora of themes, including several that would be revisited throughout its run. Categorizing the show's storytelling, one might settle on a dozen main themes — other dimensions, time travel, space travel, the power of the mind, humanity, death and dying, the devil, second chances, enchanted objects, creatures, machines, and magic.

Instead of the mundane sameness that television series usually offer, the themes and characters within *The Twilight Zone* proved the medium could offer intelligence, wonderment, and even psychology, paying heed to the human condition, our fears and corruptions, and the injustices of mankind. Serling presented a world where fate is exact and ironic, where every type of corruption or atrocity is met equally with a brilliant form of comeuppance. Consider it thematic payback time: a place where condemned Nazis spend an eternity living

Burgess Meredith stars in the classic episode, "Time Enough at Last."

William Shatner, Christine White, and Nick Cravat (gremlin) star in the terrifying "Nightmare at 20,000 Feet."

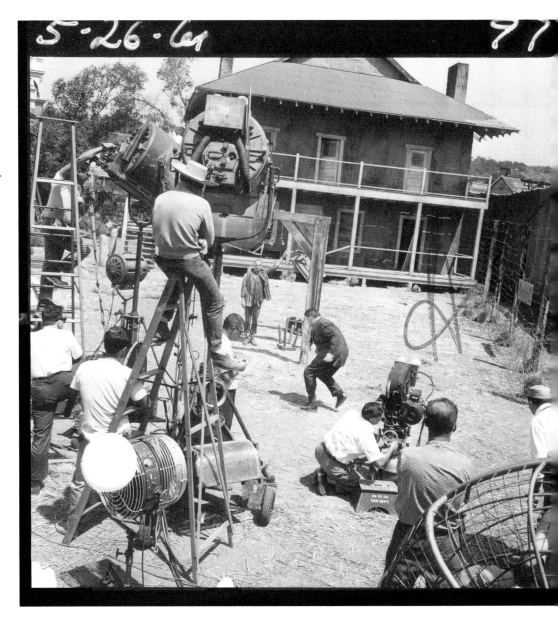

through the same horrors they inflicted upon others. Or where corrupt, power-hungry capitalists lose sight of man's worth, and either the tables turn on them in some twisted way, or insanity sets in. Great lessons abound in this endless celluloid palette that acted as a set of modern-day parables. Justice may be blind in our third dimension, but in the Twilight Zone, it sees clearly.

However, the Twilight Zone is more than just a place for the wicked. There are also second chances found between the shadows, ways to escape the stresses of modern life and return to the supposed comfort of the past. These stories are intended to yank our heartstrings rather than shock and terrorize us. It's no mystery that Rod Serling used nostalgia in his work. Having experienced the hectic life of a prominent Hollywood playwright and television icon, he imagined returning to a slower, more content past. Serling often visited the second-chance theme, as did several of the show's other writers. With classic episodes such as Serling's "A Stop at Willoughby," "The Sixteen-Millimeter Shrine," and the semi-autobiographical "Walking Distance," as well as Reginald Rose's "The Incredible World of Horace Ford" and George Clayton Johnson's "Kick the Can," the audience is brought back to simpler times, when a person could stretch his soul and have another chance at a better life.

There's no need to wish for better television here, though: *The Twilight Zone* has it all. From its deep sense of poignancy, irony, and twists of fate, to the magical and mysterious, the creepy, strange, and haunting, it opens a door with the key of imagination. Since its premiere nearly 50 years ago, *The Twilight Zone* has established itself as Hollywood's landmark television series, and its fans and critics across the board view it as the greatest television show ever created. But *The Twilight Zone* has reached the status of being much more than just a television show or entertainment. As a vital part of American pop culture, as it is regarded by audiences worldwide, the show has developed into a form of expression — when something strange or unexplainable happens in real life, people will universally hum out the notes of the eerie theme music. No other television show has had such mass appeal that it has come to define all things unexplained in real life.

The original phrase, "twilight zone," came from the early 1900s, used to describe a distinct condition between fantasy and reality. The term evolved into an entry in the dictionary defining the lowest level of the ocean that light can reach, and as an aeronautical term used by the U.S. Air Force. As noted in Marc Scott Zicree's *The Twilight Zone Companion*, when Serling was asked how he came up with the title, he replied, "I thought I'd made it up, but I've heard since that there is an Air Force term relating to a moment when a plane is coming down on approach and it cannot see the horizon. It's called the twilight zone, but it's an obscure term which I had not heard before."

Today, the popularity of *The Twilight Zone* has surpassed anything Rod Serling, the CBS executives, or anyone else who worked on the series could have ever imagined. As is the case with other classic television shows, there was little idea these creations would continuously be rerun through syndication, extending their shelf lives to countless viewing audiences. But *The Twilight Zone* towers over these other classic syndicated shows, a leader in quality and imagination. It has that same quality of memorable wonder, and place in American culture and Hollywood history, as *The Wizard of Oz* and *It's a Wonderful Life*. The series also offers a growing nostalgia for baby boomers who want to relive the magic of watching the shows they grew up on, going back to a time when it was possible to leave something to the imagination and work the brain's muscles.

Television devoid of *The Twilight Zone* would have been like rock 'n' roll without Chuck Berry, the Beatles, or Led Zeppelin, or horror films without

James Daly stars in the dreamlike fantasy, "A Stop at Willoughby."

An original *Twilight Zone* promotion piece of the time.

8

Frankenstein, the Wolf Man, or Dracula. Rod Serling's *Twilight Zone* paved the way for some of Hollywood's television creators and filmmakers, to bring us shows like *The Outer Limits*, *X-Files*, *Quantum Leap*, *Lost*, and *Star Trek*. And who's to say if George Lucas, Wes Craven, Chris Carter, J.J. Abrams, M. Night Shyamalan, or even Steven Spielberg (whose directing debut was on *Rod Serling's Night Gallery*) would have been inspired to go the routes they did. Who would have thought that the work of Rod Serling would touch the minds of so many of today's Hollywood creators? Or of the many others who became writers and teachers specifically because they watched *The Twilight Zone* as children?

Having expanded viewers' minds simply by taking them on a weekly journey into Rod Serling's imagination, *The Twilight Zone* has had such a strong influence upon the industry that it's been parodied and referenced countless times in early series like *The Dick Van Dyke Show* and *The Jack Benny Show*, as well as later shows like *Saturday Night Live*, where Dan Aykroyd did a deadpan impersonation of Serling. The series has been referenced in modern genre shows such as *Buffy the Vampire Slayer*, and several Fox series, including *Futurama*, *Family Guy*, and *The Simpsons*. ABC's hit, *Lost*, is like an extended episode of *The Twilight Zone*, while *3rd Rock from the Sun* went so far as to parody both the original version of "Nightmare at 20,000 Feet," where William Shatner played the passenger who sees the gremlin on the wing of the plane, and John Lithgow's reprise in the movie version. Here, Shatner arrives off a flight and refers to seeing a man on the wing of the plane, and Lithgow excitedly states that the same thing happened to him.

In the realm of fantasy and sci-fi on television, Rod Serling broke new ground. Prior to creating *The Twilight Zone*, he honed and polished his abilities working as a television playwright during the grand Golden Age of the '50s.

Serling's first major success came on January 12, 1955, with his sixth Kraft Television Theatre teleplay, "Patterns." In the callous setting of the corporate world, "Patterns" is the dramatic story of young executive Fred Staples, forced to replace the company's worn vice-president in a power struggle to someday overthrow the merciless company president. The press reaction to "Patterns" was nothing short of amazement, as newspaper critics across the country reviewed it not only as Kraft Television Theatre's best production to date, but also a milestone for the medium and a brilliant achievement for Serling. "Patterns" won Serling the first of an eventual six Emmy Awards, and ten days later, the big-screen version of "Patterns" was released. Now Serling had to live up to the success of "Patterns" and continue to deliver works of similar dramatic quality. "I had something to prove, first to others and then to myself. I had to prove that 'Patterns' wasn't all I had," he said.

On October 4, 1956, CBS's 90-minute live anthology series *Playhouse 90* debuted with Serling's Cold War drama, "The Forbidden Area," based on a novel by Pat Frank. Produced by Martin Manulis and directed by John

During the production of the videotaped episode, "Static," actor Dean Jagger and crew look on as Rod Serling performs his on-camera narration — an alternate take not used in the finished episode.

CBS TELEVISION

A Division of Columbia Broadcasting System, Inc.

_____

EMPLOYMENT AGREEMENT (WRITER)

_____

AGREEMENT made this 1st day of March, 1957 by and between CBS TELEVISION, a Division of Columbia Broadcasting System, Inc., Television City, Hollywood, California (herein called "CBS Television") and ROD SERLING, c/o Blanche Gaines, 350 West 57th Street, New York, New York (herein called "Writer").

In consideration of the mutual covenants herein contained the parties hereto have agreed and do agree as follows:

1. CBS Television hereby employs Writer and Writer hereby agrees to perform artistic and professional services as required by CBS Television as a writer of three (3) original scripts suitable for broadcast on the ninety (90) minute programs of the "Playhouse 90" Television series, all as hereinafter provided, it being understood that all materials furnished by Writer hereunder shall be referred to herein as the "Material." CBS Television shall broadcast or cause to be broadcast each of the three (3) scripts over the CBS Television network on a program of the "Playhouse 90" series or on such other ninety (90) minute program (whether or not of a program series) as CBS Television shall elect with respect to each such script.

4
30
57

2. The term of this agreement shall commence March 1, 1957 and shall expire on that date on which Writer has rendered all services required of him by this agreement.

3. Writer will use Writer's best talents, efforts and abilities in performing services hereunder and shall perform such services under the direction and control of CBS Television. Writer will deliver final drafts of said three (3) scripts on the following dates:

Script Number	Script Delivery Date
1st script	July 1, 1957
2nd script	November 15, 1957 if based on 2nd outline, or December 15, 1957 if based on 3rd outline

28. This agreement contains the entire understanding of the parties hereto relating to the subject matter herein contained, and this agreement cannot be changed or terminated orally.

29. Each check becoming due Writer hereunder shall be made payable to "Blanche Gaines" as agent for Rod Serling.

IN WITNESS WHEREOF, the parties hereto have executed this agreement as of the day and year first above written.

CBS TELEVISION
A Division of Columbia Broadcasting System, Inc.

By _____

_____
(Writer)

Frankenheimer, "The Forbidden Area" starred Charlton Heston and Vincent Price in what proved a substandard tale about a saboteur of nuclear bombers blown up during flight. The following week, *Playhouse 90* aired Serling's remarkably poignant teleplay "Requiem for a Heavyweight," about a weathered boxer on his last breath. To this day, "Requiem" is viewed as Rod Serling's greatest single creation outside of the popularity of *The Twilight Zone*, and it aired with a flawless performance. Regarded by Serling himself as the finest moment in his career, "Requiem" won several awards and was remade in 1962 as a feature film.

Serling's role as a leading television playwright continued over the next few years with quality *Playhouse 90* teleplays such as, "The Comedian," "The Dark Side of the Earth," "A Town Has Turned To Dust," "The Rank and File," the semi-autobiographical play, "The Velvet Alley," and "In the Presence of Mine Enemies." Amid an endless sea of traditionalism that seemed to ignore the social struggles of the time, Serling was determined to speak his mind through his work. He was an advocate of elevating the quality of dramatic television and inspiring the consciousness of the audience. Having delved deep into many social injustices of the time, like the racism of the true-life lynching of Emmett Till in *Playhouse 90*'s "Noon on Doomsday" and "A Town Has Turned to Dust," and seeing political issues toned down for *Studio One*'s "The Arena," he witnessed firsthand how censorship was costly to the integrity of his work. "By the time 'A Town Has Turned to Dust' went before the cameras," Serling said, "my script had turned to dust. Emmett Till became, as *Time* noted, a romantic Mexican who loved the shopkeeper's wife, but 'only with his eyes.' My sheriff couldn't commit suicide because one of our sponsors was an insurance firm and they claimed that suicide often leads to complications in settling policy claims. The lynch victim was called Clemson, but we couldn't use this 'cause South Carolina had an all-white college by that name. The setting was moved to the Southwest in the 1870s. The phrase 'Twenty men in hoods' became 'Twenty men in homemade masks.' They chopped it up like a roomful of butchers at work on a steer."

A magazine ad for the encore performance of the *Westinghouse Desilu Playhouse* production of "The Time Element." Notice the misspelling of Serling's last name.

Indeed, Serling came through those times frustrated with the networks' constant censoring of his work and rebellious toward the restrictions imposed by commercial sponsors. Close to the end of television's Golden Age, Serling was ready to enter the next phase of his career, one that would give him more creative control over his work. During the final reigning era of the live anthology shows, most of which were cancelled in just over a year's time, Serling's interest steered away from the practical, reality-based stories and toward the limitless realm of fantasy. The idea for a fantasy series came from a Serling script previously aired during his college days on the Cincinnati WLW anthology series, *The Storm*. "The Time Element" tells the tale of a man who time-travels back to Pearl Harbor and attempts to warn people of the impending Japanese attack. Serling reworked and expanded the script to a one-hour format, fleshing out details of the characters and submitting it to CBS with a new title: *The Twilight Zone* — "The Time Element." CBS purchased the script, likely since it was a work by Rod Serling. However, as with other conservative networks of the time, CBS was unenthusiastic about the fantasy storyline and summarily decided to shelve the property. It wasn't until a year later that "The Time Element" saw the light of day. Bert Granet, producer for *Westinghouse Desilu Playhouse*, had been scouting for scripts by prominent playwrights, and Serling was definitely at the top of his list. He bought "The Time Element" from CBS for $10,000.

Desilu Playhouse added "The Time Element" to its 1958–59 production schedule, however, Granet met much resistance from the conservative Westinghouse advertising agency and sponsor at the time, McCann-Erickson. They wanted stories with tight, conclusive endings, while Serling's tale was open-ended and let the audience use their imaginations. Granet continued to struggle over the use of the script until he got Desilu founder Desi Arnaz in his corner. Even though the sponsor remained reluctant, Arnaz supported Granet and eventually "The Time Element" was approved for production.

"The Time Element" starred two veteran actors, William Bendix as Pete Jenson, a man who claims his dreams of time-traveling back before the Japanese attack on Pearl Harbor are real, and Martin Balsam as Dr. Gillespie, the psychiatrist who tries to convince him time travel is an impossibility and that his dreams are simply a result of an overactive dream state. McCann-Erickson insisted on the need for an explanation at the end. As the conclusion of "The Time Element" plays out, Jenson does go back in time to the Pearl Harbor attack and is killed by enemy planes. The scene changes to Dr. Gillespie sitting in his office alone; he looks at his appointment book — no entries. He visits a bar and, upon having a drink, glances behind the bartender toward a picture on the wall of a guy who seems strangely familiar. He asks the bartender, played by Paul Bryar, "Who's the guy in the picture?" The bartender replies, "Oh, that's Pete Jenson. He used to tend bar here. Know him?" "No," Gillespie answers. "Just looked familiar, that's all. Where is he now?" "He's dead," adds the bartender. "He was killed at Pearl Harbor." This is where the scene should have faded, leaving the audience with an ideal prelude to the style of *The Twilight Zone* twist endings to come. Instead, Desi Arnaz appears and offers a dry explanation to the story: "We wonder if Pete Jenson did go back in time or if he ever existed. My personal answer is that the doctor had seen Jenson's picture at the bar sometime before and had a dream. Any of you have any answers? Let me know." This easy out was a nightmare that caused Serling to again question the sponsor's power over the content of a writer's work.

"The Time Element" aired on *Desilu Playhouse* on November 24, 1958, and received more phone calls, telegrams, and positive viewer mail than any of the series' other dramas that year. It was with this overwhelming audience approval that CBS owned up to the shelving of Serling's script and decided to produce a pilot for *The Twilight Zone*. William Dozier, the head of CBS's West Coast programming, assigned the task of production to William Self, who at the time was a new addition to the network and the development department. Self's first *Twilight Zone* business was to secure a good story for the pilot. As "The Time Element" had already been produced for *Desilu Playhouse*, a new script needed to be written for the pilot. Serling wrote a one-hour piece entitled "The Happy Place," which resembles and predates the *Twilight Zone* episode "The Obsolete Man," painting the dark picture of a futuristic totalitarian state where people reaching the age of 60 are considered obsolete and brought to concentration camps for extermination. Self found the story a remarkable statement, yet believed it too depressing as a pilot to sell the series. Serling agreed to write a completely new script and just a few days later, arrived at Self's office with "Where Is Everybody?"

As an ideal starting point for *The Twilight Zone*, the new script offered both a solid story and an underlying strategy to sell the series to potential sponsors. Steering clear of fantasy and sci-fi themes, which likely would have deterred the sale of the series, the pilot presented an imaginative story with a conservative ending that returns to reality. Wary of the conservative mindset of the sponsors, the pilot also avoided any plot devices like aliens, devils, and robots, which

Rod Serling on the set of "Cavender Is Coming."

would later become such a big part of *The Twilight Zone*. Still, this very first script encapsulates many other elements that the series would be known for — imagination, alienation, fear of the unknown, and Serling's exploration of the human condition. Within this safe structure, the plot is basic — a man suffering from amnesia finds himself utterly alone in a small town devoid of people. Aside from the pilot's quality of writing and sensible plot, other selling points were the direction, cinematography, music, and high production values. Hired to direct the pilot was Robert Stevens, a veteran director for several episodes of *Alfred Hitchcock Presents*, *Playhouse 90*, *Climax*, and *Suspense*, who would later direct the seminal *Twilight Zone* episode, "Walking Distance." Adding more credibility to the visual mood was cinematographer Joseph La Shelle, who also worked on *Alfred Hitchcock Presents* as well as memorable feature films such as *Laura*, *Marty*, and *The Apartment*. Along with these seasoned talents, Bernard Herrmann, one of the industry's most renowned composers, was brought aboard to create the music. Herrmann was known for scoring films such as *Citizen Kane*, *The Day the Earth Stood Still*, *The 7th Voyage of Sinbad*, and *Vertigo*. Playing the lead role of Mike Ferris in the pilot was actor Earl Holliman, who, previous to his first television job the previous year in Rod Serling's *Playhouse 90* episode "The Dark Side of the Earth," had worked in 19 films, including the sci-fi cult classic *Forbidden Planet*, *The Rainmaker*, and *Gunfight at the O.K. Corral*.

The pilot was shot in December 1958 at Universal International Studios, which offered a perfect back lot for use as the empty town in the story. The budget for the pilot was sizable for the time — $75,000, which covered a day of rehearsal and an eight-day shoot. Following the filming of the pilot, it was scored, edited, and flown to New York to be screened by the chief executive officer of CBS, William Paley. William Self, who was there to oversee the screening, told Tony Albarella in his book, *As Timeless as Infinity*: "Paley was extremely high on it. He was a big supporter of it. Strangely enough, some of the other executives at CBS were not; they didn't know what it was, they didn't quite get it. But Paley did and that was all that counted at CBS in those days." CBS signed on with Rod Serling's production company, Cayuga Productions, with Serling contracted to write 80 percent of the scripts for the first season. CBS and Serling split ownership of the series and, within just a few months, production began on *The Twilight Zone*.

However, before the series would actually see fruition, a few adjustments needed to be made to the pilot, including the first line of Serling's original opening narration: "There is a sixth dimension, beyond that which is known to man. . . ." Self asked Serling, "Please explain to me what the *fifth* dimension is," to which Serling replied, "Oh, aren't there five?" The opening was rewritten and rerecorded with the Twilight Zone introduced as the fifth dimension. The somewhat archaic opening title sequence needed updating, and for the broadcast version, a new opening was commissioned from the title company,

Actor Earl Holliman wrote this publicity letter just four days before the premiere of the pilot, "Where is Everybody?"

EARL HOLLIMAN

September 28, 1959

Hi:

Just wanted to let you know I'll be appearing on the CBS television network this coming Friday night, October 2nd ...and in not one show, but two!

First my new Western series, HOTEL DE PAREE, goes on the air from 8:30 to 9 o'clock. I play an ex-gunslinger named "Sundance", who returns to Georgetown, Colorado after spending seven years in prison. With me, is my dog (about the only friend I've got), a wonderful little mongrel named "Useless". I think the series will be a very good one. If you like it (and I hope you do) we'll be on every Friday night.

Second, Rod Serling's new "stranger-than-fiction" series, TWILIGHT ZONE airs at 10 o'clock the same night. A different actor will appear each week, but I'm lucky enough to be in the first one. It's called "Where Is Everybody?" and I play a guy names "Mike". Since it's a terrific suspense story, and I wouldn't want to spoil it for you, that's all I'll say about it.

Hope you get a chance to watch them both.

Sincerely,

Earl Holliman

P.S. The shows might be on at different times in your area, so you might check your local newspaper or TV Guide.

UPA. This new animated title sequence flawlessly matched the tone of Serling's narration.

Along with these revisions came the significant choice of narrator. The original voice used to narrate the pilot was that of Westbrook Van Voorhis, the ominous narrator behind the *March of Time* newsreels. However, at the screening it was unanimously decided that his tone was just not right for the show — Serling especially thought Van Voorhis seemed to be talking down to the audience. Other narrators were considered, including Orson Welles, but his price proved too high. It was Serling who finally suggested he'd do it himself. At first, this move was met with uncertainty, but after Serling did some vocal tests, it was clear he was perfect for the job.

With these changes in place, CBS gave the green light for production of the first 26 episodes of *The Twilight Zone*. All that was left to choose was the production team. Serling asked Self to stay on board as the show's producer. Self appreciated the offer but passed, as he was eager to continue in his executive-producer position at the network. He did, however, suggest Serling consider his production team from *Schlitz Playhouse of Stars* and *The Frank Sinatra Show*, which consisted of story editor Buck Houghton, cameraman George T. Clemens, production manager Ralph Nelson, and a few other talents. After meeting with Serling and later reading a couple of scripts, Houghton accepted the position of producer. Soon Clemens became the director of photography and the rest of the team followed closely behind. With the production team firmly set, Rod Serling's words from the pilot's opening narration described well what they were about to embark upon — "The place is here, the time is now, and the journey into the shadows that we're about to watch could be our journey."

CHAPTER TWO

Team of Wizards

*"What's going on here? Where are we?
What are we? Who are we? Who are we?!"*

— The Major in *"Five Characters in Search of an Exit"*

**Rod Serling in a *Twilight
Zone* promotion piece
for the series.**

As much as Rod Serling is remembered as the creator of *The Twilight Zone* and for his vision, writing, narration, and executive producing force, it was the team of wizards that made the series work so well. Serling's left and right hand — brilliant writers Charles Beaumont and Richard Matheson — as well as the skillful production of Buck Houghton, the cinematography of George T. Clemens, and the work of a distinct group of experienced directors and actors made this creative circle complete. For Serling, it was exhilarating working among the various artisans in an industry he helped through its infancy. And since *The Twilight Zone* was viewed as an exciting production to work on and a special series unlike any other show, the experienced crew contributed their efforts with pride.

The foundation of *The Twilight Zone* is in its writing. By the time Serling had created the series, he had already achieved the status of a television-writing heavyweight. With *The Twilight Zone*, Serling brought to the medium a storytelling approach similar to that of fantasy and science-fiction authors who wrote for books and pulp magazines. Serling had a deep respect for the work of Ray Bradbury, Isaac Asimov, and

Charles Beaumont gets a light from actor Robin Hughes on the set of "The Howling Man."

Robert A. Heinlein, as well as Theodore Sturgeon, H.P. Lovecraft, and Edgar Allan Poe. He took the quality of writing he had already contributed to early television, mixed it with the genres of fantasy, sci-fi, and the supernatural, and crossed it over into television's more conventional world. Since Serling was already spread thin with his many responsibilities for the series, a core writing team was needed to create additional stories of equal quality. Along with his appreciation for writers versed in fantasy and science fiction, Serling sought storytellers who could also easily adapt to the structure and sensibilities that were *The Twilight Zone*. Early on, an open call went out for writers, but the story submissions proved to be of inferior quality and nowhere near a good match. Serling then invited a group of noted writers to meet, including Charles Beaumont, Richard Matheson, and Ray Bradbury, and showed them nine of his scripts to see if they could adapt to his writing style.

Beaumont was considered the integral center of the Southern California Group of Writers, commonly known as the Group, which included his mentor, Bradbury, collaborators Matheson and William F. Nolan, and later members George Clayton Johnson, Jerry Sohl, Robert Bloch, and Harlan Ellison. The Group's aim was to raise the state of television fantasy and science fiction. With the *Twilight Zone* project, Beaumont was at first wary of this Hollywood player, Rod Serling, who was invading their territory. Beaumont believed the series sounded like low-budget B-movie television, but his reluctance to join the *Twilight Zone* team was also based on a trend toward failed proposed fantasy and science-fiction television shows, a strong signal that the genre was going the way of the dodo. He thought *The Twilight Zone* would likely follow suit. He then read Serling's sample scripts, including such powerful stories as "Walking Distance," "The Lonely," and "Where Is Everybody?" Beaumont recognized the high quality of the writing and dialogue tightly woven into these half-hour fantasy dramas. The approach to the storytelling was neither clichéd, nor the cheap imitation science fiction he had expected. It was clear that with *The Twilight Zone*, Serling was providing an outlet for professional fantasy and science-fiction writers to bring a high level of work into television.

Matheson and Bradbury also read Serling's scripts and felt the project worthy enough to join Serling's writing team. Even though Bradbury was considered a contributing writer, only one of his teleplays actually made it into the series, the botched rendering of his short story, "I Sing the Body Electric." As production proceeded, more and more of his scripts were rejected, purportedly because the elaborate settings of his stories were too costly for the budget. Disillusioned, Bradbury eventually accused Serling of plagiarizing his work and that of several other science-fiction writers. He summarily pulled out of both the series and his friendship with Serling.

Quite the opposite was true of Beaumont and Matheson, both of whom contributed many of *The Twilight Zone*'s most outstanding and memorable episodes. Beaumont easily met the high quality of storytelling on the series, as he had already established himself with work on *Alfred Hitchcock Presents*, *One Step Beyond*, and *Have Gun — Will Travel*. His approach to storytelling dealt with bizarre and often horrific circumstances thrown upon individual characters, whereas Serling's scripts concentrated on social commentary and poignant sentiment.

David White, Veronica Cartwright, Vaughn Taylor, and Josephine Hutchinson star in Ray Bradbury's single *Twilight Zone* contribution, "I Sing the Body Electric."

Beaumont's episodes proved that there were several doors to the imagination, not just that of Serling. Indeed, some of his episodes have reached classic status, including "Perchance to Dream," "Shadow Play," "The Howling Man," "Long Live Walter Jameson," "Person or Persons Unknown," and "Miniature." His hard-edged, eerie, and often uneasy storytelling concerned itself with the very existence of an individual, his state of mind, his perception, and the terrifying border between reality and fantasy. From Beaumont's very first script, "Perchance to Dream," Serling advised him to write the script the

Actor John Close and star Dennis Weaver pose as characters from Beaumont's superb "Shadow Play."

July 24, 1960

Buck, Rod, Del, Doug, Jack, Doc & Reggie:

Here is the overhauled version of THE HOWLING MAN, a grand script by a grand writer. Most of the suggested modifications have been incorporated, but not all. Explanation:

1. To start it in the penthouse would be to lose all of the suspense in the matter of whether Ellington will or will not open that door. It is important suspense. It makes up a great deal of the drama. Properly done, it should have the viewers divided, half urging Ellington to let the poor bastard out, half screaming at him to get the hell away from that place. Therefore I have kept the original opening.

2. I have retained the ~~original~~ *this* method of discovering the Prisoner's cloven hoof. I tried it Doug's way, but either I don't see it or I am right in believing my way better. The "Help me!" - "Help you!" dialogue, the scramble up the wall, the sulphurous figure of the prisoner etched against the night as he stands atop the wall & then vanishes in smoke.... all this strikes me as wonderful stuff. The cloven hoof coming down on Ellington's laced hands is, of course, Rod's idea, but I'll fight for it anyway.

3. The "my son" routine is retained, mainly because I like it. I realize that Buck doesn't, but since this is hardly a policy matter, I don't see why I should mumble humbly and shuffle off with bowed head. The point here is that Ellington himself is annoyed m whenever Jerome or Christophorus calls him "my son," and we make something of that.

All the other changes have been ~~made~~ *tended to. They work fine*. I must say I still *has to* like the montage and don't understand why it ~~must~~ turn out dull -- the whole truth is that I don't believe montages are ipso facto dull -- but I'm not sure of myself in this area, so I'll submit to wiser and more experienced heads.

There is a great deal of brooding terror in this script, of *I think,* ~~genuine suspense~~ palpable menace and genuine suspense, and If we can bring these qualities to the screen, ~~I think~~ we'll have them shivering for days afterward. Maybe longer.

Chuck

way he envisioned the story playing out and not compromise. Beaumont followed Serling's lead. He wrote the script exactly as he saw it and it was easily approved. To cement the fact that Serling was serious about not compromising the art, Beaumont found, when visiting the set during filming, sure enough, the episode was shot exactly as he had written it. "Nothing was changed." Beaumont said. "Not one line. Not one word." Because Serling respected their work, his writers respected him in turn.

As Christopher Conlon pointed out in his introduction to the book, *California Sorcery*, as Charles Beaumont became more involved in the series, his workload was swamped with other projects. He found it necessary to outsource some of his *Twilight Zone* scripts to ghostwriters who were also members of the Group. This started during the third season with Ocee Ritch's "Dead Man's Shoes" and continued with episodes such as Jerry Sohl's "The New Exhibit," "Living Doll," and "Queen of the Nile," and John Tomerlin's "Number Twelve Looks Just Like You." During this period, when Beaumont felt exhausted and burned out, his colleagues sensed that something else was going on with him besides his large workload. During activities with the Group, they noticed his once-motivated aura now seemed haggard and aged. His speech began to slur, he seemed forgetful and confused, and by 1963, when *The Twilight Zone* was entering its final season, he was unable to write. Much like a character in one of his stories who loses the thing dearest to him, this remarkably imaginative, energetic 34-year-old writer was slipping into Alzheimer's disease. Over his remaining days, Beaumont lived in a rest home, where the disease progressed, ultimately claiming his life on February 21, 1967. After his death, the Group continued with their work, even collaborating on some projects, but without their energetic friend at the helm, in time they slowly drifted apart. Beaumont's own *Twilight Zone* character, Prof. Walter Jameson, states, "Nothing lasts forever." But he was wrong. Words as timeless as Beaumont's do last forever, and for that, fans will be forever grateful.

Actors Kenneth Haigh and Simon Scott act out a scene during an exterior shot for Richard Matheson's "The Last Flight," filmed at Norton Air Force Base, San Bernardino, California.

Beaumont's colleague Richard Matheson was a core member of the Group and the writer of some of the most brilliant *Twilight Zone* episodes. Matheson's first contributions were two stories adapted by Rod Serling, "Third from the Sun," and "And When the Sky Was Opened" (loosely based on "Disappearing Act"). Both episodes are clear examples of Matheson's flair for storytelling and Serling's skill at adapting other writers' works. Matheson also wrote 14 original scripts for *The Twilight Zone*, preferring to create unique pieces instead of using previous work from his short stories.

His most outstanding episodes are the classics "The Invaders" — starring Agnes Moorehead as an isolated woman terrorized by small intruders — and "Nightmare at 20,000 Feet." He also wrote "The Last Flight," which was the first story he pitched, "A World of Difference," "A World of His Own," "Nick of Time," "Once Upon a Time," "Little Girl Lost," "Young Man's Fancy," "Mute," "Death Ship," "Steel," "Night Call," and "Spur of the Moment." Very much in line with Beaumont's fantasy-oriented approach to storytelling, Matheson's terror-based stories revolve around the unnerving conditions cast upon individual characters and their surroundings. A little girl falls through a portal in the wall of her bedroom and into another dimension. An old woman is terrified by a mysterious voice on her telephone calling from the great beyond. A man must overcome his superstitious nature or fall victim to a fortune-telling machine. A WWI pilot inadvertently travels forward through time to 1959, yet must go back and save a comrade to correct history. A businessman discovers his life is actually part of a movie, and struggles to get back to what he considers reality. Then there are a few lighter comedy turns, like the 1890 janitor who bor-

William Shatner, Patricia Breslin, and The Mystic Seer star in "Nick of Time."

rows a time helmet and mistakenly travels to the year 1962, or the playwright who can describe the characters in his plays so well, they literally come to life.

As the series' third major writer, Matheson delivered chilling storytelling that balanced the tones of both Serling and Beaumont. And like Beaumont, Matheson rarely featured the social commentary that Serling did. "The Invaders" and "Nightmare at 20,000 Feet" are considered two of the most popular episodes of the series.

Just as Ray Bradbury was a mentor to Charles Beaumont, it was Beaumont who became a mentor, colleague, and friend to the next primary *Twilight Zone* writer, George Clayton Johnson. A member of the Group, as well as a lifelong friend of Bradbury, Johnson began his professional writing career in television with stories and scripts for *The Twilight Zone*. He also wrote the first aired episode of *Star Trek*, wrote the story for the feature-film Rat Pack caper *Ocean's Eleven*, collaborated with Bradbury on the animated short *Icarus Montgolfier Wright*, and wrote the Academy Award–winning science-fiction classic *Logan's Run*, based on a novel he co-authored with William F. Nolan.

The themes in this artist's *Twilight Zone* range from the spirit of youth to the calming of death, the powers of telekinesis and telepathy to the worth and betterment of the individual. Johnson's early contributions during the first season were two stories Serling adapted into scripts, the unique "The Four of Us Are Dying," and "Execution." "The Four of Us Are Dying" first aired on January 1, 1960, ushering in a New Year, a new decade, and Johnson's first television credit in collaboration with the renowned Rod Serling. Both episodes clearly shined with Serling's dialogue and pacing, yet beneath the work lay the foundation of Johnson's unique angle of storytelling. Next in production was "The Prime Mover," a story Beaumont purchased from Johnson, as he had an assigned slot for a script but was short a story. Unfortunately, even though Johnson was paid

Actor Robert Redford and writer George Clayton Johnson on the set of "Nothing in the Dark."

$600 for his story, which for the most part was kept intact, he went uncredited due to a production error.

By the end of the second season, Johnson had successfully earned the status to adapt his own stories for the series, the first of which was "A Penny for Your Thoughts," starring Dick York. Here, York plays mild-mannered bank clerk Hector B. Poole, who one day accidentally gains a temporary knack for telepathy. Johnson took on the challenge of writing this script with much dedication and energy. Upon completion, he was amazed at how easily it was accepted and,

LEFT: **Jack Klugman and Jonathan Winters star as Jesse Cardiff and Fats Brown in Johnson's "A Game of Pool."**
CENTER: **Rod Serling shoots some pool after the filming of his on-camera narration.**
RIGHT: **Jesse Cardiff looks on as Fats Brown conveys there's more to life than just billiards.**

most importantly, that it was filmed as written. Then came his most exceptional piece to date, "Nothing in the Dark," starring Gladys Cooper and a very young Robert Redford. In an episode that reads as close to perfection as one can expect of a script, Johnson's ironic look at death and dying is among the best episodes in the series. Continuing his storytelling roll, Johnson then scripted the unique tale of challenger pitted against champion in "A Game of Pool," starring Jack Klugman and Jonathan Winters. One of Serling's favorite actors, Klugman would star in four *Twilight Zone* episodes.

Johnson's final penned *Twilight Zone* script is the touching "Kick the Can," starring Ernest Truex as a spirited old man who, through a game of kick the can, magically turns himself and a group of elderly folks back into children. As one of those *Twilight Zone* moments where a story of sentiment could easily go sappy, "Kick the Can" is a developed work that does quite the opposite. It's an honest glimpse into the spirit of youth and mortality, and is highly regarded as a counterpart to "Walking Distance" and "A Stop At Willoughby."

During the fifth season, Johnson made his final *Twilight Zone* story contribution with the episode "Ninety Years Without Slumbering," starring comedy great Ed Wynn. Unfortunately, the production of the episode changed hands by the time the teleplay was finished, and a rewrite was ordered, compromising the story with the addition of a clichéd psychiatrist character. Johnson felt the changes were a detriment to his original work. In recent years, though, he has warmed up to the finished episode.

George Clayton Johnson's storytelling in *The Twilight Zone* is as immortal as that of Serling, Beaumont, and Matheson. Like a painter whose strokes of contrast and color guide the eyes through visual explorations, Johnson's images take the mind's eye into a dimension where the logical mind is bent and the aching heart warmed.

10-13-59

CBS TELEVISION

A DIVISION OF COLUMBIA BROADCASTING SYSTEM, INC.

Television City • Hollywood, California • WEbster 8-3011

STANDARD AFTRA ENGAGEMENT CONTRACT

Agreement Between

Date............**September 5,**............19.**56**

Mr. Ed Wynn
c/o Kurt Frings Agency
468 North Camden Drive
Beverly Hills, California

(hereinafter called "Performer")

and
CBS TELEVISION

(hereinafter called "Producer")

Performer shall render artistic services in connection with the rehearsal and broadcast of the program(s) designated below and preparation in connection with the part or parts to be played:

TITLE OF PROGRAM:............**"PLAYHOUSE 90"**

TYPE OF PROGRAM:........................Local ( )   Network (**X**)   Sustaining ( )
Commercial (**X**)

SPONSOR (if commercial):....**Various**

DATE(S) AND TIME(S) OF PERFORMANCE*............**October 11, 1956**

PLACE OF PERFORMANCE: **CBS Theatres or Studios in Los Angeles, California**

AFTRA CLASSIFICATION:....**Actor**

PART(S) TO BE PLAYED:.............

COMPENSATION: ..**$7,500.00**

REHEARSALS*

Date	From	To	Place	Date	From	To	Place

Reasonable time and hours to be determined by Producer.

Execution of this agreement signifies acceptance by Producer and Performer of all of the above terms and conditions and those on the reverse hereof and attached hereto, if any.

CBS TELEVISION
A Division of Columbia Broadcasting System, Inc.

By............

....
Performer

....
Telephone Number

....
Social Security Number

*Subject to change in accordance with AFTRA Code.

T1 IH1 3-56 - F359

ABOVE: **Alvin Ganzer directs Ernest Truex in a scene from "What You Need."** LEFT: **Page 1 of Ed Wynn's signed contract from Rod Serling's poignant** *Playhouse 90*, **"Requiem For a Heavyweight."**

On the cusp of the series' core writing team is Earl Hamner Jr., an exceptional writer who christened his Hollywood career by penning eight scripts for *The Twilight Zone*, beginning in the third season. Hamner's distinct storytelling ranges from tales of wonderful country folk to comeuppance dished out to city dwellers. Hamner was indeed influenced by a Virginia mountain background (he

LEFT: **Mary Badham stars with Georgia Simmons in "The Bewitchin' Pool."**
CENTER: **Monty Pittman enjoys a friendly kiss from actress Elizabeth Montgomery, on the set of his episode, "Two."**
RIGHT: **Actor Jackie Cooper poses with puppet Caesar and a property master on the set of "Caesar and Me."**

is best known as the creator of *The Waltons*), at a time when fathers and grand-fathers sat on the porch after dinner, spinning colorful Southern legends and country tales of glorious raccoon hunts.

However, his background has also pigeonholed him over the years as a spin-ner of such country tales, ignoring his full body of work and his association with *The Twilight Zone*. Hamner does have a knack for that folksy style of story-telling, as he illustrated with his first *Twilight Zone* episode, "The Hunt," starring Arthur Hunnicutt and Jeanette Nolan in a tale of a hillbilly on a raccoon hunt gone wrong. "The Hunt" offers a comforting departure from the common suburban and metropolian settings, marking Earl Hamner Jr.'s entrance into the fifth dimension as a spirited, soulful writer.

With his second script, "A Piano in the House," starring Barry Morse and Joan Hackett, Hamner took a 180-degree turn from the folk theme in the story of a pretentious theater critic who gets his comeuppance through a magical player piano that brings out the hidden personalities of its listeners. With his next episode, "Jess-Belle," starring James Best, Anne Francis, Jeanette Nolan, and Laura Devon, Hamner returned to the folksy theme in a dark tale of black magic and the lengths a woman will go to win the heart of her man. "Jess-Belle" is one of the few fourth-season episodes that work in the hour-long format, featuring another of Hamner's early Virginia influences, the art of inserting song into sto-rytelling. Following this, his sole 60-minute episode, Hamner's remaining scripts were all written for the fifth season: "Ring-a-Ding Girl," "You Drive," "Black Leather Jackets," and "Stopover in a Quiet Town," Hamner's most memorable *Zone* contribution. Similar in tone to the series' pilot episode, "Where Is Everybody?" "Stopover in a Quiet Town" features a couple who wake up hun-gover in a stranger's house with no memory of how they got there. As they investigate the house and then the town, not only do they find the town devoid of any people, but they hear the laughter of an unseen little girl, and also find evidence that the town is suspiciously fake. Their discovery at the end makes this episode a fan favorite. Unfortunately, Hamner's final contribution, "The Bewitchin' Pool," closes out the series on a misshapen note. Starring Mary Badham, of the classic film *To Kill a Mockingbird*, the episode addresses the sensitive subject matter of children coping with their parents' divorce. Here, the kids escape their squabbling parents through a magical portal in their swimming pool, emerging in a warm country setting right out of *Huckleberry Finn*. Critically speaking, this plot device seems a bit corny, and ends up detracting from the more serious subject of divorce. In spite of this one episode, Earl Hamner Jr.'s soulful and sometimes harsh looks at the human spirit complement the works of the other core writers, making him a pivotal creator of *The Twilight Zone*.

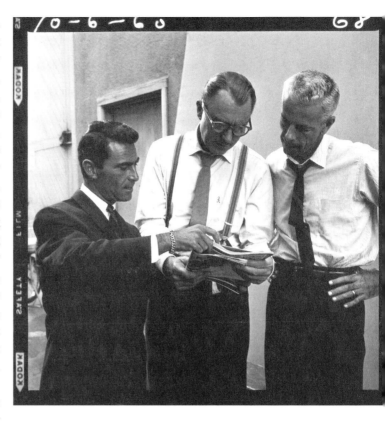

Rod Serling, actor Brian Aherne, and producer Buck Houghton reading a review of the series.

Amid the episodes created by the core writing team are groups of scripts supplied by various outside writers. Among these writers are Montgomery Pittman, who wrote and directed "Two," "The Grave," and "The Last Rites of Jeff Myrtle-bank," and Martin M. Goldsmith, who wrote two fifth-season episodes, "The Encounter" and "What's in the Box." Other writing contributions include the single episodes of E. Jack Neuman's "The Trouble with Templeton," Robert Presnell Jr.'s "The Chaser," John Furia Jr.'s "I Dream of Genie," Jerry McNeely's "The Self-Improvement of Salvadore Ross," Bernard C. Shoenfeld's "From Agnes — With Love," A.T. Strassfield's "Caesar and Me," and Anthony Wilson's "Come Wander with Me." Also featured was the remake of Reginald Rose's *Studio One* teleplay, "The Incredible World of Horace Ford," and Robert Enrico's short French film "An Occurrence at Owl Creek Bridge."

What made a good *Twilight Zone* episode was a good story. The level of storytelling in the series was made possible by the balance of quality scripts and the process that resulted in a finished product. The position of producer would later switch hands a few times, but it all started after the production of the pilot, "Where Is Everybody?," when CBS executive producer William Self connected Rod Serling with producer Buck Houghton. After sampling a few of Serling's scripts, Houghton recognized the quality of the work and agreed to sign on as producer for the series. Houghton performed many of the behind-the-scenes responsibilities, most of which entailed transferring the work from script into

Buck Houghton and actor Dean Jagger take a break during the taping of "Static."

film. His tasks ranged from securing the MGM studio facilities to purchasing scripts outside of Serling's work, overseeing the casting of actors, editing, scoring, and just about everything else. Houghton became an integral balance to Serling, helping to shape the inner workings of the series. Whereas Serling understood how to write good stories, Houghton understood the intricacies of production and how to make things come together. The two men complemented each other, contributing to the quality and longevity of *The Twilight Zone*. In fact, looking at the series in its entirety, it's obvious that the first three seasons were by far the best and most consistent years of production.

Buck Houghton started as a reader for feature-film director Val Lewton, then as a story editor for David O. Selznick, which gave him the chance to work with Lewton again at RKO. There he was involved in the production of *The Curse of the Cat People* (the sequel to *Cat People*), and two pictures starring Boris Karloff, *The Body Snatcher* and *Bedlam*. After his work at RKO, Houghton landed a job at MGM working with William Self, as the story editor for *Schlitz Playhouse of Stars*, a prominent anthology show of the Golden Age of Television. Houghton then produced a myriad of detective shows such as *China Smith*, *Wire Service*, *Meet McGraw*, the western *Yancy Derringer*, and *Man with a Camera*, which starred Charles Bronson as an ex-combat photographer. At the suggestion of Self, Houghton hired a few associates of *Schlitz Playhouse of Stars* to work on *The Twilight Zone*: Ralph Nelson as production manager, and George T. Clemens as director of photography.

With the first season, both Serling and Houghton set a standard for storytelling, to ensure that every episode remained consistent with the flavor of *The Twilight Zone*. In his book *What a Producer Does*, Houghton discusses the guidelines they created: "*The Twilight Zone* was shaped by Rod Serling. In his first few scripts his instincts led him to a pattern that he and I agreed upon as the bottom-line basis for buying stories for adaptation and for his own originals. That pattern became the rigid standard by which I did my judgmental work on story submittals." These guidelines included:

> Find an interesting character, or a group, at a moment in crisis in life, and get there quickly; then lay on some magic. That magic must be devilishly appropriate and capable of providing a whiplash kickback at the tag. The character(s) must be ordinary and average and modern, and the problem facing him (her, them) must be commonplace. *The Twilight Zone* always struck people as identifiable as to whom it was about, and the story hang-ups as resonant as their own fears, dreams, wishes. Allow only one miracle or special talent or imaginative circumstance per episode.

More than one and the audience grows impatient with your calls on their credibility. The story must be impossible in the real world. A request at some point to suspend disbelief is a trademark of the series. Mere scare tactics will not fill the bill. A clever bit of advanced scientific hardware is not enough to support a story. *The Twilight Zone* was not a sci-fi show.

During production of the 35 episodes of the first season, Houghton worked with Serling to perfect the scripts, and with casting directors Mildred Gusse and John Erman to ensure access to the best acting talents of the time. As a third element of production, Houghton met with Clemens and Serling to discuss which directors to hire. *The Twilight Zone* was to become a highlight for a select group of accomplished directors who worked on a wide assortment of Hollywood pictures and classic television series, including *Outer Limits*, *Green Acres*, *Gunsmoke*, and *Playhouse 90*. The team's top choices were Mitchell Leisen, Richard Bare, John Brahm, and Douglas Heyes, followed later by Buzz Kulik, Ted Post, Don Medford, Lamont Johnson, Richard Donner, and others. Houghton contacted the head of the CBS's West Coast music department, Lud Gluskin, who offered the expertise of composers versed in writing music for television, film, and radio such as Bernard Herrmann, Jerry Goldsmith, Fred Steiner, and Van Cleave. With these talented directors and composers, the dimension of both sight and sound were made complete.

By the end of season one's production in April 1960, this combination of production elements paid off with good ratings and several awards. Houghton won a Producers Guild Award for Best Produced Series, while Serling earned an Emmy Award for writing (his fourth Emmy to date), and Bantam Books published *Stories from The Twilight Zone*, Serling's first book of adaptations of some of his first episodes. The best news came on May 11, 1960, when CBS announced *The Twilight Zone* had been picked up for another season. The series had survived its first vital season and, even though ratings weren't through the roof, it had already started to attract a loyal audience.

LEFT TO RIGHT: **Mitchell Leisen directs actress Ida Lupino (off-camera) in "The Sixteen-Millimeter Shrine."**

Buzz Kulik directs actors Brian Aherne, Pippa Scott, and Charles S. Carlson in a scene from "The Trouble with Templeton."

Director Don Medford and actor Joseph Schildkraut on the set of "Death's-Head Revisited."

Abner Biberman directs actress' Collin Wilcox and Suzy Parker in "Number Twelve Looks Just like You."

The *Twilight Zone* crew proudly smiles for the camera during the show's third season.

The second season began on September 30, 1960, with Buck Houghton still behind the reins of production, yet with only 29 episodes on the schedule.

By the end of season two, the fan base had grown, George T. Clemens had won an award for Outstanding Achievement in Cinematography for Television, and Serling had his second Emmy for his writing on *The Twilight Zone*. By season three, which began airing on September 15, 1961, sponsors had changed a few times and Serling was fatigued from the intense amount of writing he had taken on, but Houghton remained on board and *The Twilight Zone* was reaching pop-culture status. This season saw the production of 37 episodes, with such highlights as "The Midnight Sun," "It's a Good Life," and "To Serve Man." Yet, following the airing of the season's last episode, in spring of 1962, there was still no sponsor for the series' upcoming fourth season. As a result, *The Twilight Zone* was not included in the fall CBS schedule; in its place was a new series, *Fair Exchange*. Buck Houghton was pressured to accept an offer to work for Four Star Productions and Rod Serling accepted a writing position at Antioch College in Ohio, from September 1962 to January 1963. By the time CBS decided to bring *The Twilight Zone* back mid-season that January, Houghton had already been working on *The Richard Boone Show* and Serling was engaged in teaching, enjoying his break from the stress of the series. The team of Serling and Houghton had seen its final days, and the magic of the series would slowly diminish during its last two seasons.

The production of the fourth season saw some distinct changes, the inconsequential one being the title change from *The Twilight Zone* to *Twilight Zone*. The more unusual change was that since *Twilight Zone* was scheduled as a mid-season replacement, only 18 episodes were slotted, and these were increased to an hour each. This would prove to be a mistake, as *The Twilight Zone* always worked well because of its pacing in the half-hour, two-act format. Only a few of the hour-long episodes work, while the rest just seem to drag. With Buck Houghton gone, Herbert Hirschman accepted the new role as producer, on the recommendation of both Houghton and Serling. Hirschman was no stranger to the industry, having worked as a director, associate producer, and story editor for *Playhouse 90*, as well as producing shows like *Perry Mason*, *Hong Kong*, and *Dr. Kildare*.

He came into *Twilight Zone* at a time when it was going through changes, but he adapted well, as his approach was to maintain what the remaining team had established. While Serling was in Antioch, teaching, writing *Twilight Zone* scripts, and adapting *Seven Days in May* for the big screen, Hirschman was procuring other scripts and discussing work with Serling by phone. Since Hirschman had directorial experience, he proved valuable by directing retakes himself rather than bringing the directors back on set. When he was in Los Angeles for other business, Hirschman directed the filming of Serling's on-camera narrations at the studio, in front of a nondescript gray background. Hirschman also designed and directed the new main title sequence, having supervised the making of the props as well as the idea of floating them in space. Regardless of how he adapted to this midstream production, Hirschman's contract with CBS expired at the beginning of 1963, and he was asked to produce the spy drama *Espionage*. Since this series was going to be made in London, England, Hirschman found this an inviting adventure and took the job.

Replacing Hirschman mid-season was Bert Granet, who had produced "The Time Element." In a sense, Granet was truly the guy who started *The Twilight Zone* in the first place; it's only fitting he was brought back into the series. Early on, Granet had worked as a writer and producer for countless films, including *The Locket*; later he produced television shows such as *Westinghouse Desilu Playhouse*, *The Untouchables*, and *The Invaders*. Granet finished up the fourth season of *Twilight Zone* during the spring of 1963, when CBS was just renewing *Twilight Zone* for a fifth season. The good news was that CBS was going to bring *Twilight Zone* back at its original half-hour format. The bad news was the series was beginning to tap itself out. By the fifth-season premiere, which aired on September 27, 1963, *Twilight Zone* had lost several of its most essential talents. Houghton was gone, some of the directors were gone, and at this point, Rod

Rod Serling clowns around on the set of "Mr. Bevis."

Actor Richard Basehart, director Ted Post (in baseball cap), and crew during the filming of "Probe 7 — Over and Out." Unfortunately, Probe 7 isn't the only crashed ship; just a few months later, the series failed to be renewed for a sixth season.

Serling was exhausted from writing for the series. He admitted he was burned-out and knew he was not only repeating earlier stories, but that he just couldn't tell good from bad anymore. Bert Granet persevered until, with half of the season produced and the remaining episodes in development, he too was offered a job he couldn't refuse.

William Froug, hired to replace Granet, began his role producing, with his first *Twilight Zone* episode to air, "The Last Night of a Jockey," featuring a larger-than-life performance by Mickey Rooney. Like the other producers for the series, Froug's expertise was impressive. He had worked as a writer for *The Dick Powell Show* and *Adventures in Paradise*, and would later write for *Charlie's Angels*. He produced episodes of *Playhouse 90*, and later *Bewitched* and *Gilligan's Island*. Froug brought a new perspective to working on *Twilight Zone* and Serling reciprocated by having him leave behind several scripts Granet had in development and start with new material. Froug cleverly bought the rights to Robert Enrico's short French film *An Occurrence at Owl Creek Bridge* for $10,000. As the only outside film produced for the series, it had been a winner at the Cannes Film Festival and went on to win an Oscar. For use in *Twilight Zone*, *Occurrence*. was shortened by a few minutes and given a special introduction by Serling.

By late January 1964, even though the show's ratings were moderately good, the CBS fall schedule did not include *Twilight Zone*. CBS president Jim Aubrey was tired of the show and felt the ratings weren't good enough to justify renewal of the series. In the February issue of *Daily Variety*, it was reported that Serling felt doubtful the series would be renewed for a sixth season, and was quoted as saying, "I decided to cancel the network."

CHAPTER THREE

Themes of The Zone

"I can describe any character at all . . . and by now, if I describe it well enough, completely enough, the character will come to life, real life."

— Gregory West of
"A World of His Own"

Actors Burgess Meredith and Fritz Weaver star in Rod Serling's potent episode, "The Obsolete Man."

From a psychological point of view, *The Twilight Zone* is a venture into the vast human psyche, one that delves deep into both the capacities and frailties of our makeup. It may be that in the reality of our third dimension, we humans perceive ourselves as powerful beings in control of our own destinies, but underneath the masks of illusion and time, we're as weak and lost as any other animal. *The Twilight Zone* essentially portrays man as a creature tempted by fate's darker side, ultimately outweighing his capacity for humility and potential for prosperity. The psychological dynamics of *The Twilight Zone*'s characters in turn mirror the human condition in its many themes and episodes. What follows is a catalog of those themes.

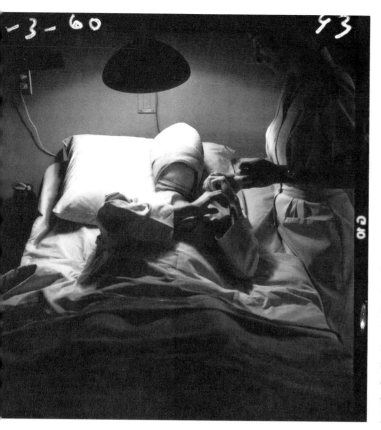

Actress Maxine Stuart stars in what is considered Serling's best episode, "The Eye of the Beholder." Stuart played her entire part under the bandages of her character Janet Tyler, and even though we're unable to see the expressions of her face, her performance is absolutely remarkable. Notice in this shot (not in the film), the nurse, played by Jennifer Howard, is seen without her "makeup."

The Individual

The theme of the individual is most notable in Rod Serling's powerful social critique, "The Obsolete Man," starring veteran actors Burgess Meredith and Fritz Weaver. This episode is a perfect example of *The Twilight Zone*'s recipe of ironic fate served with a twist. In the harsh reality of a future totalitarian state, along the lines of George Orwell's *1984*, Meredith plays timid librarian and part-time philosopher Romney Wordsworth. Weaver is the Chancellor who judges Wordsworth, standing arrogantly behind an ominous podium, symbolizing the supposed strength of the state. Through a trial, Wordsworth is deemed useless to the state, found obsolete, and is to be put to death. But in a surprising about-face, he uses the opportunity to illustrate that the state itself is obsolete. Serling's summation finds that "any state, any entity, any ideology that fails to recognize the worth, the dignity, the rights of man, that state is obsolete." Serling's "The Obsolete Man" is regarded as a "top *Zone*." Even though it's overshadowed by the more popular Meredith episode, "Time Enough at Last," the underlying theme of "The Obsolete Man" has immeasurable strength that speaks more to the soul of individuality.

In the *Twilight Zone* universe, there are several examples of alienated individuals whose very existence deviates from an underlying norm of conformity. Most pointed is Serling's " The Eye of the Beholder" (also shown with its working title, "A Private World of Darkness"). In this remarkably dark tale, we see a society where ugliness is considered a threat to the totalitarian state. Amid a superb cast, actress Maxine Stuart plays Janet Tyler, an outcast woman hospitalized for ongoing operations to her disfigured-yet-bandaged face. Here, during her eleventh and final operation allowed by the state, we find the doctor, played by William Gordon, sympathetic to her situation, although wary of Big Brother's watchful eyes. The perspective of the camera is constantly just shy of showing the identity of the doctor and nurses attending Miss Tyler. As the story progresses, a cold, haunting feeling emerges as we realize just how little of the surroundings we're seeing, and the twist at the end tells us exactly why the episode was directed in this style. Seen as a predecessor to the fifth-season episode "Number Twelve Looks Just Like You," "The Eye of the Beholder" stands out as what many consider the best episode of the series, and a perfect episode with which to introduce new fans to the show.

LEFT: **Actress Inger Stevens and Leonard Strong star in Serling's haunting episode, "The Hitch-Hiker."** RIGHT: **Richard Long and Pam Austin star in John Tomerlin's (credited to Charles Beaumont) "Number Twelve Looks Just Like You."** *A glass of Instant Smile for everybody!*

Death and Dying

Besides shocking us with ironic tales of fate, comeuppance, and the second chance, *The Twilight Zone* dealt in deeply layered themes exploring the human condition. This is present in many stories, to the point that the writers seemed in a conspiracy to fill our very idiot boxes with lessons on life. And no other lesson about man's existence in the universe makes the point quite so personally as the theme of death and dying. Unforgettable tales such as "The Hitchhiker," "Long Live Walter Jameson," and "Nothing in the Dark" remind us that we must eventually face the realization that we're all born to die. We can deny the truth and think we can cheat death, attempt to run away from it, or hide in the shadows, but eventually we must come to the soothing understanding that nothing lasts forever.

The Twilight Zone deals with death in a direct and honest fashion, sometimes it's with a gentle spirituality, other times ironically cruel, even mischievous, in a hellish chill devoid of warmth. We find death does come in many forms. The urban legend "The Hitchhiker," written by Serling and based on a 1941 Mercury Theatre radio play that featured Orson Welles, stars Inger Stevens as Nan Adams and Leonard Strong as the mysterious hitchhiker. The story begins with a mechanic, played by Lew Gallo, fixing a flat tire on Adams' car. This opening includes a line that offers a hidden lead-in clue to the story's final twist, illustrating that the dialogue could so subtly give away the ending in the very beginning of an episode, yet be so well-written that the audience remains oblivious until the ending. From this moment on in the story, during her drive out west, the woman constantly passes the same hitchhiker over and over again. Somehow he always seems to be ahead of her to the next town, hauntingly asking, "Going my way?" Every time he suddenly appears, it sends chills down your spine, but in the episode's revealing ending, we realize the hitchhiker isn't the menacing masher Adams feared he was.

Instead of the usual portrayal of death as a dark, dreary unknown, *The Twilight Zone* describes the angel of death as a sometimes-redeeming figure. There are two other *Zone* episodes that utilize this tone, "One for the Angels," written by Serling and starring Ed Wynn as fun-loving pitchman Lew Bookman and Murray Hamilton as the diligent figure of Death, and "Nothing in the Dark," written by George Clayton Johnson and starring Gladys Cooper as Wanda Dunn, the elderly woman, and none other than Robert Redford as Officer Harold Beldon. These two episodes follow suit with "The Hitchhiker," in that death is portrayed not as a dreadful end, but instead a warm beginning.

With "One for the Angels," Death is sort of a bookkeeper, here to meet the deadline on his list of those next to die. Bookman first tricks Death into not taking him, but this leads to Death having to take someone else in his place. Bookman is forced to make the pitch of a lifetime, which tests his waning skills. In "Nothing in the Dark," old lady Dunn hides in the cold basement shadows of a condemned tenement building, fearing that Death is a changeling, soon to come for her. For someone who loved living in the warmth of the sun, this is a terrible way to live out the last chapter of her life, but to Wanda, it's better to live like this than not at all. When wounded policeman Beldon tumbles down to her front door and asks for help, she is wary of trusting anyone for fear he may be Death, but she takes him in and rests him on her bed. Surprised that she still lives and convinced he's not Death, she confides in him, telling him how she has witnessed the agent of death taking people, even right in front of her on the bus. What the old woman doesn't know, but will soon find out, is that death isn't the frightening state she thinks it is, and Beldon will soon show her that death can be just the beginning of a new phase of eternity.

These few episodes do offer optimistic looks at death, but not all depictions of death and the afterlife in *The Twilight Zone* come with such forgiving comfort. The Devil never sleeps in "A Nice Place to Visit," written by Charles Beaumont, whose small-time thief Rocky Valentine finds this out for himself. Beaumont's story makes one think about what heaven and hell might be for each of us — we may think we know how we want to spend eternity, but have we really considered just how long eternity is, and whether we want to be doing the

CASTING CALL SHEET

MGM FORM 521

Todays date ___3/1/60___

METRO-GOLDWYN-MAYER PICTURES
CULVER CITY CALIFORNIA

· Page one of _____ pages   TWILIGHT ZONE SERIES

PROD. __3632TV__   DIRECTOR __J. BRAHM__   TITLE __"A NICE PLACE TO VISIT"__

CALL IS FOR – DAY __WEDNESDAY__   DATE __3/2/60__

WEATHER CONDITIONS: ___R or S___

		SCS.	LOC.
1ST SET	INT. LIVING ROOM	25	#15
2ND SET	INT. APT. HALLWAY (N)	50	"
3RD SET	INT . APT. (N)	57 thru 62	"
4TH SET	INT . GAMBLING CASINO (N)	30 thru 41	"
5TH SET	INT. GAMBLING CASINO (N)	54-55-56	"
6TH SET	TRAILER WITH ROD SERLING (N)		"
7TH SET			
8TH SET			
9TH SET			
10TH SET			

CALLED	NAME	CHARACTER – WARDROBE	GATE	MKUP	WARD	SET
X	SABASTIAN CABOT	MR. PIP		9:30a		10am
X	LARRY BLYDEN	ROCKY		9am		9:30
C	SANDRA WARNER	BEAUTIFUL GIRL		8am		"
C	PETER HORNSBY	CRAP DEALER		11:30a		12:30
C	WAYNE TUCKER	CROUPIER			"	"
C	ROD SERLING	NARRATOR	TIME LATER			
	ATMOS					
X	2 WOMEN	AS RECALLED		9:30am		
C	3 WOMEN	DRESS EXTRAS		11:30am		
C	12 MEN (35 to 55)	DRESS EXTRAS		11:30am		
X	1 WOMEN	AS SELECTED		8:30am		
C	2 WOMEN	AS SELECTED		8:30am		
	STANDINS					
X	2 MEN	AS RECALLED		9am		

CODE – "X" – INDICATES COMPANY HAS NOTIFIED. – "C" CASTING MUST CALL.

SPECIAL NOTES: _____

TIME OF YEAR _____   COLOR _____ B & W

ASST. DIR. __D. Klune/W.Jones__   UNIT MGR. __R. Nelson__

3pm/sue

Actors Lee Marvin and Lee Van Cleef star in Montgomery Pittman's episode, "The Grave."

same thing forever? This episode features one of the series' most memorable dialogue twists, and an incredible, over-the-top evil laugh by Sebastian Cabot that will give you goose bumps.

Another such heaven-and-hell episode is Earl Hamner Jr.'s backwoods tale, "The Hunt," starring Arthur Hunnicutt as hillbilly Hyder Simpson and Jeanette Nolan as his superstitious wife Rachael. "The Hunt" is one of those episodes easily remembered by average television viewers, along with other such pivotal episodes as "Time Enough at Last" and "The Invaders."

Though not regarded as a ghost-story series, *The Twilight Zone* did delve into this theme several times. From the recently dead, to the dying, to those refusing to accept death, the subject is covered pretty well. This could be attributed to Serling's firsthand experiences with death while he was serving as a paratrooper in WWII, and the fact that most men in his family died at an early age. The most prominent ghost stories include "The Grave," "The Passersby," "Night Call," "Come Wander with Me," "The Thirty-Fathom Grave," and the underrated "Ring-a-Ding Girl." Episodes featuring characters unwilling to accept death include "Long Live Walter Jameson," "The Trade-Ins," and "An Occurrence at Owl Creek Bridge."

In "Long Live Walter Jameson," veteran actor Kevin McCarthy, best remembered for the cult classic *Invasion of the Body Snatchers*, plays immortal history professor Walter Jameson. This Charles Beaumont masterpiece touches on the verity of man's mortality, as Jameson comes to realize, through thousands of years of living as an immortal, that the quantity of one's existence doesn't necessarily outweigh its quality.

In Serling's script "The Trade-Ins," starring Joseph Schildkraut and Alma Platt as elderly couple John and Marie Holt, prolonging one's life comes easily with a technology that transfers the mind and soul into a new, young body. Suffering from an agonizing illness and with enough money for only one transfer, they decide John should go ahead and undergo the surgery first. It isn't until after his surgery, and while in residence in his new body, that the shocking truth of the age difference now between them breaks Marie's heart, prompting John to make a sacrifice for her. Of the few *Twilight Zone* love stories, this one hits home in dealing with the lengths we'll go just to hang on to life. For sentient creatures governed by both science and divine law, who's to say whether cheating death isn't in itself unnatural? And could one really trust technology well enough to believe it able to differentiate between mind, body, and soul? Ultimately, the episode seems to suggest that it's logical to accept the course of nature rather than prolonging life's path.

Mob Mentality

Delving even deeper into the soul of the human condition, *The Twilight Zone* taps into the darkest recesses of mankind's unkind ways, examining bigotry and mob mentality. Take, for instance, the paranoid neighbors who so blindly turn

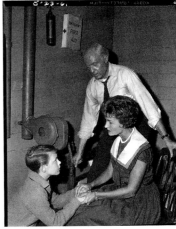

against each other in another of Serling's key episodes, "The Monsters Are Due on Maple Street." Starring Claude Akins and Jack Weston, this episode is an honest representation of how easily we can become bigoted, much like "frightened little rabbits." A similar Serling episode, "The Shelter," which aired during the Cuban missile crisis, stars Larry Gates, Peggy Stewart, Jack Albertson, and Sandy Kenyon as neighborhood friends attending a birthday party. When they learn of an impending missile attack and fight for entry into the only fallout shelter on their block, fear takes hold quickly, tearing at their friendships. In the final moments, they discover that what they've done to each other is far more destructive than what a bomb could do.

A more literal example of man's darker side is the often-misunderstood Serling script, "I Am the Night — Color Me Black," starring Michael Constantine, Paul Fix, George Lindsey, Terry Becker, and Ivan Dixon. In a backwoods small town where the morning sky remains in darkness, the murderer of a bigot faces execution for his crime. After the hanging, this mysterious darkness, fueled by the murderer's and the townsfolk's hatred, intensifies, and appears across other bigoted areas of the world. These morality plays teach us to understand and respect the diversity and rights of the individual, and to observe life not through blinders that obscure perception and truth, but through an optimism that the sooner we learn to truly come together, the better off we'll be. Yet there is an overpowering weakness in our nature that holds us back — a primitive part

LEFT: **Terry Burnham, Shepperd Strudwick, and the wonderful Janice Rule star in the chilling psychological drama, "Nightmare as a Child." Rule's character Helen Foley was named after Serling's own middle-school English teacher.**
CENTER: **Christine White, Dane Clark, Jane Burgess and Buddy Ebsen star in "The Prime Mover."**
RIGHT: **Actor/comedian Shelley Berman stars in the comedy "The Mind and the Matter." Serling wrote this episode specifically for Berman.**

of the brain designed to protect our basic territorial needs, and unfortunately one that also hinders our evolving into a civilized people.

The Human Psyche

By exploring the human psyche, *The Twilight Zone* addresses the struggle of man's conscience by allowing the inner self to surface and resume the role of the individual. Sometimes presented as another form of the second chance, the strength of the conscience is explored in episodes such as the unnerving "Nervous Man in a Four Dollar Room," starring an anxiety-ridden Joe Mantell, in "Nightmare as a Child," featuring the wonderful Janice Rule, and even in "King Nine Will Not Return," starring Robert Cummings. These stories offer opportunities for the better inner self to take over, or to simply open the eyes and perception of the soul. However, it's not always for the best, as in the case of "The Last Night of a Jockey," starring Mickey Rooney as a jockey whose only wish is to be big, and boy, does he get his wish.

On the other side of the psyche coin, delusions of grandeur run rampant in wicked stories like "The Little People," starring Claude Akins and Joe Maross, and "Four O'Clock," starring Theodore Bikel. In these psychological tales, if a character's psyche has gone over the edge, a psychoanalytical character is often introduced to help rationalize things. With reason and logic at hand, it's easy to assume what's going on is simply a delusion, illusion, identity crisis, or some such other rational occurrence.

In these limitless powers of the mind, we see secondary themes of mental breakdown, telepathy, mind over matter, and the mysterious world of the dream state. Considered one of *Twilight Zone* writer George Clayton Johnson's special-ties, the powers of telekinesis and telepathy find their way into episodes such as "A Penny for Your Thoughts," starring Dick York, and "The Prime Mover," starring Dane Clark, Buddy Ebsen, and Christine White. There's also Richard Matheson's "Mute," starring Frank Overton, Barbara Baxley, and a young Ann Jillian, and even Serling's "What You Need," starring tough guy Steve Cochran and Ernest Truex. These episodes look at some of man's untapped powers of the mind, questioning what it would be like to hear the thoughts of those around you or to move objects with a mere thought. We've heard how science has measured the energy of one person's mind, and that a single brain has enough power to light an entire city. Imagine the limitless powers that have gone untapped and the abilities we've overlooked in ourselves.

No other episode portrays this theme more succinctly and brilliantly than Serling's "The Mind and the Matter," starring actor-comedian Shelley Berman. Specifically written with Berman in mind, "The Mind and the Matter" tells the story of how one misanthropic man gains insight into the ultimate powers of concentration from the pages of a book. With his newfound ability to concentrate, Achibald Beechcroft first wishes his landlady away, and then continues until everyone is gone. As Beechcroft becomes bored and lonely, he learns something about his fellow man, but is it too late?

Just as *The Twilight Zone* offers stories on the limitless powers of the mind, it also explores how the mysteries of the fifth dimension can sometimes be too much for the primal stability of the psyche to handle. Enter the mental break-down, which was established in the show's very first episode, "Where Is Everybody?" starring Earl Holliman as Mike Ferris in a town that appears to have been abandoned. In what Ferris jokes must be an unbelievably detailed nightmare, he goes from one empty building to the next, unable to shake the feel-ing that he's being watched. Fearing he may be the last man alive, the pressure mounts until he frantically breaks down at a traffic light, pushing the button of a crosswalk over and over again, an action that brings forth the twist ending, and finally explains why Ferris is all alone. Other mental-breakdown episodes include "One More Pallbearer," "The New Exhibit," and "Sounds and Silences."

As a sub-theme to the mental breakdown, the series explores the identity cri-sis in "A World of Difference," starring Howard Duff, and "Person or Persons Unknown," starring Richard Long. Long plays David Gurney, a man who awakens one morning to a reality where everyone in his life, including his wife and coworkers, have no idea who he is. Gurney struggles to regain his identity, escapes from being institutionalized, and again awakens as if it were only a dream. But once awake, he's met with a greater horror that twists his identity crisis even further.

Obviously, things are not always as they appear, particularly in a dimension where dreams and nightmares invade the glowing rays emitted into your family room. Within the vast surreal imagination and the peculiar recesses of the sub-

Actor Howard Duff stars in one of the series' most intense identity crisis episodes, "A World of Difference."

conscious mind, the dream state contains shifts of inner perception, and a perspective that pits reality against a dream world. As philosophers have speculated, who's to say if reality is what it appears to be? Maybe there's something more to our dream state than science understands. In *The Twilight Zone*, when things appear to start out "normal," we sometimes find we've lived through someone's endless nightmare. These stories certainly make it difficult to determine where the line between reality and unreality resides.

The series visits this question in episodes such as "Shadow Play," featuring a brilliant performance by Dennis Weaver, "Perchance to Dream," starring a feverish Richard Conte, and Serling's burning tale of "The Midnight Sun," starring Lois Nettleton. Television never seemed so surreal and terrifying as it does with Weaver's portrayal of convict Adam Grant, who must live the same dream of being executed, night after night after night, or with Conte's hypnotizing turn as Edward Hall, who must stay awake for fear of dying from his nightmares (a concept Charles Beaumont developed long before the days of Freddy Krueger). Conte's performance in "Perchance to Dream" is almost enough to make you fear going to sleep at night, no matter how sultry Suzanne Lloyd's Maya the Cat Girl may be.

Two dream-state episodes that also fall under the theme of the second chance are Serling's classic "A Stop at Willoughby," starring James Daly and Howard Smith, and "Twenty-Two," starring Barbara Nichols, Jonathan Harris, and Fredd Wayne. With these stories, we see that through the dream state, characters are able to gain insight and the means to escape their dreadful fates.

Supernatural Ability

The characters of the *Zone* are indeed unique, and some possess mental abilities stretching even farther into what the mind can accomplish. Take, for instance, the mind-powered character in "A World of His Own," Gregory West, played by Keenan Wynn. West, a playwright, has the ability to describe the characters in his plays into a tape recorder so well that they come to life. Think of the power that suggests — one could simply create the people in one's life exactly how one thinks they should be. However, West finds

LEFT: **Burgess Meredith stars as librarian Romney Wordsworth (a Serling character name that plays on the *worth of words*), in "The Obsolete Man." Meredith had an obvious knack for playing bookworm characters, as he also played Henry Bemis in "Time Enough at Last."** RIGHT: **Keenan Wynn stars in "A World of His Own." Wynn also starred with his father Ed Wynn in Serling's *Playhouse 90* "Requiem for a Heavyweight." Ralph Nelson directed both "Requiem" and this episode.**

that those he creates can sometimes take on a will of their own. For this, the last episode to air in the first season, writer Richard Matheson had the brilliant idea to stretch West's powers even farther, and for the first time, Serling actually becomes part of the drama in a very tongue-in-cheek, postmodern ending.

Other supernatural-ability episodes include "The Self-Improvement of Salvadore Ross," written by Jerry McNeely and starring Don Gordon, Gail Kobe, and Vaughn Taylor; and "The Four of Us Are Dying," with a story by George Clayton Johnson and scripted by Serling, starring the stunning cast of Harry Townes, Ross Martin, Beverly Garland, Don Gordon, and Phillip Pine. Townes plays Arch Hammer, a con man with the ability to change the appearance of his face to look like anyone. By impersonating three men — a musician, a gangster, and a boxer — he's able to get the girl, the money, and a means of escaping some goons. But Hammer finds out the hard way that if something happens to one of his identities, it may affect them all.

Antisocial Behavior

Where "The Four of Us Are Dying" taught viewers to just be themselves, *The Twilight Zone* frowned upon being *by* yourself. Why socializing is important is best examined through bookworm Henry Bemis, from "Time Enough at Last." This is not to say that readers are antisocial, or that reading can't offer a great break, but Bemis takes it just a little too far. He's much more concerned with escaping reality by reading than he is with his duties as a bank clerk, husband,

or friend. This social misfit's only concern in life is to attain absolute solitude and enough time to do nothing but read. But in the fifth dimension, that's just asking for it. The lesson here is to acknowledge the basic human need for companionship — and make sure that if you have a serious vision problem, purchase a backup pair of reading glasses, just in case.

Two other episodes dealing with antisocial characters are "The Silence," starring Liam Sullivan as Tennyson, and "A Kind of Stopwatch," starring Richard Erdman as McNulty. Both Tennyson and McNulty are considered antisocial because they just don't know how to shut the hell up. They're loudmouths who boast about how to do things, yet are the last to accomplish anything themselves. But let's move on — I'm sure Tennyson doesn't want to talk about it, and McNulty's audience is completely frozen.

Malevolence

Comeuppance is the series' most potent form of retribution in dealing with characters who could be considered evil. This is demonstrated in such extremely powerful episodes as "Death's-Head Revisited," starring Joseph Schildkraut and Oscar Beregi, "Judgment Night," starring Nehemiah Persoff, "A Quality of Mercy," starring Dean Stockwell and Albert Salmi, and "He's Alive," starring Dennis Hopper. It's not surprising that Serling wrote all of these episodes, for one of his specialties was making Nazis and similarly evil characters pay for their atrocities.

Serling's social commentary in these episodes holds as strong a message against aggressive behavior today as it did in the 1960s. In the closing narration for one of the series' most heartrending episodes, "Death's-Head Revisited,"

Serling states why the concentration camps must remain standing, "because they are a monument to a moment in time when some men decided to turn the Earth into a graveyard. Into it they shoveled all of their reason, their logic, their knowledge, but worst of all, their conscience. And the moment we forget this, the moment we cease to be haunted by its remembrance, then we become the gravediggers." Upon rendering the sentence of insanity on former Captain Lutze, played by Oscar Beregi, Joseph Schildkraut's ghostly Dachau caretaker, Becker, gives this final statement on the subject: "This is not hatred, this is retribution. This is not revenge, this is justice. But this is only the beginning, Captain, only the beginning. Your final judgment will come from God."

With "A Quality of Mercy" and "Judgment Night," we witness two stories that maintain a similar tone about man's accountability for tormenting the innocent. With Dennis Hopper's neo-Nazi character Peter Vollmer from "He's Alive," we see how evil still inspires those ignorant enough to believe in segregation and the supposed purity of the white race.

Malevolence in *The Twilight Zone*, however prevalent in these few stories of Nazis and other evil-doers, is not confined to the militant-minded. We also find forms of evil in stories that deal with the Devil himself, such as "The Howling Man," "Printer's Devil," "Escape Clause," and "Of Late, I Think of Cliffordville." In these episodes, we learn that the Devil is not only evil and despicably crafty, but in some cases, can also have a heart. In "Escape

ABOVE: **A young Dennis Hopper stars as neo-Nazi Peter Vollmer in "He's Alive."**
LEFT: **Thomas Gomez and David Wayne star in the comedic episode, "Escape Clause."**

Clause," the Devil, played by Thomas Gomez and using the quirky name of Cadwallader, tricks hypochondriac Walter Bedeker (David Wayne) into exchanging his mortal soul for immortality. In a series of violent acts that challenge the limits of his newfound immortality, Bedeker eventually realizes the downside to eternal life, and the Devil steps in to spare him from his wretchedness. The same goes with Julie Newmar's Miss Devlin in "Of Late, I Think of Cliffordville," who regardless of her trickiness, still has a heart for her victim's plight. However, the Devil is not so easily mocked, as we find in "Printer's Devil" and the popular episode, "The Howling Man," in which H.M. Wynant plays David Ellington, a lost traveler who finds shelter in a mysterious monastery where the Devil himself is apparently imprisoned. With a flare for the dramatic, John Carradine plays Brother Jerome, the monastery's caretaker, who

TOP: **Julie Newmar has her devilish prosthetic horns applied by a makeup artist for "Of Late I Think of Cliffordville."**
BOTTOM: **Robin Hughes in his full Devil makeup in "The Howling Man." Beaumont was always opposed to this more literal representation of the devil.**

claims to have captured the Devil and locked him away with the Staff of Truth. This is one of the series' most visually dramatic episodes, directed by Douglas Heyes, who also directed such top episodes as "The Eye of the Beholder," "The Invaders," and "The After Hours." "The Howling Man" presents one of those rare occasions when the audience can actually share the uneasy feeling the main character is experiencing. If you suffer from motion sickness, you may want to take some Dramamine before you watch this episode.

Self-Destruction

Greed and corruption pervade episodes such as "The Fever," starring Everett Sloane and Vivi Janiss, in which hypocrite Franklin Gibbs falls for the very gambling bug he so intensely preaches against, and "The Rip Van Winkle Caper," starring Oscar Beregi and Simon Oakland. In this category, we also have "A Most Unusual Camera," starring Fred Clark and Jean Carson, which also falls under the enchanted-objects theme, and the previously mentioned telepathy-based episode, "What You Need." Episodes based on the theme of behavioral corruption include "The Silence" and "Queen of the Nile," starring Ann Blyth and Lee Philips.

Self-destruction is often brought on by tainted power, as in episodes like "I Shot an Arrow into the Air," starring Edward Binns and Dewey Martin; "The Arrival," starring Harold Stone and Fredd Wayne; "A Piano in the House," starring Barry Morse and Joan Hackett; and "Sounds and Silences," starring John McGiver and Penny Singleton. However, no episode drives home the behavior of self-destruction so well as the fourth-season hour-long episode, "On Thursday We Leave for Home," written by Serling and starring James Whitmore as Captain Benteen. A group of lost space colonists have been stranded on a dead asteroid for 30 years and are finally visited by a rescue ship to take them home to Earth. However, their leader, Captain Benteen, must let go of his control over them or face the consequences. The question is, can he?

Redemption

The series features several liberating stories of man's opportunity for redemption, proving that the Twilight Zone isn't just a place to punish the wicked and those who succumb to self-destruction. We find redeeming characters in such Serling classics as "Mr. Denton on Doomsday," "A Passage for Trumpet," "The Changing of the Guard," and even "Showdown with Rance McGrew." Through these characters, we see that if a person is receptive enough, there can be capacity for recovery and self-improvement. Of course, no one said surviving in society was going to be easy on any level, be it business, relationship, or otherwise. And as reality can be harsh, sometimes a person longs to return to the softened memories of the nostalgic past, when times were simpler and more slowly paced. Such is the case in reflective second-chance episodes like Richard Matheson's "Young Man's Fancy," Reginald Rose's "The Incredible World of Horace Ford," and

Serling's semi-autobiographical "Walking Distance." With "Young Man's Fancy," in which Alex Nicol's character, Alex, leaves a lovely bride behind to return to his childhood and the sheltering arms of his mother, we find the exception to the rule that one cannot go home again.

The opposite is true, of course, in the endearing top episode "Walking Distance." Here, Gig Young plays ad agency vice-president Martin Sloan, who one day escapes his stressful career in a drive that winds up at a service station outside of New York, within walking distance of Homewood, the small town where he grew up. Reminiscing about the innocence of his youth, he decides to walk to Homewood. Sloan visits his old neighborhood, which appears unchanged. Upon a visit to the park, he notices how things are exactly the same as when he was a kid. Remembering how he had carved his name in the post of the bandstand, he sees his younger self doing just that, and realizes he has actually returned to his childhood. But can he interact with the people of his youth, or will that cause a chain of events to take place? Or can Sloan come to appreciate living life to the fullest, humbled by the fact that a person has only one summer to live?

With a flavor reminiscent of the film *It's a Wonderful Life*, "Walking Distance" is by far one of the warmest examples of the second-chance theme, and of redemption. There are a few weaker redemption episodes, such as Serling's "Mr. Bevis," starring Orson Bean, Henry Jones, and Charles Lane, and "Cavender Is Coming," starring Carol Burnett and Jesse White. Both episodes boast marvelous casts, but fall way short of the bar, demonstrating that even with the help of "guardian angels" watching over a script, not all turkeys are just for Thanksgiving. With

LEFT: **Everett Sloane stars as hypocritical Frankin Gibbs in "The Fever."**
CENTER: **John McGiver stars in "Sounds and Silences."**
RIGHT: **James Whitmore stars in one of the fourth season's better episodes, "On Thursday We Leave for Home."**

"Passage on the Lady Anne," starring Lee Philips, Joyce Van Patten, and veteran English actors Gladys Cooper, Cecil Kellaway, and Wilfred Hyde-White, writer Charles Beaumont conveys that within the human spirit lies the power and perspective for a fresh start in life. We need not count on intangible beings from beyond to guide and shape life's meaning, whether these be angel, devil, or alien.

Alternate Universes

Although there is a vast variety of psychological subject matter in *The Twilight Zone*, the show is thought of as a fantasy series first and science fiction second. But while there are ample stories arranged in the genre of science fiction, one couldn't classify *The Twilight Zone* as a pure science fiction series, like *Star Trek*. *The Twilight Zone* is not considered a monster-fest either, like *Outer Limits*, which boasted a monster-of-the-week theme. Still, the series does delve into several science-fiction themes, such as other dimensions, parallel universes, time travel, space travel, and creatures both alien and monster. With *The Twilight Zone*, themes of fantasy and science fiction again disguise underlying questions of the human condition.

But *The Twilight Zone* does offer many fantastic rides beyond the unknown boundaries of both time and space. There are stories that feature dimensional portals, such as Richard Matheson's classic "Little Girl Lost," where we get an actual glimpse of the fifth dimension when an unknown portal opens in a little girl's bedroom wall. This story reminds us that our third dimension is the tangible separation between the second and fourth dimensions, but the fifth dimension quite surely exceeds the limits of science — which even today, we're still in the infancy

of understanding. In Earl Hamner Jr.'s "The Bewitchin' Pool," we find that dimensional portals in *The Twilight Zone* can lead to parallels of our own reality.

A more literal depiction of the parallel-universe theme appears in the appropriately named "The Parallel," written by Serling. In this episode, lone astronaut Robert Gaines, played by Steve Forrest, survives an experimental space mission. However, upon his return, he finds he's mysteriously crossed over into a universe parallel to his own. Vera Miles gives a downright paranoid performance as Millicent Barnes, in Serling's episode "Mirror Image," the eerie story of how a doppelgänger has crossed over from a parallel universe to invade her life. This story focuses on the possible outcomes of the theory of parallel universes — that for every action in our universe, there is an unlimited number of possible counter-reactions created in alternate universes, and for every person in our universe, there are counterparts in these other parallel universes. In "Mirror Image," Millicent comes to the conclusion that her double is trying to take over her life, yet she is unable to convince anyone else that she's not simply crazy. Reminiscent of *Invasion of the Body Snatchers*, this episode is an ideal example of how the series often touches on the alienation of individuals. *The Twilight Zone* tried to broaden our thinking about the scope of existence, showing us that there may be more to existence than what we assume.

Time Travel

No science-fiction idea twists the theoretical boundaries of science like that of traveling through the fourth dimension of time. Time travel is perhaps the one concept physicists have trouble grasping as a scientific possibility. However, in

LEFT: **Rod Serling brandishes a laser gun prop, another reuse from the film *Forbidden Planet*.** CENTER: **Burgess Meredith poses with Venusians Donald Losby and Greg Irvin, in the quirky "Mr. Dingle, the Strong."** RIGHT: **Tracy Stratford stars in the mysterious Matheson piece, "Little Girl Lost." This was brilliantly parodied in an episode of *The Simpsons*, where Homer enters a portal into the next dimension in animation — 3D computer graphics.**

the Twilight Zone, it's best to leave any doubt at the door of imagination, because once inside it we find anything is possible. Time travel is sometimes played out by natural means, as in episodes like "A Hundred Yards Over the Rim," "The Last Flight," "The Odyssey of Flight 33," "Spur of the Moment," and "Back There." Written by Serling, "Back There" stars Russell Johnson (best known as the Professor from *Gilligan's Island*), Bartlett Robinson, and John Lasell. Johnson plays social-club member Peter Corrigan, who, after a discussion about the impossibility of time travel and altering the past, finds he's mysteriously traveled back in time and been given a chance to stop the assassination of Abraham Lincoln. His plans are thwarted, but when he returns to his present, he finds some things are possible to change, while others are not.

More science-based time-travel stories include episodes like "Execution" and "No Time Like the Past," whose outcome is similar to that of "Back There," in that the fate of historical figures proves much harder to alter than trivial things. So, there may be no going back to assassinate Hitler, but as in Matheson's quirky "Once Upon a Time," starring silent-film great Buster Keaton, one can discover a long way round to helping the chicken cross the road.

Space Travel

Within the limits of television storytelling, there's really no better way to escape the doldrums of reality than through adventurous trips into outer space. Space travel was no stranger to *The Twilight Zone* — as a lead-in to some of the more outwardly explorative stories, there's Rod Serling's bizarre "And When the Sky Was Opened," based loosely on Richard Matheson's short story "Disappearing Act." The action takes place after a space mission, when three astronauts disappear from existence one by one, victims of an unknown intelligent force. What separates this episode from others is that it's mysteriously open-ended — for we never learn what unknown force has taken the astronauts, or why.

Representing other space-exploration themes, there are crash-landing episodes such as "I Shot an Arrow into the Air," "People Are Alike All Over," and "Death Ship," and stranded episodes like "Elegy," "The Little People," "On

Thursday We Leave For Home," and the memorable "The Invaders."

But not all space exploration ends in tragedy, as proven in episodes like "Probe 7 — Over and Out," and "Third from the Sun," where people are given a second chance for a new life on a new world.

Alien and Creatures

Alien episodes — in which, due to budget restrictions, the aliens are all humanoid — are aplenty in *The Twilight Zone*, including "Will the Real Martian Please Stand Up," "The Fear," "The Fugitive," "Stopover in a Quiet Town," "The Gift," "Black Leather Jackets," "Mr. Dingle, the Strong," "Hocus-Pocus and Frisby," and the memorable "To Serve Man."

Written by Rod Serling and based on a short story by Damon Knight, "To Serve Man" is a story reminiscent of the classic film *The Day the Earth Stood Still*. Earth is visited by "Kanamit" aliens who claim to want to serve us with technologies to end famine and war, just as they've offered to other planets throughout the galaxy. But the twist reveals that the aliens have an ulterior motive, and an uncanny understanding of the multiple meanings of English phrases. Director Richard Bare admits that to this day, of his entire Hollywood career, people comment more on this episode than on any other piece. And so they should: it's a brilliant piece of work, even voted No. 11 in *TV Guide*'s 1997 "100 Greatest Television Episodes of All Time" poll.

Among the many alien creatures in the series, there are two creature/monster-oriented episodes that fall outside the space-travel theme — "It's a Good Life," starring Bill Mumy as omnipotent Anthony Fremont, and "Nightmare at 20,000 Feet." Both are also regarded as classic moments in television and have been parodied in shows ranging from *The Simpsons* and *3rd Rock from the Sun* to the cartoon *Johnny Bravo* and the syndicated comic strip *Robot Man*.

Man Versus Machine

Primarily designed to ease the labors of man's existence, *The Twilight Zone* acknowledges that with technology's convenience may also come grave conse-

quences. Such is the case with Rod Serling's "The Brain Center at Whipples," starring Richard Deacon as a factory owner who, after replacing all of his employees with machines, comes to find his own position of authority in ironic jeopardy.

On the theme of man versus machine, there's also Serling's "A Thing About Machines," Beaumont's "In His Image," and Matheson's "Steel." When it comes to the powers of computer intelligence, there are episodes like Serling's "The Old Man in the Cave," Beaumont's "Valley of the Shadow," and Bernard C. Shoenfeld's "From Agnes — With Love." However, not all robots bring malevolent consequences, as we find in Ray Bradbury's "I Sing the Body Electric" and two Serling episodes starring veteran actor Jack Warden, "The Mighty Casey" and "The Lonely." In "The Lonely," considered a love story between man and machine, Warden plays James Corey, an innocent man convicted of murder and sentenced to spend 50 years alone on a distant asteroid. Visited periodically by a supply ship, Corey is brought an android woman, Alicia, played by Jean Marsh, to help him cope with the isolation. At first Corey finds her a mocking reminder of what he left behind, but he soon grows emotionally involved and falls in love with her. Eleven months later, the supply ship arrives with news that Corey's been granted a pardon and can return to Earth, but due to weight restrictions, Alicia must stay behind. Will Corey choose to stay in his new life with his machine or return to a life with real people?

Another episode that taps into the moral implications of artificial intelligence is Serling's "The Lateness of the Hour." Inger Stevens plays Jana, the daughter of Dr. Loren (John Hoyt), inventor of android servants that tend to his family's

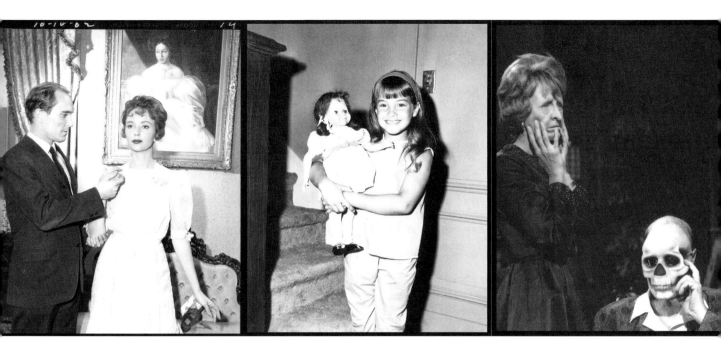

every need in an estate kept private from society. Jana finds living in this antiseptic environment intolerable and demands that her father dismantle the androids or she'll leave home. Dr. Loren attempts to persuade her of the androids' purpose in their household, but, seeing her despair, submits to dismantling them. In a house now free of any android influence, Jana is ecstatic . . . until she discovers that her father decided to keep one of his androids after all.

Enchanted Objects

Some of the show's most unique and terrifying characters are enchanted objects with a life all their own. They come in the form of dolls and mannequins, domestic devices and vehicles, and various items of everyday life. Enchanted dolls are found in episodes like "The Dummy," starring Cliff Robertson, "Miniature," starring Robert Duvall, "Caesar and Me," starring Jackie Cooper, and Charles Beaumont's terrifying "Living Doll," starring Telly Savalas. In "Living Doll," a little girl's Talky Tina doll, voiced by June Foray of *The Bullwinkle Show*, protects her from an abusive stepfather. With this episode, and "The Dummy," *The Twilight Zone* has seriously terrorized some viewers by capitalizing on their fear of dolls and puppets. Proving that when it comes to subject matter in the series, no stone goes unturned.

Such is the case with the wide range of domestic-device stories in episodes like "A Most Unusual Camera," "Static," "Long Distance Call," "The Mirror," "A Piano in the House," "A Kind of Stopwatch," "A Thing About Machines," "What's in the Box," and "The Fever." Characters aren't even safe from their vehicles, such as the haunted car in "The Whole Truth" and the car with a con-

LEFT: **Robert Duvall stars with Claire Griswold in Beaumont's touching escape from reality, "Miniature."**

CENTER: **Tracy Stratford costars with Telly Savalas and Mary LaRoche in "Living Doll." June Foray supplied the eerie voice of the Talky Tina doll, which was a Vogue Brickette doll of the early '60s that the prop department altered by installing a motor to make its arms and head move.**

RIGHT: **Virginia Gregg and Robert Keith star in the unique Serling episode, "The Masks."**

LEFT: **Malcolm Atterbury stars as peddler Henry J. Fate in "Mr. Denton on Doomsday."** There was a small production error in the episode: the potion supplied to Denton comes in a small plastic bottle, at a time when there were no plastics.

CENTER: **George Grizzard and the lovely Patricia Barry star in "The Chaser."** The address of Professor Daemon is 22, as in *Catch 22*.

RIGHT: **Joseph Ruskin, Luther Adler, and Vivi Janis star in the intriguing genie episode, "The Man in the Bottle."**

science in Earl Hamner Jr.'s "You Drive." Here, Edward Andrews plays a hit-and-run driver whose car forces him to turn himself in to the police. Even a pair of shoes has the ability to haunt the living, as in Beaumont's "Dead Man's Shoes," starring Warren Stevens as Nate Bledsoe, a bum who, while wearing the shoes of a dead gangster, is inhabited by the vengeful gangster's spirit.

Two memorable Serling episodes feature humanoid objects. In "The After Hours," Anne Francis plays Marsha White, a shopper in a department store who comes to understand she's not who she thinks she is. In "The Masks," Robert Keith stars as a dying elderly man with plans to get back at his greedy family who have come to inherit his estate. During a Mardi Gras celebration, and as a prerequisite to their inheritance, he forces them to wear ugly masks containing "special properties," which in turn give them exactly what they deserve.

Magic

The Twilight Zone is a magical show, enchanted by sensibilities that widen the scope of the mind's eye. It only follows that the series should offer stories on the subject of magic. Within the show's supernatural arsenal are literal forms of magic, such as potions, black-magic items and genies, and psychological forms of magic with voodoo and wishes, all of which cover this lost art quite well. Magic potions turn up in the third episode of the series to air, "Mr. Denton on Doomsday," written by Rod Serling and starring the full cast of Dan Duryea, Malcolm Atterbury, Martin Landau, Jeanne Cooper, Ken Lynch, and a young Doug McClure. Duryea plays washed-up gunslinger Denton, who attempts to use a quick-draw potion to redeem himself. Another lighter magical-potion

LEFT: **Actor John Dehner's Employee Personal Information form.**

RIGHT: **John Dehner stars as a nonbeliever of voodoo in "The Jungle."**

episode is "The Chaser," where George Grizzard plays Roger, a man so obsessed with lovely Leila, played by Patricia Barry, that he uses a love potion to win her heart, without realizing the consequences.

The dark art of black magic is examined in "Still Valley," "Jess-Belle," and "The Bard," and genies appear in "The Man in the Bottle" and "I Dream of Genie" (no relation to the television series). Among the few voodoo episodes is the Charles Beaumont classic "The Jungle," where John Dehner plays an engineer in charge of constructing a dam on ancestral land in Africa, and suffers the consequences upon his return home to New York.

In "Mr. Garrity and the Grave," Dehner plays an Old West con man who claims he can raise the dead from their graves. He goes from town to town fooling people with his con, unaware of his hidden talent underneath the guise of a con man. Another such con game turned magical is Serling's western episode, "Dust." Here, a father whose son is about to be hanged for running over a child buys dirt from a peddler who claims it's a magic dust that will turn hate into love. The father spreads the dust out into the crowd, hoping its "magic" will stop the death of his son.

Sometimes it's a *belief* in magic that's important, and not necessarily that an object has magical properties. In George Clayton Johnson's poignant episode, "Kick the Can," the title game turns a group of elderly folks back into children, but they don't realize it wasn't the can that made the magic work.

Proving that some wishes do come true, *The Twilight Zone* offers two hopeful episodes, "The Big Tall Wish," starring Ivan Dixon, and "The Sixteen-Millimeter Shrine," starring veteran actors Ida Lupino and Martin Balsam. Lupino plays aged and out-of-work movie queen Barbara Jean Trenton, who hides away as a celluloid hermit watching her old films, longing for the Golden Age of Hollywood. Trenton so passionately wants to reunite with her old friends up there on the screen that she magically wishes herself into the world

Movie queen Ida Lupino
stars in Serling's nostalgic
"The Sixteen Millimeter
Shrine." Lupino also
directed the episode,
"The Masks."

of her films. In the case of movie queen Miss Trenton, she was careful what she wished for.

The characters of the *Zone* exist as immortal icons of yesterday's black-and-white celluloid dreams, kept alive by qualities of a time unparalleled. Everlasting entities projected by light and shadow, they continue to offer their hard-earned lessons to generations of viewers from the limitless boundaries of the fifth dimension and into our own.

CHAPTER FOUR

Comic Relief

"It's to laugh. I swear it's to laugh."
— Max Phillips of "In Praise of Pip"

One rarely thinks of *The Twilight Zone* as a comedy series — it's so much closer to tragedy. However, the formula for comedy offers relief and balances the more prominent and serious themes of comeuppance, alienation, and conformity. Most audiences enjoy a good comedy, something to soften the blows of a sometimes harsh reality. *The Twilight Zone* understood this, as Rod Serling and the other writers aimed to not only shock and terrorize, but also amuse viewers with the lighter sides of storytelling. Out of the dozen or so comedy episodes, there are certainly a few gems that do just that, but *The Twilight Zone* will never be in the same company as classic comedy series of the time, such as *I Love Lucy*, *The Dick Van Dyke Show*, or *Bewitched*.

Patricia Breslin and William Shatner goof around during a break from the filming of "Nick of Time."

The tendency of most critics and fans of the series is to write off the comedy episodes as forgettable; even Serling referred to a couple of them as "turkeys." Like the poor delivery of a punch line, the series does have its share of missteps, which has led to the perception that *The Twilight Zone* was better suited for portraying tragedy. Although it may feel sacrilegious to call any *Twilight Zone* episode a turkey, the turkey prize clearly goes to both "Cavender Is Coming" and "From Agnes — With Love." This dubious honor is based merely on their weak material and flat humor, and is not meant as a poke at the talented cast members. Jesse White, Carol Burnett, and Wally Cox are all class acts with great bodies of work, and it's a delight that they appear in the series. But "Cavender Is Coming" is dreadful, almost as bad as that "hippie" episode of the original *Star Trek*. In this corny installment, White plays Cavender, a cigar-smoking, undisciplined guardian-angel-in-training, assigned to fix the life of misfit Agnes Grubbs, played by Burnett. As in "Mr. Bevis," the character to be *saved* is given opportunities for a new and improved life of fame and fortune, but in the end she decides to stick with the meager life she already has. There is only one seriously funny moment in this episode — when the bus driver makes that unexpected dive out the driver's-side window, it seems right out of a *Monty Python* sketch. The other pratfalls seem like fillers in an overall weak comedy episode that just isn't funny. To make matters worse, a forced laugh track was used over the episode, a decision that CBS executives made to promote this episode as a possible pilot for Jesse White. There's nothing more insulting than a laugh track.

"From Agnes — With Love" also falls flat due to the main character, James Elwood, played by Wally Cox, who is written as such a clueless nerd, it's no won-

der the only action he can get is from a computer. "Agnes" does, however, have its moments, such as the unique close-up wide-angle shot of Don Keefer in the opening sequence, and the animated look of insanity when Elwood finds out that supercomputer Agnes is in love with him. These brief moments are this episode's only respite, and they aren't nearly as interesting as the little moral lessons we get from other episodes. Though there *does* seem to be an ironic lesson in both of these episodes: never name a main character Agnes.

Unfortunately, there are a few other *Twilight Zone* comedies that end up offering more comic grief than comic relief. Poorer episodes — based purely on bad material and not necessarily the casts — are Serling's "The Whole Truth," "Showdown with Rance McGrew," and "Mr. Bevis." The latter was originally meant as a pilot for a comedy series starring Burgess Meredith as Bevis, but after Meredith turned the project down, Serling ended up salvaging the script for *The Twilight Zone*, not once, but twice. Two seasons later, in a decision that defies logic, the weak "Mr. Bevis" was remade as the weaker "Cavender Is Coming."

Richard Matheson's "Once Upon a Time," starring silent-film comedian Buster Keaton, Stanley Adams, and Jesse White, begins to show how *The Twilight Zone* could indeed honor the tone and timing of classic comedy. Producer Buck Houghton and Matheson had the idea to do a comedy that featured Keaton and old-school director Norman Z. McLeod, who was known for directing comedy greats such as *Topper* and the Marx Brothers' *Monkey Business* and *Horse Feathers*. The payoff in "Once Upon a Time" comes with the homage of filming the beginning and end in the style of a silent film. The crew, not coincidentally, used a street on the back lot that 40 years earlier was built for

LEFT: **Raymond Bailey stars with Wally Cox in the flat episode, "From Agnes – With Love."**

CENTER: **Larry Blyden and Arch Johnson star in the silly "Showdown with Rance McGrew."**

RIGHT: **Orson Bean and Henry Jones star in "Mr. Bevis."**

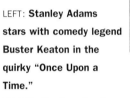

LEFT: **Stanley Adams stars with comedy legend Buster Keaton in the quirky "Once Upon a Time."**

CENTER: **Keaton stands on his mark for the next shot while the lighting of the special effects takes place.**

RIGHT: **Keaton plays around with the camera during a break.**

a Buster Keaton comedy. Even though the genius of Keaton's comic timing is tapped into, other elements keep this episode from being a comedic masterpiece. For one, the gags aren't all that funny. This may be due to budget considerations — some of Matheson's more elaborate slapstick chase sequences had to be cut, replaced with the rather normal repair-shop scene, directed later by Les Goodwin. Although Keaton is best known for his outrageously choreographed chase sequences, it is a special treat that during the "talkie" repair-shop scene, we get to hear this silent-film icon speak his lines. The opportunity to see the great Buster Keaton in a *Twilight Zone* makes this episode worth watching.

Looking closer, we see several gems that offer pure comic relief and do indeed prove that *The Twilight Zone* could succeed at featuring some good laughs. Confirming that Serling could do comedy are solid comedic episodes like the quirky "Mr. Dingle, the Strong," starring Burgess Meredith as a vacuum-cleaner salesman given superhuman powers by visiting aliens. Other such Serling scripts include "A Most Unusual Camera," "Escape Clause," "The Mighty Casey," "A Kind of Stopwatch," "Mr. Garrity and the Graves," and "The Mind and the Matter." Other more serious episodes feature hints of comedy designed to offer a tone of normality. A certain element of humor in the script helps ground characters, as we find in episodes such as "Time Enough at Last," "One for the Angels," "Elegy," "A World of His Own," "Five Characters in Search of an Exit," "Nick of Time," and even "A Passage for Trumpet," in which, despite the suicidal tendencies of Jack Klugman's character, he still has the ability to poke fun at himself.

Another comedy gem worth noting is the whimsical "Hocus-Pocus and Frisby," based on Frederick Louis Fox's unpublished story and adapted by Serling. Here, the viewer is taken along on a journey of a boy who cried wolf.

Except, in the *Zone* universe, we find an enjoyable Andy Devine, with that high-pitched crackling voice of his, playing backwoods liar and spinner of tales Somerset Frisby. Costarring are some familiar faces from television history, including Dabbs Greer, who appeared in several episodes; Howard McNear, most remembered as Floyd the barber in *The Andy Griffith Show*; and Milton Selzer and Larry Breitman, playing the two aliens. In this story, grocery-store owner Frisby is known to burn the ears of his customers with exaggerated claims that range from having invented the first rear-engine automobile for Henry Ford, to being able to predict the weather. It's Frisby's overconfident claims of multiple degrees in engineering that cause two human-like aliens to abduct him, thinking he's an optimal human specimen. Back in their spaceship, the aliens divulge their plans for putting Frisby in their alien zoo, to make use of his superior intellect. Frisby, fearing for his life, finds himself forced to con-

fess he's just a liar and a country bumpkin with a big mouth. Yet the aliens have
no concept of dishonesty and proceed with their plans. Frisby panics and
punches the commanding alien in the face, which cracks apart and reveals the
creature's true alien identity, hidden under a human mask. What makes this so
funny is the audience's knowledge that if Frisby ever does get himself out of this
pickle, he'll finally have a story for the ages. But will anyone believe him? The
obvious lesson here is not only that honesty is the best policy, but also, it might
be wise to keep a harmonica handy, just in case.

The brightest comedic turn by far comes in the tongue-in-cheek quality of

Look out! There's a man behind the wheel of this cart!

Serling's hilarious episode "The Bard." The last of the fourth season's hour-long episodes to air, this was one of the few that actually worked. Starring a witty Jack Weston as Julius Moomer, character actor John Williams as William Shakespeare, and Burt Reynolds as Rocky Rhodes, a Marlon Brando knockoff, this gem offers fine comedic timing. Hack wannabe television writer Moomer mistakenly misuses a book of black magic to conjure up a writing partner in the form of *the* William Shakespeare. Moomer, who seeks fame even though he has absolutely no idea how to produce good writing, is able to convince "Will" to

A guy walks into a barber shop . . .

A dimension of sight . . .   **A dimension of clowns.**

help him write a television pilot. At times, the dialogue is flavorful, and, through the playfulness of Moomer's quirky Bronx dialect, we see how Serling had a talent for animating his characters with a touch of authenticity. We're even witness to hearing William Shakespeare's final goodbyes to Moomer in a round of proper Shakespearean vernacular, followed by an outright hilarious, "Lotsa luck!" "The Bard" clearly shows that Serling was capable of writing comedy, not just the drama he was most known for.

But one of the things that makes this comedy episode work so well is Serling's parody of his own bread and butter, the television industry. He shows how a television play can be butchered under the steely knives of network executives who cower before the nonsensical edits of the commercial sponsors. And as an extra treat, Reynolds is priceless in his cool parody of Brando, with his beatnik summation on the meaning of acting: "What is my tertiary motivation?" "The Bard" proves to audiences and critics alike that comical regions of the fifth dimension were present and accounted for.

When all is said and done, if you ever wished away any of the 156 *Twilight Zone* episodes, even if it were one of the two comedic turkeys, there would be an empty black hole in its place. Instead, one ought to look at the series as a matched set, where each piece has its place. Sure, there are a few that can be a little painful to watch, but for a television series, that's not a bad average. And again, the comedy episodes were chosen to simply balance the more intense tone of the series, and for the most part, they do that well. This *is* entertainment, not rocket science, and no one said it was a perfect medium.

CHAPTER FIVE

Beyond Dimensions

"I do believe I may have left my mark. A few gauntlets of knowledge that I've thrown down that may have been picked up."

— Professor Fowler of "Changing of the Guard"

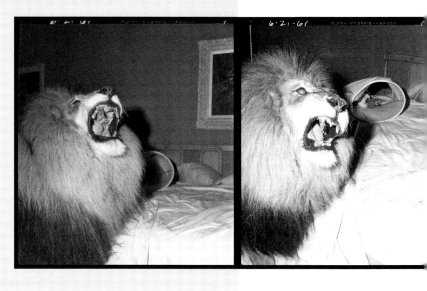

The MGM lion plays himself in "The Jungle."

As the adage goes, all good things come to an end. By the end of *Twilight Zone*'s fifth season, the series had worked through its own boundaries, doing almost everything it could. In the eyes of the CBS network executives, *The Twilight Zone* had run its course — it was beginning to repeat itself, even — and they did not renew it for a sixth season. It was time for the roaring MGM lion to move on to greener pastures. This was quite all right with Rod Serling. Buck Houghton had already left the ship two seasons earlier, and for Serling, who had enjoyed his experience as a writing teacher, it was time to step outside of the realm of fantasy and science fiction.

Up next for Serling's television work was the short-lived black-and-white western *The Loner*, starring Lloyd Bridges as William Colton, a Civil War veteran tarnished by the idea of killing. The series, which ran 26 episodes during the 1965–66 season (15 penned by Serling), aired on CBS, the same network home of *The Twilight Zone*. Serling's take on the television western was quite different than your average bad-guy-versus-good-guy scenario; it was a thinking man's western that revealed the real

conditions of the West. The lack of barroom brawls and gunfights led to fairly low ratings, and the series was canceled.

No matter where Serling's path had taken him as a writer, the actor side of him still had a desire to play — but he was no Cary Grant. Realizing that his inimitable voice was one of his selling points, Serling took on several narration projects, most notably on television's nature series, *The Undersea World of Jacques Cousteau*. He even did television commercials and public service announcements, despite drawing criticism that he was a sellout for doing so. Serling hadn't sought out the commercials; it was the insistent sponsors who had approached him with offers of big dollars and luxury cars for a simple afternoon's work. For Serling, it was honest work, and as Carol Serling pointed out, "He laughed all the way to the bank."

Serling then straddled the line between television and feature film by offering his hand at made-for-TV movies, adapting Irving Wallace's novel *The Man*, starring James Earl Jones as the first African-American U.S. President, and *The Doomsday Flight*, the story of a crazed ex-airline mechanic who plants an altitude-sensitive bomb on an airplane.

Perhaps one of Serling's finest contributions to movie magic is the popular film *Planet of the Apes*, based on Pierre Boulle's novel. With this unique story of a planet run by sentient simians, Serling brought into the film social issues

concerning mankind and the nuclear age, much as he did with *The Twilight Zone*. Serling penned three drafts of the screenplay, but when his scripts got caught in limbo after a few years of involvement, his interest faded and he decided to part from the project graciously. Michael Wilson was hired on to take control of the screenplay, sharing a credit with Serling, which has sparked much debate over what parts of Serling's work made it into the finished film. However, when one views the film, it's obvious that Serling's overall tone, dialogue, and classic twist ending remain intact.

Following the cancellation of *The Twilight Zone*, of which Serling was 40 percent owner, and despite the fact that he had grown tired of the show, he was still interested in doing another anthology television series. Unfortunately, the networks weren't interested in revising *The Twilight Zone* series, partly because of the low market value of an anthology that lacks recurring characters from which to milk spin-offs and products. Following the advice of his agent, Ted Ashley, Serling decided it best to get whatever profits remained by selling his *Twilight Zone* rights to CBS, giving them full ownership of the property. This proved to be a big mistake. Serling made the deal before television syndication, and no one knew the show could ever make serious money again after its initial run. Shortly after the deal, CBS put the show into syndication, and *The Twilight Zone* went from being an unmarketable property to an immortal one.

ABOVE: **Patricia Barry in a candid shot from "The Chaser."**

BELOW: **William Schallert plays a policeman in "Mr. Bevis."**

Serling continued to pitch the idea of an anthology show to other networks as *Rod Serling's Wax Museum*, and where NBC passed, ABC insisted on a horror series, which Serling didn't want, so the project was canceled. Still determined to revisit the genre he had first brought to television, Serling wrote some *Twilight Zone*–like stories and packaged them for NBC. The network bought the pilot and made it into a two-hour television movie.

On November 8, 1969, the made-for-television movie *Night Gallery* aired, with Serling introducing it in his inimitable style: "Good evening, and welcome to a private showing of three paintings, displayed here for the first time. Each is a collector's item in its own way — not because of any special artistic quality, but because each captures on a canvas, suspends in time and space, a frozen moment of a nightmare." The premiere of this two-hour special saw ratings high enough to sell the series to NBC, and earn Serling a Mystery Writers of America Edgar Allan Poe award.

NBC signed for six more installments and produced it as a short series in late 1970, titled *Rod Serling's Night Gallery*. Jack Laird took over production of the series, and Serling passed on the position of executive producer, thinking he would naturally have creative control over the direction of the series. Regrettably, though, as the series progressed, Laird ended up rewriting some of Serling's scripts and it became clear that Serling's role was merely that of story contributor and host. With this lack of creative control, Serling couldn't exploit his talents, and it was apparent the series was developing into something far from what he had established with the television movie.

Nonetheless, *Night Gallery* was an artistic series, with good production values and some amazing talent, using directors like Steven Spielberg, Jeannot Szwarc, John Badham, Gene Kearney, and Jeff Corey, and actors Joan Crawford, Orson Welles, Edward G. Robinson, Vincent Price, Mickey Rooney, Burgess Meredith, Agnes Moorehead, and Ray Milland. *Night Gallery* lasted into a third season, in 1972, by this time cut out to a half-hour show. By this final season, it was obvious Serling was being used simply for his name and stature as a host, but he couldn't leave the series, since he was contractually bound to stay.

Upon its cancellation, and due to insufficient episodes needed for syndication status, Universal combined *Night Gallery* with the series *The Sixth Sense*, starring Gary Collins. As part of the syndication package, numerous edits were made to *Night Gallery*. Scenes were replaced incoherently with filler stock footage, which weakened some of the storytelling beyond comprehension. Luckily, with the release of the series on VHS and the first season on DVD, Universal presented beautifully restored masters without the dreadful syndication edits. In a strange twist of fate, the Season One DVD box set was released as *Night Gallery* instead of *Rod Serling's Night Gallery*.

It's hard to believe that it's been over 30 years since the death of Rod Serling, and yet his work still shines on. Since his exit from this dimension, Hollywood has tried to remake *The Twilight Zone* four times, but these imitations naturally pale in comparison to the original series. The first attempt, *Twilight Zone: The Movie*, played in theaters in the summer of 1983. The movie featured narration by Burgess Meredith, an opening intro, one new story, and three remakes of original episodes. Steven Spielberg headed up the project and assembled the direction team of John Landis, Joe Dante, and George Miller. Veteran *Twilight Zone* writer Richard Matheson penned the screenplay for the three remakes, and Jerry Goldsmith, one of the original series' conductors, was also brought on board to create the film's music. The film features original *Twilight Zone* alumni such as Murray Matheson, Kevin McCarthy, Patricia Barry, William Schallert, and Bill Mumy, and used some of the same character names and locations from the original series.

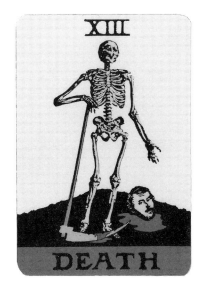 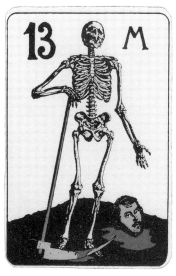

The prop Death playing card used in *The Twilight Zone* [1985] episode, "Dealer's Choice," as well as an alternate unused version.

_____

The film does have a few good moments that *sort of* feel *Twilight Zone*–ish, but overall it's a disappointment. It might have stood a better chance if some of the direction had not felt so cartoony, which was such a departure from the original series, and the use of color instead of black and white diminishes the mystery and starkness.

The second attempt at revising the fifth dimension came about when CBS decided to return to their *Twilight Zone* license by creating a new series, unofficially referred to as *The New Twilight Zone*. This *Twilight Zone* ran for two seasons, from 1985 to 1987, with a third direct-to-syndication season in 1988. During this same time, joining the trend of revising the television anthology, NBC and ABC spawned Steven Spielberg's *Amazing Stories*, and a revamping of *Alfred Hitchcock Presents*. This installment of the *Zone* universe was simply a return to the anthology format, with the title of *Twilight Zone* attached to its surface. If you hadn't seen the intro sequence telling you it was a new version of *The Twilight Zone*, you wouldn't know what show you were watching. If the series had aimed at actually continuing where the original had left off, it probably would have been more successful.

A third attempt, CBS's *Twilight Zone: Rod Serling's Lost Classics*, was actually more directly related to Serling's original creation. This television special, which aired in 1994, was hosted by James Earl Jones and featured two stories, the half-hour "The Theatre," a Richard Matheson script based on a Serling story treatment, and the 90-minute "Where the Dead Are," an unproduced Serling script. "The Theatre" stars Amy Irving and Gary Cole in a classic story of the foretelling of one's own demise and the inability to stop it. "Where the Dead Are" stars Jack Palance as a chemist who has discovered a drug to bring the dead

A *Twilight Zone* [1985] concept painting for the episode, "The Shadow Man."

to life and has kept the people of his island alive by administering it. Both stories play as lost treats, but again, cannot quite recreate the past.

The most recent attempt to remake *The Twilight Zone* debuted on UPN network for a single season of 43 episodes in the fall of 2002. Creators of the series, Pen Densham and Ira Steven Behr, assembled a crew yearning to pay homage to Serling's original, but unfortunately, production fell under marketing demographics and limitations set by the network. The result was a new style of *Twilight Zone*, marketed to a younger, hip-hop, trend-conformed audience, in what turned out as something that should have been called *MTV Zone*. Critically speaking, this remake, or revisit to the title, is by far the weakest. It again misses the style and spirit of the original — stark lighting, a mysterious sensibility, superior writing, uneasiness, and brilliant performances in a palette of wonderful character actors playing unforgettable parts.

As we find in other modern television series, this new installment features some fine production values, technical effects, and some decent stories. Hosted by Forest Whitaker, a fine actor somewhat miscast, this hipper updated version feels too far from the scope of the original to carry the title. And like its 1985 predecessor, most of the attempts to redo some key original episodes offer only average renditions and with far less impact. The remake of "The Eye of the Beholder" involves mutated people instead of a race of conformed "normal" people who look exactly alike, and the threat in "The Monsters Are Due on Maple Street," simply ends up as U.S. Army mock-terrorist civilian war-games, instead of an otherworldly event.

One highlight of the series is the episode "It's Still a Good Life," based on the original episode, "It's a Good Life." This revisit to the small, secluded town of Peaksville, Ohio, features reprising roles by Bill Mumy as the grown-up omnipotent Anthony Fremont, Cloris Leachman as his mother Agnes, and Liliana Mumy as Anthony's daughter Audrey. The story takes place 40 years after the original, and Anthony has grown bored with the dynamics of his ultimate powers. He has wished everything but Peaksville into the cornfield, and finds that his young daughter has the same powers — and even more. She's able to wish things *back* from the cornfield and into reality, a power Anthony never achieved. Anthony's mother reveals her hatred toward Anthony, and in trying to convince Audrey he's a monster and should be wished away into the cornfield, she herself is wished away when Audrey decides to protect her father.

Rod Serling at a book signing for *Rod Serling's Twilight Zone* (1963), a book that features urban legend tales, coupled with a few Serling stories adapted from his scripts.

However, the real twist is revealed when we discover Audrey's powers might be more dangerous than Anthony's.

Despite this one good episode, this new and yet still unimproved *Twilight Zone* seems much as it did before — a remake in the format of an anthology, with *The Twilight Zone* title stamped on it. Yet, isn't it altogether better to leave well enough alone? As we've come to see with all of these remakes, the answer would be *yes*.

But at least J.J. Abrams got it right in January 2000, during the second season of his television series *Felicity*, when he paid an amazing homage to the original *Twilight Zone* with the episode, "Help for the Lovelorn." This one episode, which partly recreates the original *Twilight Zone* story "Five Characters in Search of an Exit," features the elements of storytelling, direction, cinematography, setting, wardrobe, score, and sound that recapture the feel of the classic series. Showing how exacting this single homage was, Abrams not only hired Lamont Johnson, of the original "Five Characters" to direct, but also shot with a Mitchell, the same type of camera used for the original. Take heed, all you future *Twilight Zone* remake wannabes: study this single *Felicity* episode well, for it fully demonstrates the essentials needed for perfecting the art of how to *Zone*. The most important factor, besides quality storytelling, is that it's done in black and white. *Do you hear?* Black and white!

The original *Twilight Zone* will remain television's timeless series. This is proven time and again, as new fans of the show are born every day. American fans now spend more time watching *Twilight Zone* marathons on Independence Day than they do lighting fireworks. And because of its growing popularity and fandom, all five seasons of the series have been made available in their original

airing order, in the Definitive Edition DVD box sets. Young fans of film and science fiction who are unfamiliar with *The Twilight Zone* are undoubtedly impressed with the show's high quality and artistry, and how well it holds up, even today. In fact, *The Twilight Zone* only gets better with age. Even high school teachers of English and social studies are known to run episodes in their classrooms and build lessons around them. Rod Serling himself used his own *Twilight Zone* work to analyze in class, taking the shows apart to critique both

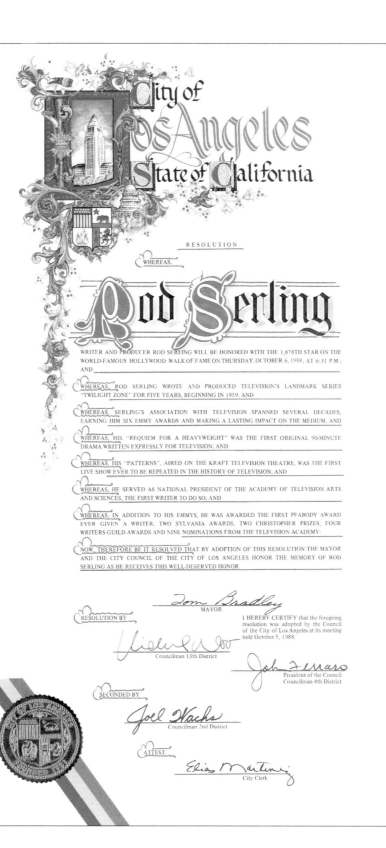

The official Hollywood Walk of Stars Certificate (1988), awarded with Rod Serling's star on the Walk of Fame.

the writing and the filmmaking. An old adage goes, "Those who cannot do, teach," but Serling put the lie to that. He could do better than most, and then teach it to others.

In the annals of television history, Rod Serling truly is an immortal figure. This suave, dark-suited gentleman with such a perceptive understanding of the human psyche will forever reign as the king of imagination and terror on television. He was a profound writer and a founding member at television's very beginnings, who introduced literature both poignant and terrifying into the campfire glows of family rooms. Though *The Twilight Zone* became a huge success for Serling, he treated fame in a self-effacing way, which in turn made him approachable. Whereas other celebrities can let fame go to their heads, Serling acknowledged his worth with dignity. Hollywood historians often refer to Rod Serling as Television's Last Angry Man, and that may well be, if they mean the passion he had for television's potential. He was a lone voice striving for quality and honesty. He was angry, yes, but it was out of frustration with the censorship of the times: the McCarthy era that now seems so distant and archaic. Serling wouldn't sit back and allow television's censorship to dictate the kinds of stories one could tell — he spoke for the artist's right of expression. He was not only an invaluable asset to the growth of early television, but his work continues to show a creative influence on current television creators and filmmakers who entertain in Serling's style of storytelling.

Rod Serling died on June 28, 1975, of complications during open heart surgery. He said he just wanted to be remembered as a writer, but he was so much more. He was a genius, in the true sense of the word, and not the way the term is thrown around so easily today, like cheap bubblegum. He was a humanitarian, a prolific thinker, a role model, a mentor to many in and out of the film industry, and he remains one of the greatest fantasy writers of the 20th century. Serling commented late in his career that he felt he had gone dry and needed to replenish the well. With all due respect, Mr. Rodman Edward Serling, your well is quite full. You may have left this existence so many years ago, but your art lives on, not only in the reality of this third dimension, but forever lasting in the fifth dimension known as . . . *The Twilight Zone*.

Sight, Sound, and Mind

Earl Holliman

Earl Holliman starred as Mike Ferris in the pilot episode "Where is Everybody?"

Do you have any mementos from the pilot episode of *The Twilight Zone*?

I have a wonderful letter, it's all framed, that Rod wrote me when I was in the hospital. I had done the pilot, in December of 1958, and it was the first filmed television I ever did. I had just finished the last day of shooting on a picture for Hal Wallis at Paramount called *Visit to a Small Planet*, and I got acute hepatitis. I was in the hospital for a month, and one day I get a letter from Rod. It's a wonderful letter. I'm very proud of it.

How did you get involved with working on the *Twilight Zone* pilot?

My association with Rod went back to the year before. I had started out in motion pictures and I wanted badly to be able to do good live television, like *Playhouse 90*, and so I changed agents, I went to MCA, and they took me immediately. My very first *Playhouse 90* was written by Rod Serling — it was called "The Dark Side of the Earth," about the Hungarian revolution. I was playing a young Russian officer, Captain Volodney, who had great admiration for this general played by Van Heflin. And in the end, of course, I have to turn him in, and these other people, they're

all blown away, you know, standing there watching my idol being killed. During the rehearsals, Rod was there with the script and at one point I went up to him and I said, "You know Rod, there's no scene where I actually express my admiration for the general, something to the effect of 'I know what you did at Stalingrad, and I was there, and I know about . . .'" etc. And Rod would begin tinkering with his pencil, writing all this down. And the speech comes back in his words, but not unlike what I had said to him, and I just found that very interesting, because a lot of writers are so protective and possessive of their talents, and the idea of some actor suggesting a scene — a lot of people wouldn't go for that at all.

So he was perceptive with the actors.

Yes, he was indeed. I didn't see him again until a year later; I was doing my second *Playhouse 90*, "The Return of Ansel Gibbs," and I ran into him in the parking lot and we got to talking and I asked, "What are you doing? What are you up to?" And he said, "Oh, I'm doing this science-fiction pilot over at Universal. We offered it to . . ." I'm pretty sure he said Tony Curtis. But, he said, "They can't work out the deal." So he said, "I'm going to send you the script." And I said, "Great."

I had done a picture at Metro that turned out to be a big cult film, *Forbidden Planet*, and all my scenes were with Robby the Robot. I played the cook who was kind of comic relief, but I had not wanted to do that picture. The

ROD SERLING
1490 MONACO DRIVE
PACIFIC PALISADES, CALIFORNIA

October 21, 1959

Mr. Earl Holliman

Dear Earl,

I am an admitted shmuck, but an abject one. I intended
to visit you in the hospital; I intended to send a box of
Mother See's candy; I intended to send a long and hysterically
funny telegram to make you feel better - but I was immersed
in this here series called The Twilight Zone and while
dripping with intentions, resolves never saw fruition!
This note is by way of an apology and a simple re-state-
ment of what I've already told you - your performance was
outstanding, full of dimension, shading and a fantastic
believability. In short, Holliman, you're one hell of
an actor!

Some rich and gracious producers send wristwatches and
things like that as expressions of appreciation. Gracious
I am - rich I ain't, so accept these few clippings as
evidence of my thinking about you. You probably already have
a service, but remember that these were sent by hand!

It strikes me that you ought to close down the hotel
for the season and come back to the shady zone. To this end
I will lend my efforts! All best, Earl, and bless you.

Cordially,

Rod Serling

RS:prt
Encls

The letter Rod Serling sent to Holliman when the actor was in the hospital.

Serling shares a conversation with Robby the Robot, famous for his role in the classic sci-fi film, *Forbidden Planet*. For his appearance in the *Twilight Zone* episode "Uncle Simon," Robby was fitted with an alternate headpiece, to appear more human.

director just had to have me in his next picture, and his next picture just happened to be *Forbidden Planet*. So he offered it to me and I read it and I thought, "This isn't right for me, I wouldn't be good at this." And they offered me more money, and so I finally said yes and did it, but I was never comfortable in it.

When Rod said it was a science-fiction thing, I thought, "Oh god, it's another thing with 30 guys on a spaceship." So I got it either that night or the next night, and I sat down to eat. And I turned the first page and I went

right to the script before I ate anything. I was just so fascinated with this — the hair was standing up on the back of my neck. No matter where this character went, there were remnants and indications that people had been there, but there was nobody around. But it was a chilling thing, it was fascinating. So I immediately said yes. And they paid me a nice sum at that time; they gave me $5,000 to do it. And today that's not a lot of money, but in those days it was nice. They were paying guest stars on big shows to do things like that, but I had never made that kind of money.

I'll never forget the first read-through. I felt, there again, rather uncomfortable because I wasn't used to acting by myself. And I sat down at a little room at Universal, with Rod and Bill Self, who was executive producer, and Robert Stevens, who was the director, whom

Earl Holliman stars as Mike Ferris in the pilot episode, "Where is Everybody?"

On the set of "Escape Clause," Rod Serling discusses the shooting script with director Mitchell Leisen.

I'd never met. We went through the script and they read the directions and I read the dialogue. And the next day we started shooting. Rod was on the set back and forth a bit, he wasn't permanently there all the time, but he was there quite a lot. But we worked very hard the next day, it was a cold December day. We worked all day long, and just as it was turning dark about five o'clock — I was really tired, because I was in every shot — suddenly I heard the loader of the camera, he was changing the film, and I heard him say, "Uh-oh." Something had been wrong with the camera all day long and they had not noticed it, and they didn't have one single shot. Everything we shot that day had to be reshot. And I went home and it turned out I had the flu, I had 102 degrees of fever and crawled in a hot tub and began to take aspirin and all kinds of stuff. So, if you notice it, it's not so bad so much anymore, but I used to be very aware that I was hoarse in some of the beginning shots, because

I was not well. But I went over to the set the next day and eventually we reshot all that stuff and we started out again down the road and back into the café.

But seeing it now, I mean, god almighty, I'd love to do it all over again, because I had never had to work totally alone. And a lot of the dialogue, it didn't fit my mouth as well as it fit Rod's, you know. It was definitely Rod Serling speaking. When Mike stands in front of the mirror and is making himself an ice-cream soda, or hot-fudge sundae, whatever he made, he gets to talking about, "There's more about you, were you a piece of pork, an undigested piece of beef," or something, he's talking about stuff from Dickens. And you know, it was a little foreign to me, but I'd love to go back and really play all those moments again. And especially at the end of the first act, when I come running out of the jail and run right up into the camera yelling, "Where is everybody?!" I didn't have the experience to really *look* in that camera. I was a little intimidated by it.

It was quite an experience. I had a wonderful time. I wanted to get together with [director] Bob Stevens, and every time I went over to talk to him, he would get up to answer the phone. And he said, later on, that he was just one of those guys that just didn't know how to talk to you about acting. Bob was a wonderful, adorable sweetheart of a guy, and everybody who worked with him loved him, but they also said he was a nut.

Getting to know Rod was fun. He was a great, fun guy, and very sure of himself. He could be quite cocky if he wanted to be, but not in a negative way, just a fun way. If I went to him and made a suggestion he didn't like, he would contemplate it for a second and he would say, "Let me put it to you this way. You're wrong." He was so talented and really a sweetheart of a guy. They're not all like that, you know.

On location for "Mr. Denton on Doomsday," director Allen Reisner joins in on a conversation with actor Dan Duryea and Serling.

I've heard he respected actors and that if he needed to rewrite a line, he would go off set and rewrite it.

There's the scene where I'm in the telephone booth. Now, in the one that's released, I don't know whether it's still . . . In the original version, the phone rings in the telephone booth, I run to it, slam the door, and pick up the phone and say, "Hello," and start talking to the operator and it turns out to be a recording. And then finally, in frustration, I hang up and next thing I turn around and I try to get out and the door is locked. And I think somebody is playing a joke on me. But before that happens, I begin to frantically turn through the phonebook, looking for something, anything. And I'm running through names and I mention various relatives of mine, just throw in their names. But I said to Rod after the scene, "Rod, what if I tear a page out of the phonebook,

and it ends up in my pocket. And after we find out this whole thing took place in my mind, at the end of the thing, if somehow out of my pocket, at last, falls this torn page from the phonebook out of limbo." And he said he liked the idea, but he said he couldn't do it because CBS wanted realism. That was before they really got into the more bizarre, more interesting stuff. Actually, everything that happens in "Where Is Everybody?" takes place in my mind; there's nothing occult or bizarre or strange really that happens. It's all realistic.

When Rod wrote the novelizations of his scripts, he changed the ending so your character still had a ticket stub from the theater in his pocket.

Ah, that was it! Well, see, he added all that later — I mean, after we did the show. I'm not taking credit for something . . . but that was my suggestion at the time. There were two things, by the way, that really were chilling in the script that were not chilling when I saw it. There's nothing in the world that would make me think that there was a real person sitting in that truck. I wish there had been some way of shooting that to make it a little more real. If they had used a real person sitting there very quietly, dressed in the same stuff, and then when I open the door this mannequin falls out, so it looked like a real person but it was really a mannequin, that would have been something that would have been more surprising. As it was, it was not surprising.

And the other thing, because Rod wrote it wonderfully, but it didn't come off the way . . . After coming out of the theater, I trip over the bicycle and fall on the sidewalk. I look up, and in the script there's this big eye looking at me and that was very spooky. Well, in the film, of course, it's obviously just a big painted eye on the sign from the oculist, and it didn't have the same effect. But those little shortcomings, if there were shortcomings, were not Rod's.

Future Colombo Peter Falk stars as Ramos Clemente in the episode, "The Mirror."

The scene where you run into the mirror at the base of the stairs is particularly shocking to watch.

What they did was they tied the camera down so that it was immovable, and they shot me coming down the stairs and running into the mirror and then falling. Then they shot the whole thing without me, and the cameras looking into the mirror at all times. And then at a certain period they said, "Now," and a guy with a sledgehammer behind the mirror hits it and breaks it, and it all shatters. So, they then take the two films and put them together and they blank on the one where I'm not coming down the stairs, and they black my figure out where my figure would be. It's almost like putting a shadow on the other film, so that I'm not ethereal coming down, you can't see through me. And they put the two strips together, and then make a cutout of the one, and they just follow me down the steps.

Why weren't you ever called back to work on another episode?

You know, I never quite understood that. Because as I just shared this letter to you where Rod says, "It strikes me that you ought to close down the hotel for the season and come back to the shady zone. To this end I will lend my efforts!" Yeah, I don't know why I never came back. Jim Lister was a casting guy who later was a friend of mine, and I once asked him, "Why did they not have me back?" He said, "Well, I think for one thing they're offering about half the money and I think they were embarrassed to offer it to you." Something to that effect, and that just wasn't a good reason for me. I have no idea, because everybody really liked me. It wasn't like, "Oh god, he's a pain

In this sequence of shots during a break on "Mr. Denton on Doomsday," Duryea stepped out and Jeanne Cooper leaned forward, covering Reisner just as the picture was snapped. Duryea stepped back in, laughing, and they all broke up over the fact that Jeanne messed up Reisner's big chance to have his picture taken.

in the ass," or, "He did a terrible job." I don't know, it just never happened.

What do you think makes a good *Twilight Zone*?
Well, the hook, the twist. They're like O. Henry short stories in many ways. And Rod had a knack for that. He had that great imagination. It put people, Mr. Everybody, Mr. Joe America, Joan America, in a situation that any of us could possibly wander into. It was a big hit mainly because it was tremendous entertainment. It was an engrossing show. It was almost always a surprise. There were so many wonderful moments that you reflect on in *The Twilight Zone*. Yet, from time to time I hear somebody discussing a *Twilight Zone* I never saw. I unfortunately didn't see every episode. But there's hardly anybody you know who doesn't know what *The Twilight Zone* is.

As a matter of fact, I went to an agency interview a few years ago and I was switching from one agent to another, and my manager took me over to meet these people. And of all my credits — and I did a lot of motion pictures — the one thing they were really impressed

about was that I did the *Twilight Zone* pilot. The other stuff didn't mean anything to them. People are always saying to me, "Didn't you do the original pilot for The *Twilight Zone*?" And I cleverly nod and slyly say, "Yep."

I've got to tell you something about the *Twilight Zone* pilot. I personally feel very, very lucky to be chosen by Rod personally to do it. Because that's a part that almost any actor with a soul could have done and probably done better. The point is, I'm the one who got it. But I'm not the only one who could have done it, you know, and everybody would have brought something different to it. I just feel very lucky to have been chosen to do it. And here we are talking about it nearly 50 years later.

Did you ever see Rod Serling after that?
The last time I saw Rod, we were both in the audience for a live show, and we hadn't seen each other for years, and we stood and talked for a while. It couldn't have been more than a year or two before he died, but at that time he started doing some commercials and I don't remember what else he was doing.

I once asked him how he got started writing, and he said it was when he was in the service in WWII. He was in the hospital, and he had all this time in the hospital, and they came around offering them things to do, and he said it was either basket weaving or learning how to write. And he said he decided he'd try and learn how to write. Otherwise he might have been a hell of a basket weaver.

Lamont Johnson

Lamont Johnson started off acting in television shows such as *Alfred Hitchcock Presents* and *Gunsmoke*, and then became a television and film director. He directed *Twilight Zone* episodes "The Shelter," "Five Characters in Search of an Exit," "Nothing in the Dark," "One More Pallbearer," "Kick the Can," "Four O'Clock," "Hocus-Pocus and Frisby," and "Passage on the Lady Anne."

Having worked on *The Twilight Zone*, what were your impressions of Rod Serling?
An extraordinarily wired man and obviously hugely sensitive guy; very prickly, but also a very gentle person. Obviously a bundle of nerves — I'd never seen anybody chain-smoke so intensely as he did, which of course killed him. Nerves like you wouldn't believe. When he was confronted with having to do the lead-ins, the famous Serling lead-ins, which everybody loves, it drove him crazy. He would break out in a deadly sweat and he dreaded that, he really hated it. I think he was pretty vain, but the complexities were just amazing about the guy.

So I played some tricks on him, I did a couple of the lead-ins for some of my shows, and I knew how nervous he was, so I would say, "Just run it, Rod, and just talk to me, they're still setting up." So he would do it more improvisatorially, sort of freely, and I usually would like it. I would say, "That's it! We've bought it." And he'd say, "Okay, when do we have to do it?" I said, "We just did it." And he was so relieved that he said, "Oh, I want you to do all of these. That's terrific!" And so I did quite a few of them from shows that weren't mine. But that showed you how just a little deflecting from the normal procedure saved his nerves.

What did you think of the fourth season's hour-length format?

I didn't like it. I thought that it was a natural, absolutely in its right element, in the half-hour. Rod's whole idea, the whole feeling of suspending disbelief for a certain period of time, then having a wonderful snapper come along, worked magnificently, classically, in the half-hour, and didn't work nearly as well in the hour. I'm not just talking the one I did, "Passage on the Lady Anne," but the ones I saw. There was a certain kind of time capsule that was perfect for *The Twilight Zone*, that would suspend disbelief for so long, and then would cause a wonderful snapper and you had the *Twilight Zone* experience. But somehow with the hour it lumbered, it didn't stay afloat.

What do you think makes a good *Twilight Zone*?

First of all, a naturalistic setup starting out with something that seems extremely natural, very normal, and then seeing it turned upside-down. This is what I think is so universal and such a great appeal to people. We all have these nightmares, we all have our own Twilight Zones — we live these seemingly plateau lives a lot of the time, but there are things that are unaccountable, or totally deranged in the normal forms of things that suddenly come up, so that everybody's nerve ends are all attuned to a

Jack Albertson stars as Jerry Harlowe in his first of two *Twilight Zone* episodes, "The Shelter."

more placid or normal thing, and we love when we know it's fiction, to see discomfiture, that twist, that makes your imagination work and gives you prickles.

While you were working on The *Twilight Zone*, what did you think of its production?

Well, it was always a turn-on. It was always a delightfully refreshing kind of experience. It had wonderful actors who wanted to work on it, you worked with really good, imaginative writers, and Buck Houghton was a great guy to work with. I would look forward to it. Whenever I'd get a call for a *Twilight Zone*, my agent would say, "Well, I'll get a script and send it to you," and I'd say, "I don't need it. If it's *The Twilight Zone*, I want to do it!" The last two before "Lady Anne" are hazy to me. These weren't my favorites. I love "Kick the Can." And I love some of the other classics, like the one where the guy looks out the plane window and sees the gremlin, and the great one with Burgess Meredith and the glasses! That's the all-time classic *Twilight Zone*.

Jerry pleads with Doctor Stockton (Larry Gates) to allow entry into his fallout shelter.

The cast of "The Shelter" cracks up during a run-through for the argument scene between character Marty Weiss (Joseph Bernard) and Henderson (Sandy Kenyon). Also seen here are Moria Turner, Jo Helton, John McLiam, and Jack Albertson.

How did the production values of *The Twilight Zone* compare to other television shows you had worked on?

You went in and picked a set with a scene designer, and you knew there wasn't going to be much to do anything with, there was no money for the budget, you would pull together and that was part of the joy of the show, you'd do it with odd lighting, and for that reason my favorite was "Five Characters in Search of an Exit," because all it was, was that tube they were all in. But that really called upon your imagination, and it was a great joy for that reason. You even relished the fact that you didn't have a lot of money to play with, because there was so much imagination that was part of the equation.

Do you recall if any other episodes were in rehearsals or being shot while you were working on your episodes?

No. You see, in those days, I was really busy earning a living and I was doing a lot of shows. I would come in and do a brief preparation and kind of wing it as I went along, which was great fun. Usually with excellent casts. And then I would get a minimal day of editing, and that was it maybe. There were no frills on *The Twilight Zone*. But because the material is so stupendous — you know, the basic creative talent — you just said, "Okay, it's worth it."

What was Buck Houghton like?

A thoroughly delightful guy, a good business-man who had a great appreciation for the creative talents. He wasn't an enormously creative person himself, but he had the imagination to go with his business sense and his production sense. He appreciated what it took to have the creative process go. He had a huge respect and

This shot reveals where the crew was able to film within the limited space of the tube set in "Five Characters in Search of an Exit." Actors Murray Matheson and William Windom run through dialogue for the next scene as a crewman readies their marks. Notice the camera has been named "Fink Rat."

consideration for Rod's feelings, and so it was a great complementary relationship. I had usually superior cameramen that I loved working with on other productions, and Buck again — from everything in terms of the director's cut, the discussion of things — was a real gentleman and a guy I got to be friendly with later on, too. I certainly miss him. Sad that he wasn't better used in his later years.

How was it working with director of photography George T. Clemens?

He was wonderful. I worked with him on a couple of other things, too. Always a very conservative guy with a tremendous technique, but when you challenged him, when you want-ed to do something different or offbeat, he loved it and would find a way to do it. He was a very quiet guy. He would not say a lot when you'd take him through a scene and show him things, but his questions were always very appropriate, and if he had to demure about something, he would express it always in a cre-

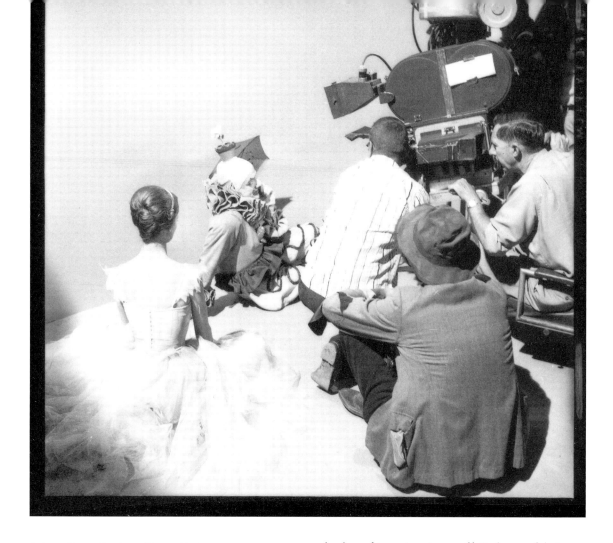

Actress Susan Harrison, Murray Matheson, and camera-men work on a close-up shot of the Clown.

ative way: "Is it possible we could do this instead of that . . . ?" But he would never flat-ly say, "Oh, let's not do that, I don't want to do that." He would never pull a master cam-eraman on you.

I know the scripts were fairly tight. Was there an opportunity to direct differently than how the scripts were laid out?
Interesting question. I know that everybody's imagination and all of their reflexes were con-siderably more alert — you were on a kind of good adrenaline, a happy adrenaline that creat-ed a lot of imaginative stuff. I always felt I was doing my best work when I was doing that.

From a directorial point of view, what would you say is the look and feel of *The Twilight Zone*?
Well, what makes it all the spookier is it had an illusioned height of reality. It was highly theatri-cal, but it had an illusion of being very real, and yet bizarre, almost nightmarish things were happening to you and to it. Therefore, the light-ing and the look ought to be fairly normal, so that when you saw a face coming in the plane window, from "Nightmare at 20,000 Feet," you knew that that was something that looked so real, but "My god, that's impossible!"

You must have had much input into the casting.
Oh yeah, to a certain degree. A lot of times,

The full cast from "Five Characters in Search of an Exit": Susan Harrison, Kelton Garwood, Murray Matheson, William Windom, and Clark Allen.

they were giving you a script and would say they wanted so-and-so for this, and I would usually concur because they were usually wonderful choices. I had brought to them Gladys Cooper, with whom I worked in the theater and summer stock and even some television, and really wonderful great old stars, British and American theater, and movies, and she was perfect for that old lady in "Nothing in the Dark." So then we had to get a young guy to play Death, the policeman. So I saw the people and then called up Ethel Winant, who was the casting director, and I said, "I saw this terrific guy on your cast —" She was also casting director for *Playhouse 90*. "Who is that good-looking kid who played the scene with Charles Laughton last night [in Serling's 'In the Presence of Mine Enemies']?" She said, "His

name is Bob something, I don't know what his last name is, let me look it up." She comes back and says, "Well, his name is Bob Redford, but he doesn't have an agent. I'll have to try and reach him for you." She called me back and said, "I can get a hold of him. Where do you want him to go?" So I said for him to come and read. He read for me and he's perfect! And I don't think Bob had done anything but live television and theater before that time. He had done a movie, certainly, and hadn't done any filmed television. So then I said, "Okay, I want you to come in and read for Ms. Cooper," who

British actress Gladys Cooper stars as Wanda Dunn in George Clayton Johnson's touching episode, "Nothing in the Dark."

A young Robert Redford stars as Harold Beldon. Redford comments, "I was a young actor for hire, loved working with Gladys Cooper and R.G. Armstrong, they were very fine actors. I enjoyed working with director Lamont Johnson and the writer, George Clayton Johnson. It was a short, sweet, and wonderful experience."

was a great star, and I wouldn't dream of casting anyone opposite her that hadn't read with her, and he said, "I'd be delighted." And he came on back and read with her, and I said, "Thank you, Mr. Redford, we'll let you know." And when he left, the door had barely clicked when she clutched my arm and said, "Oh, darling, get him for me!" She was a sexy old babe. I could see her looking at him, sort of cruising him like crazy.

What was Robert Redford like, working in that part?

Well, a very sensitive, excellent, wonderful performer. He did a couple of episodes of *Kildare* after that. Then he went on doing films, and the rest is history.

What did you think of George Clayton Johnson's work on the show?

I liked him, he was a very imaginative guy, I loved working on "Kick the Can" with him, and also on this one. You know, a very opinionated guy, but then most writers are. Working with Rod, who did "Five Characters," was absolutely a joy, too.

How was it directing that episode? Was it a difficult shoot?

No, it was extremely simple, as a matter of fact. The limitations of space and set put you in such an imaginative plane. So that I did it very simi-

Dunn confides in Beldon and tells him of her fear of death.

---

larly, but — and this is almost subconscious — it came out practically choreographed like a ballet. William Windom was excellent, and I loved old Murray Matheson, good people, and the girl that was just delicious, Susan Harrison.

Did you have any other options for that tube-like set?

Well, no, that's actually one of the few sets that were built, because it had to be something that we could tilt on its side for them to crawl up. So that was one of the very few cases where the production budget went for building this big tube. But that was all there was to it — there was no dressing, there was no anything else about it. So it was not an expensive set, but superbly useful.

Could you tell me about the episode of *Felicity* you directed — "Help for the Lovelorn" — that used the framework of *The Twilight Zone* as an homage to the original series?

That was fun; I had a great time doing it. I was the hugest doubting Thomas you'd ever seen. J.J. Abrams [the creator and executive producer of *Felicity*] sent my agent a couple of tapes and I thought, "This is fairly charmingly done. I mean, it's not a dumb thing." So I told J.J. I would think about it and he said, "Come down, I'll pay your way, I want to talk about it." So he brought me down and I expected at least this middle-aged kind of guy who had always followed *The Twilight Zone*, and I walked into his office on his ticket and he was younger than my grandson, and it was fascinating. So he was very persuasive, very bright, excellent, and so we put that thing together, and I had a great time doing it. I was shocked that it could have worked, and it did.

They had a very special, very hip, very up-to-date, pretty sophisticated camera technique for *Felicity* — all long lenses, even masters, and so on. It had a particular look, a style to it. But what Michael Bonvillain, the cameraman, was crazy about was when he saw three or four of the *Twilight Zone* episodes, he kept pumping me about it and I've never seen anyone so conscientious. He wanted to drain my mind for what lenses we used, under what circumstances, and he went out and found a Mitchell camera of that period. And the difference in forty-some odd years — the weight, the heaviness of that camera. He made his camera operator and assistants learn how to use that old cumbersome piece of machinery, because he felt that would have something to do with it — you know, the way we moved, the way the dollies worked — and in a way he's right, but it was his conscientiousness about it that was just so charming. The whole crew was really taken over by the idea of recreating *The Twilight Zone*.

I invited Carol Serling to the showing at UCLA that we had of the *Felicity* episode, and told her how conscientiously they went along with my intention to be so close to the original concept, and she came out to UCLA to see it, and she was absolutely delighted by it and surprised, which is terrific.

Were you involved in any of the updated *Twilight Zone* episodes?

My favorite cameraman — or one of them, at least — Bill Wages, had been so impressed with the ones I had done, and loved talking about it as a cameraman, so when he got this chance to direct a new version of *The Twilight Zone* [2002], he thought he'd like to get me in, in an advisory kind of capacity. To his shock and horror, he found out they had absolutely no interest in bringing back the qualities of it, or the atmosphere, or anything about it, they just cashed in on the title. He didn't like it either. He's a considerably younger guy and he just found it kind of offensive, because he really values what the original thing was. They're cashing in on the great cult fame of the thing and a kind of automatic response to the name *Twilight Zone*. But they had no interest in exploring it like J.J. Abrams did; he was very conscientious about that.

Richard Bare

Richard Bare is a television and film director who directed *Twilight Zone* episodes "Third from the Sun," "The Purple Testament," "Nick of Time," "The Prime Mover," "To Serve Man," "The Fugitive," and "What's in the Box."

What were your impressions of Rod Serling?

The day I first met Rod Serling, I was astound-

Lloyd Bochner (Chambers in "To Serve Man"): "So many people seem to remember 'To Serve Man' and remind me 'It's a cookbook!' It's really a delight that those segments of our lives have not been forgotten. The making of 'To Serve Man' was really an adventure."

ed. Instead of meeting someone whom I had imagined to be a tall, thin, and bespectacled and somewhat introverted writer, Rod barged into Buck Houghton's office with the energy of a whirlwind. He grabbed my hand and said he had heard some good things about me. He was short and stocky and looked like he had been a quarterback at Notre Dame. He had a grin a mile wide, told me, "Welcome aboard," and then ducked out.

Rod was often on set. Do you have any anecdotes of him to share?

The only time Rod was on my set was when he had come down to do his intros. No matter where we were in the shooting, we moved the camera over and shot his "talking head" and the assistant director let everybody know that the "master" was ready. And he was always ready. He never flubbed his lines, which, of course, were written by him. He had boundless energy and could come up with ideas faster than he could write them down on his Royal.

What would you say is the look and feel of *The Twilight Zone*?

Stark black-and-white photography and the feeling that if it were a book it would be a page-turner.

Actors William Reynolds and Dick York pose with Rod Serling on the set of "The Purple Testament."

Director Richard Bare, director of photography George T. Clemens, and a cameraman set up the next shot.

How did you come to direct *Twilight Zone* episodes? Did Buck or Rod contact you?

Neither. It was my agent who lined me up with Buck Houghton. I had not been known as a particularly esoteric director. My credits had been lots of comedy and westerns, although I did win the Director's Guild Award for Best TV director in 1958 on Warner Bros.' *77 Sunset Strip*. I would bet that since they always had a budget problem on *T-Zone*, Buck found out that I could shoot fast and put some quality on the screen. The year after *T-Zone* folded, I was signed to direct the wacky comedy series *Green Acres*, and I still hold the record for the number of continuous episodes directed by a single director — 168. I was the only director they had.

How did the production values of *The Twilight Zone* compare to other shows you had worked on?

Shooting at MGM, with access to their fantastic scene dock, we were able to provide a rich look to the show. And the back lot with its streets and countrysides helped a lot.

What was it like working with director of photography George T. Clemens?

George was fantastic and agreeable to almost anything a director could ask for. For instance, on "Third from the Sun" I got an idea that wasn't in the script, that the production department wasn't prepared for. I told George to put the camera on the center of a bridge table and get a close-up of each of the players as they had dialogue. That necessitated bringing in a "fourth wall," but neither the grips nor George complained, [they] merely went about fulfilling the director's vision. Since I started directing at a young age, I always had a certain amount of friction with the camera-

Bare proudly takes the experienced stance of the director for *The Twilight Zone*.

men — until they found out that I had gotten started as one of them.

Was the average workweek of an episode one day of rehearsals and four days shooting?
Shooting schedules varied, as some episodes were more complicated than others. I didn't do a lot of rehearsing — it was more of a reading where we all sat around the table and talked things over. I like to rehearse on the stage, and not to the point that the actors lose

their energy. There is an old saying I used to use, "A perfect rehearsal is a wasted take."

Was there an opportunity to direct differently than how the scripts were laid out?
What? And get fired?

Did you have a need to do storyboards for any of your episodes?
I have made over 500 television films and a dozen theatrical movies and have never felt like using a storyboard. Storyboards can lead a director into using camera setups that someone else has conceived. It's much better to have the freedom on the set and allow the actors to contribute, and believe me, most actors can do something that no artist had preconceived.

Besides, storyboards can slow you down, adding hours to the shooting schedule and limiting a sudden inspiration a director might have on the set.

An incredible shot looking down on the entire crew and cast of "The Purple Testament."

"To Serve Man" is one of the top episodes of the series. Any comments about that?
"To Serve Man" is the episode I hear most about when the subject of *Twilight Zone* comes up. Everybody shouts out, "It's a cookbook!"

You mentioned that Rod said "Third from the Sun" was one of his favorite episodes. Did you both talk about it?
I invited Rod and Carol to a party up on Mulholland Terrace and got to know him better that night than I ever had at the studio.

Alcohol does loosen one up, and Rod confessed that the job I had done on "Third from the Sun" was exemplary, and that of all the shows to date, he liked that one best. And I know why he liked it. I used wide-angle lenses on every shot; even close-ups were made with a 28 mm. I tilted and cocked every scene to give a sense of uneasiness since the cast was making plans to fly to another planet and avoid an impending H-bomb attack. Working with actors like Fritz Weaver, Edward An-

Another great shot of the entire set during filming.

drews, and Joe Maross is a pleasure because they need no direction, only instructions to position themselves for the camera — and, of course, avoiding bumping into one another.

Were you pleased with the overall shoot on "The Purple Testament"? Anything you would have done differently?
No, I was pleased with the episode, otherwise I would have done it differently. I've always been a confident director, and once I say, "Cut

and print!" I know what I've got in the can. My films have always been easy to edit, as I virtually cut them in the camera. The editor's job is to splice the scenes together, cutting in reaction shots, etc.

Anything notable happen during filming?
Bill Reynolds was cast at the last minute, and I can say in this respect I did muddle in the casting. The actor who had been cast to play Fitzgerald after the reading went into Buck's office and said he didn't want to do the part — he didn't think a soldier who looked into the face of another soldier could cause him to die, and therefore was unbelievable. Unbelievable? That was what made *Twilight Zone*. But I had to scramble and find another actor who could

play Fitzgerald. Bill Reynolds had played the lead in a pilot I had just completed at MGM, *The Islanders*, and I knew he would be perfect. A couple of weeks after shooting, I convinced MGM that if they would let me take a small crew down to Jamaica and shoot some action sequences, the pilot would have more chance of being picked up by one of the networks. After 10 days of shooting, we packed ourselves into the Grumman Goose seaplane and headed for Miami. Twenty minutes later, both engines quit and we crashed in the Caribbean, killing George Schmidt, our cameraman. Bill Reynolds and I had three broken legs between us and were about four miles off Jamaica, swimming for our lives. After an hour or so, I yelled over to Bill, "Hey, you know what's

A wonderful shot of William Shatner and Patricia Breslin during the setup of a scene in "Nick of Time." Richard Bare watches along with the cameramen as Shatner and Breslin stand on their marks readying for the next scene.

playing on CBS tonight?" "Yeah," Bill said, "'The Purple Testament.'" And I said, "Please don't look at me!" [In "The Purple Testament," Reynolds' character sees a glow on people's faces when they're about to die.] It turned out that CBS pulled the show after reading the headlines, in deference to Bill Reynolds, that he might be dead.

Actors Buddy Ebsen and Dane Clark during a scene in "The Prime Mover," in which Ebsen's character Jimbo levitates a bed by using his power of telekinesis.

Any memorable moments working with actors William Shatner and Patricia Breslin on "Nick of Time"?

I remember Bill Shatner as a kind, gentle actor who always knew his lines, unlike the reputation he has today. Pat Breslin was a doll and

very professional. Due to the limitations of the set, this was one episode where I sent the crew home at 5 PM. As far as the devil atop the fortune machine, I thought it was a good touch.

"The Prime Mover"?

Charles Beaumont was asked by Rod to come up with a story, quick. Having none at the moment, Beaumont paid George Johnson $600 for a script about a man who could move things by telekinesis, such as dice on a table. This was the second time I had worked with the amiable Buddy Ebsen, the first being

J. Pat O'Malley and Susan Gordon star in the sci-fi episode, "The Fugitive."

Northwest Passage, also at MGM. Later, when he was doing *The Beverly Hillbillies* and I was directing *Green Acres*, we became close friends and he tried to get me to come over to Stage 1 and direct *Hillbillies*. I told him I didn't want to break Eva Gabor's heart, as she truly loved me. As far as Dane Clark was concerned, dropping down from starring roles at Warner Bros. to half-hour television didn't sit well with him and he let us all know that *T-Zone* was beneath him. What little did he know.

One of the two leading ladies, after I had asked her to go to the window and look out, asked, "What is my motivation?" "Motivation? It's your paycheck, honey."

"The Fugitive"?

I probably had some influence in the casting of this one, as I ended up with two of my favorites, the irascible J. Pat O'Malley and the indefatigable Nancy Kulp, who went on to a running part on *Hillbillies*. Both of these actors had worked for me at Warner Bros., both in the Joe McDoakes series of one-reel comedies, and hour shows like *Maverick*, *Cheyenne*, and *77 Sunset Strip*. They always lifted a scene beyond the intentions of the writers and producers. Again, Charlie Beaumont came through with a delightful script.

"What's in the Box"?

With a new producer, William Froug, the show stuck to its format all through its final year. I was impressed by the cast, two veterans of the major studios during the golden years, Bill Demarest of Paramount and Joan Blondell of the many, many Warner Bros. hit pictures. Neither one took, or needed, my direction, as I have always bragged that I wasn't running an acting school. Without arguments about how a scene is to be played, life on the set was a happy place indeed, and the assistants didn't have to order in dinners. I do remember asking for the odd-beat Sterling Holloway to play the all-knowing television repairman, who engineered the set to play a heretofore unknown channel that revealed Demarest's extramarital affair, causing his wife to blow her top. Although this episode got mixed reactions to Martin Goldsmith's script, I was fond of this show, perhaps because I worked with such a fine group of actors.

Richard Donner

Richard Donner directed *The Twilight Zone* early in his career with "Nightmare at 20,000 Feet," "From Agnes — With Love," "Sounds and Silences," "The Jeopardy Room," "The Brain Center at Whipple's,"

and "Come Wander with Me." Afterward, he directed for *The Fugitive* and *Tales from the Crypt*, as well
as numerous films, including *The Omen*, the *Lethal
Weapon* series, and *Timeline*.

What were your impressions of Rod Serling while working on the show?

Very far out, kind of a mind like a computer
before its time really, a bit of a genius, everything was always flowing. Actually, you got
the feeling like the cigarettes he was smoking
were grass. I mean, he was always coming up
with these crazy far-out ideas — couldn't be
someone who hadn't been stoned before, I
think. This man was extremely prepared for
everything he did. Extremely creative person.

How did you come to direct *Twilight Zone* episodes?

I was directing quite a bit of television and I
was doing a lot at MGM. I think my first one
was the Bill Shatner one, "Nightmare at
20,000 Feet." It was either my first or my last,
but anyways the producer was Bert Granet,
and they called me and asked me if I wanted to
do one. I read the screenplay and jumped.

How did you compare *The Twilight Zone* to some of the other early television shows you worked on?

Well, the early television shows were phenomenal. I mean, MGM especially was extraordinary;
they treated every little television show like a
feature. Most of the studios, with the exception
of Universal, or MCI or whatever the hell they
called it, had a great deal of pride in their work.
Television at Universal in those days, all they
cared about was the dollar, and they cared very
little about what the picture looked like. As for
the production values in all the shows, MGM —
probably more than any other place — put a lot
of value into the look of the piece, and the size
of it. They were extraordinary.

Did you have much input on set design and locations?

Yeah, of course. The set designer would come
in and do drawings; you'd talk about what
was going to be done. If I remember, everything I did with them was studio; there were
no locations. A lot of the sets were constructed
from other sets, that was the beauty of MGM.
They had scene docks, and as I was laying
them out and putting them together, you
would discuss whether the door should go
there, the window should go there — "I like
the bed on that wall because I want the
windows here." There was one show, "The
Jeopardy Room," where a Russian politician

On the set of "Death's-Head Revisited," actors Oscar
Beregi and Joseph Schildkraut go over a part of the script.
An info sheet notes: "There is a photo feature
possibility in that the Beregi and Schildkraut families are
old friends, but the two have never appeared in a show
together [before now]. As a boy in Vienna, Beregi lived
in the house the Schildkraut family had vacated to come
to U.S. But over Oscar's bed was a picture of Joseph
as a boy."

During filming of an outside scene in "Death's-Head Revisited," we're given an example of the vast selection of environments made available at the mighty MGM back lot.

was fleeing the country, played by Martin Landau, who was wonderful to direct. And I remember designing that very carefully, because I had to film from another hotel room into his room from across an alley. Yes, a lot of input went into those.

Your assistant director on that was Marty Moss.

Marty Moss used to ride a bicycle to work every day. Little, bald-headed Marty Moss, wonderful wonderful. If nothing else, you could sit and listen to his stories for the rest of your life.

Do you know if you had any scenes cut from "Nightmare at 20,000 Feet," due to the logistics of the shoot?

I think that was a three-day shoot, and it was the water tank at MGM where they had this air-

As the crew film this scene, Don Medford directs Beregi (off-camera) as Schildkraut speaks his off-camera lines.

plane already there. A lot of things were written for sets that were available also. I think that was Richard Matheson, yeah. A lot of times the producers would take the writers around and show them existing material and they'd come up with stories to fit it. Anyway, we were shooting on a second day — I believe it was Bert Granet who came to me and said, "You have to be out of here tonight," and I said, "What are you talking about?" and he said, "The feature department needs the airplane." And so we stayed up and shot until the sun came up. But they were wonderful, just great challenges.

That's one of the most memorable episodes in the series.

I wish they had taken a little more time and effort when they redid it in the film.

How do you feel about how the gremlin worked out?

I thought he worked out great, phenomenal. They used the acrobatic champion Nick Cravat, who was Burt Lancaster's circus partner. I loved the costume; the wardrobe was great as long as you didn't show the back with the zipper. The way we lit it, the way we shot it, I thought the face was wonderful in the window. Well, sorry, Mr. Matheson, but at least the public liked it and that's all that counts. As I remember, I liked the gremlin a lot; scared the hell out of us when Shatner looked out the window and he moved the curtain. It was great working with Shatner, we had a lot of fun. His wife was played by Christine White, who was a protégée of Loretta Young, and Asa Maynor played the stewardess.

Do you have any behind-the-scenes memories of working on that episode?

On that show, they set me up. It was that late night, when somebody said Eddie Burns had come over because he was pissed off at Bill for moving in on Asa. Anyway, I was just below the wing of the airplane talking with special effects and somebody yelled, "There's a fight in the plane," so I started up the wing of the plane, to get inside, and I saw the window that eventually Shatner was supposed to open was open. So Shatner is in the window — remember, this was about 40 feet off the concrete — and then he went inside and then all of a sudden he came shooting out the window, sliding out the window, and then he hit the wing and fell to the ground, 40 feet below. And I said, "Oh my god!" and I ran down, and when I got there the crew had gotten to him and it was a dummy. They had set it up to try and scare me. I was ready to kill them both. On my sets you usually have a lot of fun. We're lucky to be doing what we're doing. If we don't have fun doing it, get out of it.

One of the episodes was "Sounds and Silences," with John McGiver. How was it directing him?

On that series, I rarely ever had any problem with actors. John McGiver had a great sense of humor; he was a delightful person to be with. I also did one that was the first I did, believe it or not, with Wally Cox, called "From Agnes —

Wally Cox stars in the episode, "From Agnes – With Love."

with Love." I remember [in that episode] he was in love with a computer operator. The computer he was working had the woman's name Agnes, and she had a crush on him and screwed up his relationship with the girl. He was Marlon Brando's roommate as kids in New York; I used to bleed him of stories, I'd sit him down and have him tell me this and tell me that, all these wonderful stories. He died very young.

Another one of them was "The Brain Center at Whipples," with Richard Deacon.

Oh yes, the computer takes over. That was a prop that belonged to MGM, Robby the Robot, and so they wrote a show around that prop; they were smart in those days. I'm sure a lot of work went into them, and there was a very creative group.

Rod Serling on the set of "A Game of Pool."

Were you pleased with how you directed "Come Wander with Me," with Gary Crosby?

Yeah, I assume so. I had a good time doing it, and it was really interesting. I can remember the song, I can hear it right now, it was a musical, and I thought Bonnie Beecher was going to become a very important actress. In Marc Zicree's *Twilight Zone Companion*, Bill Froug says he "interviewed this frightened little girl, Liza Minnelli, and that he chose Bonnie Beecher." He didn't choose her; I did, because I knew Liza. I thought Bonnie was incredible.

What are some of your favorite *Twilight Zone* episodes?

It's like people today say, "What's your favorite film?" Each one individually has so much importance to me. I don't know my favorite episodes — I loved making each one; they were such a delight and such an enjoyment to do, and they were such a feeling of fulfillment. I couldn't pick it out and say, "This was my favorite." I remember that "Nightmare at 20,000 Feet" got a tremendous amount of reaction and play. There were some great ones made. It was a very prestigious show, and if you got the chance to direct a *Twilight Zone*, it was like you had made it. It was the thing.

Ted Post

Ted Post first directed *Twilight Zone* in the first season with "A World of Difference," and then did three more episodes later in the fifth season: "Probe 7 — Over and Out," "Mr. Garrity and the Graves," and "The Fear."

How did you get involved in the series?

"A World of Difference" was, to me, one of the most imaginative. Richard Matheson wrote that. I was supposed to do the pilot, but I couldn't. So they got Bob Stevens to do it. After "A World of Difference," Rod wanted me to do some more and I couldn't. I kept get- ting too busy, my agents kept me occupied. So Rod called me and said, "I'm going to close shop; I'm not going to do any more. I've got three of mine. You want to do them?" So I didn't even check with my agent. I said, "I'm going to do them." Of the four episodes I did, it was the best one, and that's what Rod told me. He said, "I wrote some bad ones, Teddy, I want you to know that. I'm tired. I didn't want to do any more. I had lost my patience and I

Howard Duff stars as Arthur Curtis, and Frank Maxwell as Marty the director, with cast and crew during a scene in Richard Matheson's bizarre episode, "A World of Difference."

had lost my desire to really fix things. So you're gonna get not the best of me." I said, "Ah, I'll do the best I can. But not the best of you is far superior to most." So the ones he gave me, I did the best I could, and he was right, they were nothing anywhere near what Matheson did. He had said, "Matheson is going to give you something that's way up your alley."

What about Rod Serling? What was he like?

I just loved him. They used a quote from me on the *Twilight Zone* DVDs, except they removed one word and changed the meaning. The quote is this — "Rod Serling's works were not beyond the realm of conjecture. His subtext is about humanity and not special effects." And they left out the word not. They said, ". . . *and* special effects." That really makes me sick. I said, "Rod strove to inform, enrich, nourish, and revive the dead," which he did. I did that story where he revived the dead ["Mr. Garrity and the Graves"]. "He saw the invisible, felt the intangible, and achieved the impossible." That's my quote.

What kind of person was he?

Lovely, wonderful, warmhearted, talented, brilliant, locked into his dream. When he came up with the idea, we spoke about it. I said, "It's unusual, it's different, and it should keep a lot of people awake, because it's going to be oddball, really eccentric, way away from the norm." He said, "That's what I want," and I said, "How do you feel about it?" And he said, "Because you're doing it, I feel good about it." In the early days, when he wrote those scripts, they were brilliant, they were just outstanding, and he was the guy who spent time to communicate, and he did the best he could. The only thing wrong with his writing — and he was aware of it — is that every character sounded intellectual. You could switch dialogue and you would not know, it wouldn't make any difference.

Seems he wasn't opposed to changing dialogue and such.

He'd fix everything very quickly. Some of the scripts that came in were good ideas, but they were not that well structured. He would restructure it. Or the dialogue was not superior enough for him, or rich enough for him, and he would fix it right then and there. He was wonderful. I mean, there may have been one or two writers that Rod didn't quite like, because he would do that rewrite, and they wouldn't like to be retouched as much as they had to be retouched — really be rewritten almost, some of them. But they didn't like him for that reason. But that's a handful, or less than a handful, because many of the very important writers loved the idea of sharing, of feelings and thoughts and ideas, and lifting the scene and the dialogue and the characterizations to a higher level.

Another shot of Duff and Maxwell while crewmen figure out the actors' marks.

This shot from "A World of Difference" is a *Twilight Zone* in itself, as it represents a set within a set on a soundstage where we wonder which camera is which. No wonder Jerry Raigan, I mean Arthur Curtis, is so confused.

"A World of Difference" is one of the better episodes. Viewers get a glimpse of the behind-the-scenes look of a real crew. What about any special shots?

I did something very tricky. I invented it right then and there, and Buck Houghton didn't want me to do it, he didn't approve it. I said I wanted to do this in one shot. I want Howard Duff to come into the office, first shot as he comes into the office. Gail Kobe is the secretary, she's got her feet on her desk, right? She puts her feet down quickly and behaves like a secretary. He asks for any phone calls, she gives him whatever papers, and then in one shot, I follow him into his office. They had the set arranged so that he goes through the secretary's office door, and I dolly with him into his office and then as he walks to the desk. The desk is on the other end of the stage, and I curve around with him and have him sit into the chair. His back is to me, but as he came in, I panned him over to the window. In other words, I pan him over to the window, and he opened up the window shades and let the sun in, and that's all in one shot. Never did a cut. And then I sit him down at his desk, in one shot. His back is to me, he puts his case down, there's a picture of his wife on the desk, and then he decides to make a call and picks up the phone. The phone is not working. He tries it again, it's not working. I'm still on his back a little bit, he gets up, and I still go with him on his back about halfway down, just a little beyond his shoulders. I have him walk right to the middle of the room and he hears the word, "Cut!" and he gets confused. As he turns to the left, my camera goes to the left over his shoulder, and where the window was, there's a crew. In one shot.

I was told by Matheson, "You revealed exactly what the character's problem was. The schizophrenic problem became clear just by a production concept which helped underscore and make that point." And Matheson, to this day, has never gotten over his reaction to that. It was not written, I just invented it and I felt that it would state immediately what the difficulty was going to be with this gentleman, who didn't know whether he was an actor or a businessman. It's one shot.

And for some reason Houghton thought that was going to be a costly shot?

Yeah, that's exactly right. He said, "You can't do that shot." I said, "Here's what you do. We'll put that particular wall on wheels, and as I pan him away from the window and sit him down, we roll the wall out. That's all it was, rolling the wall out. Rod said, "That's tremendous, Ted!" And that's what a good director does. He helps visualize the concept the story is rooted in. You have to make things happen like they're the most natural thing in the world. You mustn't make it look as if you're shooting your movie and make the audience aware that, "Oh, we're watching shooting now." A director must at all times make sure that he never violates that principle of keeping the audience totally engaged *in* the story, and never make them aware of the fact that there's ever a camera there.

So what did you think of *The Twilight Zone* at the time of production?

I thought it was a very imaginative experience that kept you at the edge of your seat. Because most of the stuff I saw was the kind of subject matter that really hooked you, and you couldn't get your eyes off the screen, because you wanted to follow every second of it to see where it was taking you and what the solution would be and how would it go about solving the problem. That always kind of hooked me, and I couldn't take my eyes off the set. I really was extremely caught up with it, like you, probably. And fascinated and trying to guess the answers myself as to what kind of solution they'd have to arrive at to resolve this problem. It was so uniquely worked on, so that very few people ever came to figure out the kind of ending that was always unexpected.

Did *The Twilight Zone* have a certain visual style that you didn't have an opportunity to utilize in other series?

There were some wonderful directors who knew how to attack the issues visually. They were terrific in terms of how they made the subject matter that much more interesting in the way they staged and used the camera. The lighting was different too, very much metaphysical.

On your *Twilight Zone* episodes, you mentioned you had two days for the shoot. Did you have much time for rehearsal?

Maybe a day, and sometimes those rehearsals would start in shooting. It depended on the time they gave us and what was allotted to us. But when you measured Rod Serling's *Twilight Zone* up against all the other crap that was on television, this was a miracle that it ever saw the light of day.

And not only does it still hold up, but it also stands as a groundbreaking piece. It's timeless.

That's right, it doesn't age. That says a lot about it. And the subject matter, of course, is timeless. With *Twilight Zone*, I did it so quickly, including even the one with Howard Duff, because I was being pushed like crazy by my agents to get off and get into the next project, or some other things they were pushing down my throat. So my reputation has always been, no matter what I do, I'm going to do it as if I'm playing a Stradivarius, and I had to make the best music I could possibly make. Even under the most limiting conditions.

With *Twilight Zone*, I respected Rod, and I was very happy to be a part of it. Rod Serling

Actual filming of the scene where Marty confronts the man who, in his reality, is actor Jerry Raigan.

makes me very happy. That he was there, and he was the inspiring force that really gave you the feeling that this was worthy of your time and your spirit. To be totally engaged and involved in making it the best possible thing you can do under the very limiting circumstances.

From what's been mentioned, Serling did treat people in a good way that made you feel the work you did meant something.

That's the point! Meaningful work — it had meaning. It had human significance. A thrill you feel, as if you are really joined in hands with life to do something of value with it.

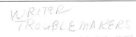

CBS TELEVISION

A DIVISION OF COLUMBIA BROADCASTING SYSTEM, INC.

6121 Sunset Blvd. ● Hollywood 28, Calif. ● HO. 9-1212

EMPLOYMENT CONTRACT—INDIVIDUAL SCRIPT

Agreement Between   Date........ **November 14,** 19 **57**

┌ **Mr. Rod Serling**
c/o Ashley-Steiner Agency
449 So. Beverly Drive   (herein called "Writer")
Beverly Hills, California ┘

and
CBS TELEVISION   (herein called "Producer")

1. Employment: Producer hereby employs Writer, and Writer hereby accepts such employment, as a script writer for the preparation of television script material described as follows: **Polish of a television script entitled "The Troublemakers" by George Bellak for the television program series entitled:**

"PLAYHOUSE 90" – air date November 21, 1957

2. Compensation: Producer will pay Writer, as compensation in full for Writer's services hereunder, all rights in said material and Writer's other agreements herein contained, the sum of $**750.00** ....payable **upon delivery of a satisfactory polish to be acceptable to CBS Television acting in the reasonable exercise of its discretion. Plus auto expenses to be accounted for.**

3. Special Provisions: **None.**

Execution of this agreement signifies acceptance by Producer and Writer of all of the above terms and conditions and those on the reverse hereof and attached hereto, if any.

_____
Writer

CBS TELEVISION
A Division of Columbia Broadcasting System, Inc.

By _____

_____
Telephone Number

086 -18 - 5427
Social Security Number

W-1 3/55 F-425

A signed contract for Rod Serling to polish the _Playhouse 90_ script "The Troublemakers," by George Bellak.

Del Reisman

Del Reisman was an associate producer and story editor for *The Twilight Zone,* and an associate producer for several other shows, including *The Untouchables* and *Rawhide.* He also wrote for many television shows, including *Peyton Place, Kung Fu,* and *The Six Million Dollar Man.*

What were your impressions of Rod Serling when you first started working on the series?
I knew him in some of the early days of live television, I'd run into him a few times, and I always liked him. I found him a very amusing guy, he loved jokes, and then I worked with him. I was story editor on *Playhouse 90,* and Rod wrote five or six scripts for that show. And then when *Twilight Zone* was in the middle of its first season, Rod called me and said he would be interested in getting some script help, because it was just him, and Buck Houghton was producing. Buck wasn't a writer and I was tied up. Anyway, when I was free at the end of that television season, I said, "Boy, I'd love to have joined you."

So I went over to *Twilight Zone* as we developed season number two, and Buck was still producing, and my impression of Rod, which I got very, very early, was that he was highly intelligent and very passionate about what he did. He had a tremendous intensity to him in terms of his personality, and he was very professional and did things in his way. I mean, it was his voice, which I don't think was imposed on material, it's just the way instinctively and naturally it came out of him. And I liked him very much. He was really a decent person, a person of tremendous goodwill and generosity. So I was attracted to him as a person who was significant as a human being — that, and above and beyond, his talent. I found it a very intriguing experience to be around Rod. We were not social pals ever, but I would run into him a great deal because we frequented the same places. The same restaurants and the same movie houses, so we'd see each other a lot and talk a lot and that was always enjoyable to me.

Do you have any anecdotes about Rod?
Rod was a marvelous joke storyteller, and his great pleasure was to go over to CBS, to the dress rehearsal of *The Red Skelton Show.* Red was a wonderful ex-vaudeville comic who really specialized in a great deal of pantomime, and Red's dress rehearsals were legendary. I went with Rod once or twice, and Red would know he was out there. In the classic way of vaudeville, Red Skelton would not use the actual punch line of the joke in the sketch. He would do mumbo jumbo, because all of those comics who were trained in vaudeville, they'd botch up the timing if they actually rehearsed the punch line. Jackie Gleason was like that. They wanted the punch line to be fresh, and so he would do mumbo jumbo. It was dress rehearsal and the cameras were moving

Rod Serling and director Mitchell Leisen going over the jail sequence in the script for "Escape Clause."

A "Time Enough at Last" photo, autographed by Burgess Meredith.

Thomas Gomez and David Wayne star in "Escape Clause." Seen here is the filming of the scene when the Devil, Cadwallader [Gomez], stamps his signature on the contract for Bedeker's soul [Wayne].

A special-effects man on the extreme left created the smoke.

around and so on, but it would be absolutely filthy, whatever Red would say, absolutely filthy. And, of course, Rod would fall on the floor laughing. Rod was a great fan of comedy, a great, great jokester. If I would run into him at a café or something, he'd come right up to me and say, "Okay, two guys walk into a bar . . ." He'd just start.

So you became story editor and then you were also assistant producer to Buck.

Actually, my official title was associate producer. But my title kind of obscured a lot of sins. Rod wanted me on the show because he wanted somebody else in story other than himself. He wanted, in effect, a classic old-fashioned story editor, someone whose job was to find material, work with writers in developing it, and so on. And that was the thrust of my job. I was also assisting Buck in many of the production details. So the title was associate producer, but the job was to find the stories.

What was involved in being story editor for the series?

There was a great deal of material that was submitted to us. The agencies submitted material to us, individual writers would call up, but mostly on *Twilight Zone*, it was my specific search for story ideas. Buck and I would drive out into the vast MGM back lot, and it was just extraordinary, it was like a city. They had everything. They had a magnificent French village street, which they used in everything, and they would simply redress it from one movie to the next. They had every conceivable thing. And one time we were out there, we were driving past this one area and we both said at the same time, "Boy, that looks like the post-holocaust, it looks like the nuclear war has hit this place." So we began to talk about it, and out of that, and long discussions with Rod, came the story that Burgess Meredith was in, "Time Enough at Last."

The other side of my job was to work with the

Cast and crew during the filming of a scene from "The Trouble with Templeton."

writers. I remember a young writer who was really fascinated with science fiction named George Clayton Johnson, and George was presenting a lot of ideas and so on, and Rod said to him directly, "You've never written a screenplay before, a teleplay before, and I don't want to start you on *Twilight Zone*. Show us your stories, but we'll have to have somebody else write the teleplay, because it's complex." I'm putting it in crude terms; Rod was very courteous. And George was close with Charlie Beaumont and Richard Matheson, so he came with professional credentials in terms of his professional associations. So one day, he submitted a story, and Rod called Buck and me and said, "I want Del to work with this guy and get a teleplay out of him." I said,

"Absolutely." So George came in and was as much of a character then as he is now, and we sat down to work together and it was not easy. And the reason was a very favorable one for him, because he didn't know it at the time, but he had a particular voice, he really did. And it was just instinctive with him, and I would tell him with "A Penny for Your Thoughts," "You make up the rules for this story. In other words, whatever you say, you have to stick with it, you have to stick with the rules. Can he overhear the guy next to him? Can he overhear the people out in the street? You know, what does he overhear? And whatever you decide, that's the rule, and then you stick with it. You create your universe for this story." So we worked that way, and it was a struggle. But finally he got the script out and it was his, and I want to emphasize this — every word was his. I would not touch it. I worked as a guide for him. I wouldn't touch it. Every word was his and it turned out to be a very good show, and then of

Inger Stevens in the car rigged for running shots from the back seat, while the crew prepares for the next scene.

course, George went on for many others. But essentially, that's a story-editing situation.

So it was common for you to meet with Rod and Buck and the other writers?

Generally speaking, we divided it up. Rod worked mostly with Richard Matheson, Charlie Beaumont; I worked somewhat with Richard. It was really weekly television and you just couldn't let the ball drop. If you were busy with something, somebody else had to do it. Essentially, Rod worked more as one who heard the idea and then encouraged people. He didn't work on the details, he didn't do that. Buck and I would work with writers on those things. But eventually, when you get a guy like Richard Matheson, Richard was so comfortable with it, essentially it was his work. That's the way that worked out.

So, what would you say is the look and feel of a *Twilight Zone* episode?

First of all, it was unique in its time. There was

nothing on the air that had the look and the feel. I'd say start with the feeling first. The tone of the show really was intense story-telling. In other words, the show reflected more than other shows of the time — what happens next, what happens next, what happens next? Really the craft of telling a story in 26, 27 minutes, or whatever it was. And so, it had the feel of a driving story. Now, a lot of times, as in the good movies and good television, we're sitting in the audience, and we pretty well know the story that's being told. We know what's going to happen. It's how they get there that's interesting. In *Twilight Zone*, generally speaking, you didn't know the ending, or didn't guess the ending, and how they got there was also interesting. So we had a kind of double whammy in *Twilight Zone*.

The look of the show was essentially the production design and the cinematography of George Clemens, and that had an otherworldly look that was really worked on very carefully. That was where Buck was very, very prominent, in setting up that look. It wasn't necessarily tricky camera angles. It was the lighting, it was the whole classic mise-en-scène, the way that it really came across. And so it had a different physical appearance than other shows that were on television at the time, or really other feature movies. It had its own look, and that had a lot to do with George Clemens as cinematographer — the lighting particularly and the camera angles — which were not necessarily director's choices, it was just the style of the show. So the look was unique for its time.

Did you visit the set when episodes were being filmed?

Not often, but I did visit the set for professional reasons. I was only on the set because there was a problem — a story problem, a script problem, a line wasn't working, something of that type. There were a couple of exceptions to

In a scene from "The Eye of the Beholder," the doctor (William D. Gordon) and nurses (Jennifer Howard and Joanna Heyes) attempt to calm an upset Janet Tyler (Maxine Stuart).

that. The show that we used to open the second season was "King Nine Will Not Return," and this was very rare, we shot it on location, interiors and exteriors. We went up to Edwards Army Air Base up in the Mojave Desert, we drove up there — it was an intense heat, by the way — and this was the story of a lost WWII B25 bomber which had been covered up by the shifting sands. It starred Robert Cummings, who was a prominent actor of the time, and I was with it every shot for the entire shoot. Bob was having problems in the

tremendously intense heat, and he had to get into this mock-up of the plane, which increased the heat. And we had a nurse there with a towel wrapped in ice, and she would go up to Bob and put the towel on his neck between shots, and she did it to all of us. She cooled off all of us. But that was a time when being there all the time was important, because Bob Cummings would have a lot of problems with the fact that he was in this intense heat and he would say to the director, a fellow named Buzz Kulik, "Look, I've only got one or two of these takes in me, then you've got to get me out of here." And so there were some line adjustments, and so on. So I was, with that, on set all the time.

Generally, Buck would call me and he'd say, "Listen, get down to stage so-and-so, there's a problem with such-and-such," and that was when I was on the set. But that was not often. Generally speaking, both Buck and I stayed away from the actual shooting. Buck would go down at the end of the day's shooting to talk it over with George Clemens, the cinematographer, and after we saw dailies, then usually Buck would go down and talk to the director.

What was Buck like?

Buck was tall and lean and he had a kind of country-boy air about him, although he was a city boy. He used a lot of barnyard similes all the time, you know, "Like a rooster hopping on a junie bug." But he had a kind of all-American country-boy quality, and very intelligent, very well read. Buck had come up through the production side. He started out at Paramount when he was very young and he went into various departments. He went into the budget department, he went into this department, that department, so by the time Buck left Paramount and went into the producing of television films, he was a very knowledgeable producer. He knew production design, he knew enough about cinematography to talk to a cinematographer, and costuming, and so on. He was really fully grounded in all of these aspects, just a terrifically knowledgeable man, and he was all over that lot all the time. I would walk in to his secretary and say, "I've got to talk to Buck," and she'd say, "He's on Stage 33, he'll be there ten more minutes." He had a schedule like an airline. So he worked terribly hard.

Despite having a low budget, you had the sets at your disposal, the properties.

Yes, exactly. We had a lot of things there, mostly the back lot, where you could get, "Okay, let's use this street," you know, the Andy Hardy street, that little room, and redress it and use part of it and use another

Rod Serling graciously signs books for fans at a bookstore.

part of it, and that was the great advantage because they had all the stuff there. Now, naturally we were charged — that was expensive stuff — but it was there, it was available. So we were fortunate in that way.

Would you say Rod liked the celebrity status, yet remained humble toward the public?

It was that strange paradox. There was that café up on Sunset Boulevard, Villa Nova was the name of it, an Italian place, it's kind of a hangout. And I would see him there occasionally, and after he would come in, he'd greet everybody at the bar, he'd make jokes and everything else, he'd go off to a booth with whoever he was having dinner with, and be in absolute isolation. He'd be in a back booth and he wouldn't want any contact after that. So there was always that paradox. I think it fed him with a lot of dramatic storytelling that he liked, but he was an interesting guy that way, because he reveled in the celebrity status.

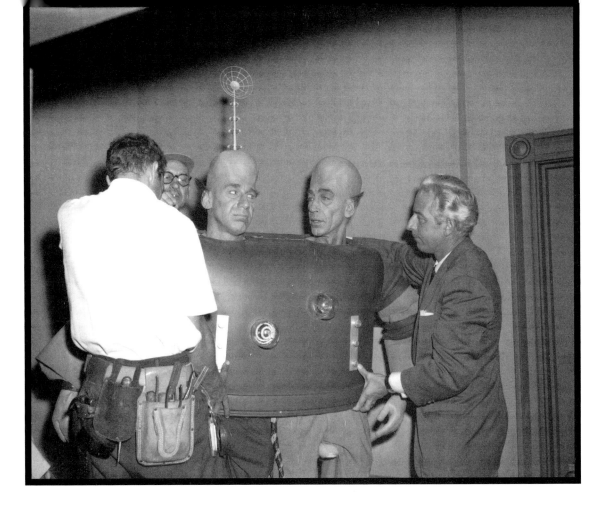

Actors Douglas Spencer and Michael Fox are fitted into their Martian suit for "Mr. Dingle, The Strong."

Hollywood kind of gave him the boot later on, didn't they?

Yeah, yeah, it was bad. It was really a strange thing. Part of it was Rod's fault, because he was ubiquitous — I mean, on television every time you turn your set on, he was doing a commercial, you know. And he was good at it, he was terribly good at it. He was selling every conceivable product, and so he was all over the place and I think that kind of wore out the welcome a little bit. But what troubled me in those days was that the way television thinks and works, he was considered old hat about

three, four, or five years after *Twilight Zone*. And that just didn't make any sense — it was this industry, this town. You know, "Bring me the next person, bring the next hot person." It's a deeply impersonal, indifferent field that is constantly looking for the next Orson Welles to come in and save us all.

And in years after that, again, I was never a social pal of Rod's, but I would run into him so much and we were very friendly when we'd see each other, and I would see him occasionally during this time, and during *Night Gallery*. And I said to him, "Look, with no comment on the show, but what are you doing up there?" And he told me, "Look, they're using me simply as the host, just using my name and getting me up there as the host." He said he had no input into the content of the show at all, and he was pretty bitter about it. But on the other hand, why did he make the deal?

Vera Miles, director John Brahm, property master Jack Pollyea, assistant director Edward Denault, and an unknown woman, on a break during the production of "Mirror Image."

Director of photography George T. Clemens on location during the shoot of "The Bewitchin' Pool."

Well, Serling did turn down the offer to be executive producer for *Night Gallery*, fearing it would reach the stress level of *Twilight Zone*. In hindsight, it's really a shame *Night Gallery* producer Jack Laird didn't make use of Serling's talents and experience beyond his script contributions and role as host.

Well, I knew Jack Laird, and I knew him when he was struggling as a writer. He'd been an actor as well. I think that Jack suddenly thought, "I want to do what Rod did with *Twilight Zone*. I want this to be mine." And it was a huge mistake, because Jack was not that kind of a talent. He had talent, but it was not

Martin Milner behind the scenes of "Mirror Image."

A shot during filming of the scene when Millicent Barnes speculates that a double from a parallel universe is trying to take over her life.

really the original voice that Rod was. And I think that a lot of that came from Jack himself, who wanted some kind of identity and I think messed it up because of that. If he'd been smart, he would have used Rod for everything that Rod had to offer, and then he himself would have prospered.

Were there any multiple *Twilight Zone* productions going on? Or was it always one episode at a time?
Oh, we had one episode shooting, one in development — that is to say, a director was already working with a location manager and with us if necessary, in terms of the script. And then the third area was that the next script was in a near-ready position. In other words, we tried to do it that way, that script one was being shot, script two was written and being prepared, and script three was being completed in the writing. So we always had a lot of balls to juggle, particularly if there were significant makeup problems. Or, you know, we had aliens, and testing the lighting, there was

always that need to have George Clemens and maybe his camera operator or somebody shoot the look of some makeup or a monster face or something, so there was a lot of testing going on. So it was sometimes things worked, and sometimes they didn't.

Had you submitted any of your own stories?
Well, to tell you the truth, when I went to *Twilight Zone*, Rod said, "I want you to really work with the writers, you know, if you have any idea," but what he was saying to me was, "I'm not hiring you to write these, I'm hiring you to work with the writers." And I had a number of ideas that I passed on, when Buck and Rod and I had our meetings. And Rod would take them and use them in some way. So I never had an idea that completely became an episode. It would be a character from this one, an incident in that one, and so on. And that was the job; it was a story meet-

During the taping of "The Lateness of the Hour" (the first of six taped episodes), preparations are made for the emotional scene when Inger Stevens's character Jana breaks down once she finds out who she really is.

ing, and I was very facile in those days, and I presented a lot of ideas.

I gave Rod one of his big laughs from the whole second season. We were talking about an alien story, and an alien in my favorite setting for *Twilight Zone*, a diner. You know, there's a diner, a dozen people are in there, and a guy serving coffee and hamburgers and whatever, small town. And a guy comes in, takes his hat and coat off and puts them on the rack, comes in and sits down, orders some coffee and pie or something. And I remember Rod said, "Well, how do we know which one is the alien?" And I said, "It's the one with the big green antennae." And Rod fell on the floor, and that was the one that sustained us through a lot of problems, so I was proud of that little remark.

These were very, very creative meetings, and I look back on them very fondly because no-body demanded credit for anything, nobody said, "Wait a minute, that's mine!" It was an exchange of views. And it was very serendipity-like. I mean, you'd go this way, and then that way, this way, that way, and so it was one of the best creative experiences of my life.

So you might have been in a meeting and collectively come up with an idea for a story, and then he would have gone off and written it.
Exactly, and he would come back x number of days later and toss a first draft on our desks, and it would have used that idea, but in his way. In other words, he would take the idea that we started with and he would turn it and twist it. He was remarkably fast, just remarkable. As you know, he dictated into a machine, and I used to ask him, "I have to see the words on the page. How do you do it?" He said, "I don't know, I have to play every part." It was just amazing. And I know his secretaries would come in the next day, take the tape, and type it up. They were always amazed.

What was George T. Clemens like?
I may have had a different view than Buck, but George Clemens to me was a tyrant of the set [laughs]. In other words, he was looking at the clock like any good cinematographer — "Are we going to get it done?" In other words, "If this camera setup is the setup the director wants, it's going to take me 45 minutes to light it, and it's my responsibility." George, I'm sure, said to himself, to inform the director, "Okay, I'll do the shot that you want and come back in 45 minutes, I'll have it lit." And the director would then say, "Well, wait a minute, wait just a minute. We've got to finish the day's work. So what about this and this and that?" It would be a very simple camera move, and George would say, "Fine, come back in five minutes, I'll have it lit." So he was a tyrant of the set, and when he saw blood, he

Buzz Kulik directs Brian Aherne and costars Pippa Scott and Charles S. Carlson in a scene from "The Trouble with Templeton."

was like a shark. He went right for it. If he had a director who had a sense of hesitation about him, or a director who was not quite sure, he just fed on that director. But Buck, who had the chore of dealing with George all the time, probably had a more benign view. But I saw George in action a lot and I thought George is really kind of running the set, because of the need to move, to get going, to complete the shot and go on to the next, because of the horrendous pressure of the schedule. When you have a director like Doug Heyes, who was very experienced, Buzz Kulik, who was very experienced, that was a different thing on the set. Because those guys would say, "Okay, George, thank you very much for your help, but this is what we're going to do, and we're going to do this, and that and that." So the experienced guys would take over, which is really the way it should be.

It must have been something to see some of these directors, like Buzz Kulik, Douglas Heyes, and another one was John Brahm.

John Brahm, who was a venerable older director with a certain reputation. Which was of highly stylized horror films and mystery films and so on, out of the German Expressionist tradition, the tradition of F.W. Murnau and all of the great prewar German directors. And John was a very interesting guy. He was very skilled with lighting, camera, and so on, because he had done those horror pictures, those melodramatic pictures. He was very interesting and very able.

Did you only work on the second season of _The Twilight Zone_?

That's correct, that long second season. At the end of the second season we did not know we would be renewed, we had no way of knowing. And Jim Aubrey kept everybody hanging, and Rod called me one day, and he said, "Listen, I don't know what's going to happen. You better tell your agent, just don't wait." So that's what happened, and I went on to do something else. Then a week or two later I found out they were renewed. And I was delighted for them, you know, and Buck recommended a fellow I knew to work with him on stories, Dick McDonagh, good guy, able guy. So I would have loved to have stayed with the show, but CBS and Jim Aubrey tormented Rod with that. I mean, they just held out till the last minute, in terms of renewing it, anyway. I really wished that I'd been able to stay with it, but I took Rod's advice, and I was glad he was interested in my welfare.

What did you think of _The Twilight Zone_ at the time?

I thought it was great. I had no idea in the world that it would last beyond its time. But I knew that I was working on something very good, and I was really excited about that fact.

I knew it was good while we were doing it. That's why, when there's a marathon on or something, I tune in now and then and I'd look at something, and I would remember all of the agony of getting that show done.

A full shot of an MGM sound stage, during the filming of "Cavender Is Coming."

Although it never really had high ratings when it first aired.

No, it didn't. That's why Jim Aubrey was after us all the time, because he wanted higher ratings for the show and it just didn't sustain them. But the interesting thing, and it's one of the first times it happened in television, was that the impact of the show on the audience that did see it was far greater than the impact of shows that had higher ratings on their audiences — far greater. And that's what built it through the years: the people who did watch it were deeply affected by it.

Bert Granet

Bert Granet was a Hollywood writer and producer who worked in film before producing television shows like *The Loretta Young Show*, *The Untouchables*, and *The Intruders*, as well as later seasons of *Twilight Zone*. He was the producer for *Westinghouse Desilu Playhouse*, where the beginnings of what would evolve into *Twilight Zone* were first seeded with the Rod Serling teleplay, "The Time Element."

Do you have any mementos from "The Time Element"?

I can read you a couple of letters Rod sent me. Here is a fax dated June 17, 1960:

Dear Bert,
I can't give you residuals for doing our "pilot," but you can have use of the Emmy three days a week, and every other weekend. Bless you for your cordial note. See you soon.
Cordially, Rod

Another one from May 22, 1961:

Dear Bert,
Your note was a delight and it reminds me that I owe you another thank-you for the gracious ad in the trades a couple of weeks ago. Talented people, I suppose, are at somewhat of a premium around here. And when the talented people were as gracious as you are, it makes for quite a combination. Again, thank you, Rod

Were you on set for your productions for *The Twilight Zone*? Was that a common thing?

No, you're very seldom on set because you're developing scripts, you're editing the previous week's pictures. The set is a very bad place for a producer to be, whether it's moving pictures or television. Why? Because sets are built big

and cameras' views are limited, it's best for you to see the picture in the rushes, to see if you're getting the story you wanted to get. To see the actual film, what the director is struggling with, and the glamour of so-called sets, which is minuscule, a lot of technical people doing a lot of technical work, and your presence on the set only creates fear, since you're the boss. You have only one way to behave if you ever become a boss: say something nice before you blam past somebody or you'll get two days' bad work.

Did you have any multiple productions during your episodes?

One at a time. You had a crew that stayed with you for the year, so that was the best way. Some shows, because of their economics, do two at a time, but we did one at a time.

Did you scout any of the outside locations yourself?

Generally, if there was something special,

Producer Bert Granet visits the set during the filming of "**Of Late I Think of Cliffordville.**"

you'd go out and look at it. If not, you'd send a man out with a Polaroid camera and have him come back, and you'd say, "That's fine." Television didn't lend for very much going on in the studio; it was expensive to send the whole crew out.

A shot of the crew seconds before filming a scene in which Burgess Meredith displays his ultimate strength in "Mr. Dingle, The Strong."

Any input on the types of sets or backgrounds being used?

Yes, you saw them, but at a certain point the communication becomes easy, the people understand you and you understand them — well, you get different working arrangements. Time is at a great premium in television because you're developing scripts, you're developing casting, you're cutting others' pictures, you're scoring them, you're putting in sound effects, you're looking at prints which go on the air, and your day is pretty much occupied. I would always tell my secretary to put the dirtiest work there is early in the morning, to get it over with. And it's repetitious, it's very hard, and frequently you go to bat with a show that you don't want to do, because there is nothing else available. It would be great if good writing were available to you at any given moment. There weren't many guys that could write like Rod, but he wasn't always the best writer on the show.

There are all sorts of production problems that are devoid of having anything to do with the creative quality of a *Twilight Zone* story. I have never known anybody that started out to make a bad picture or a bad television show. Whether you're in television or pictures, there are systematic demands. You've started out to get a big star, but the big star says, "I like it, but I've got something better." So you immediately compromise with some lesser personality. You start out going for this director, but he's already got a job. So, frequently, you can't do exactly as you want, but you have to go, because that show's got to be on the air two weeks from now.

Were you happy with "The Time Element" and what it achieved?

Well, it didn't particularly achieve anything for me; it achieved a hell of a lot more for Rod, who made a lot of money on it. I never forgave Rod for not offering me a partnership when he established it. Now, *The Untouchables* I owned, that's a little different. I still get paid after forty-odd years for places from Madagascar to Timbuktu.

That's quite an achievement to have your work still showing and appreciated by so many people.

Except that you turn it out like baloney. You know, it's hard to identify what's good and what's bad, it's "Let's just do it" — as is the history of any television show, comedy or drama. So much has to do with what's beyond your control, where you finally reach a point where you have to make a decision and go! You can have as much integrity as you want, but if the gods aren't with you, you're in a corrupt situation where the true matter would be to say, "No, let's not make it because this isn't right." But television doesn't behave that way.

In a subway scene from "The Mind and the Matter," actor Shelley Berman stands on his mark alongside director Buzz Kulik.

What did you think of *Twilight Zone* at the time, while you were working on it?

It was a living. You know, it's a business. Like anybody else, you can have talent, you can have a lot of things, but once it's maximized to the point where it's repetitious, it becomes a living. You do it to the best of your ability, with all the uncontrollable forces that are constantly working against you, where actors get drunk, and you've got to replace them, and things like that. It's a complex business that you've got to develop a stomach for; it's not near as easy as it looks.

I think the best episode was not written by Rod Serling. It was "Nightmare at 20,000 Feet," written by Richard Matheson, who for this kind of story was much better than Rod. Dick Donner directed "20,000 Feet," who was a very good director for it.

Was that a difficult shoot?

No, we used to go through Metro and look and see what standing sets they had of an airplane set; the story was written around the set. I thought Dick did a better job than Spielberg when Spielberg did *The Twilight Zone* as a picture. George Miller directed the episode in the film, and he tried to clamp on to a few things, but it didn't work. I was disappointed in it, though I think Spielberg is a talented man. He obviously wanted to put his own imprint on it. When the original turns out good, it's very hard to put an imprint on it with a remake, because it usually turns out lousy.

With the gremlin, it's how little you see of it, and not how much you see of it. I had to recut it and even cut short shots because supplementary ideas are much more vivid and frightening. That way you have a chance to examine what causes fright.

Another great episode you produced was "On Thursday We Leave for Home," with James Whitmore, and directed by Buzz Kulik. What did you think of Kulik's work?

Buzz worked for me several times, and he worked for me at Desilu too. He was a very competent director. Matter of fact, he shot one of the funniest scenes I've ever seen. It was Joseph Cotton, who was a drinker, he was playing a scene opposite a woman. It was a two-shot in profile and he came back from lunch drunk, and as he played to her — this was a western scene — his breath got her and she had to move back a little bit, so they looked like they were on a ship and it wasn't straight. I remembered Buzz directed that shot; when I saw it, I snickered.

There was an episode that Ida Lupino directed, "The Masks."

Yeah, "The Masks" was a pretty good one. Toward the end of the show, it just got repetitive. I find in science fiction there's a limitation to what you can write and what you can imagine, and that starts from Jules Verne on. Once you've been there, the second time — no matter how good it is — it's not quite . . . It's like reading *The War of the Worlds*, which I read as a child, by H.G. Wells, and to me, that's still the most vivid conquest of the Earth by Martians.

The interesting thing about Rod is he's a frustrated actor. If life had been what he wanted, he would have been a movie star. He loved the Hollywood scene. That appealed to him.

Actor Milton Selzer, in full prosthetic makeup, proudly displays his mask of "avarice" from the episode, "The Masks." The masks were designed by makeup artist William Tuttle, crafted by Tuttle, Charles Schram and the makeup team, and were constructed from a papier-mâché Styrofoam material.

Actress Barbara Nichols receives direction from Jack Smight during the taping of "Twenty-Two."

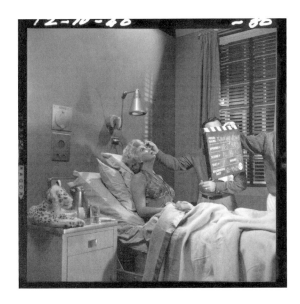

Nichols is given some glycerin drops for a teary-eyed scene.

"Stopover in a Quiet Town" was a story written by Earl Hamner. Did you know Earl well?

I never got to know Earl; Earl developed the script, brought it in, it was workable. If the script was workable, I had little to do with the writer, because why screw up something that's good? To put your own identification mark? Being a producer also means exerting tact when somebody is a better writer than you'll ever be.

I think some producers today have a tendency to mess with the mix a bit too much.

Well, they'd be so stuck with ego and insecurity that they have no contribution. It's like criticism. I see a lot of things that are at the expense of some writer; the critic has made marvelous satirical jokes at their expense with their criticism. They seldom realize that criticism is also considered good work. The talent gets fucked up if you listen to critics. You should do your work with a minimum outside help; there's only one person who deserves to see your work — that's the publisher. Don't give it to a thousand people to read, because most people think of criticism as criticism, otherwise they'll just give you a fair shake, a "very good," meaning it stinks. I also learned to never show a pilot that I made to anybody except those who can buy it. There's an inherent jealousy amongst creative people, because they see their own career merited against your own.

On *The Twilight Zone*, do you recall having to do any big changes to your productions?

No, they either went out good or fair or bad. You didn't have much time to change it once you made it. It wasn't like a motion picture, where you can come back and say, "Let's do some retakes on that." You were too close to the line of being on the air.

Whatever I worked on happened for better or worse. When I left *Twilight Zone*, strangely,

Wonderful behind-the-scenes shot of the crew rigging a lifeboat during the filming of "Judgment Night."

I was still at CBS. They had a series called *The Great Adventure*, and Rod couldn't conceive of me ever leaving. There was a lot of hostility between the two of us, except I was getting $25,000 an episode on this new show; this was when John Houseman saw it went way over budget and I was brought onboard. So I insisted CBS show me Houseman's contract, and I saw it. Ultimately, they said, "We never show anybody our contracts." But they gave me a great deal. I think I got $250,000 for 10 episodes; it was a lousy show.

And Rod was not too happy that you had left.
No, he thought I was deserting the ship. He took it personal as a vindictive betrayal between the two of us.

It can happen in the business.
Yes, it does, but at last analysis, I'm not decorating the Sistine Chapel, I'm only making a television show. When people begin to take themselves too seriously — I can understand the motion picture, that you'll work on a picture a year, year and a half — of being highly principled, and I generally did the best with what little ability I had. But a television show is baloney being sliced by the dailies. You're lucky if a good script shows up, you're unlucky if a bad one shows up, you always have one script in the drawer in case some writer who promised you something good turns up with something lousy, and then you do the lousy one in the drawer. That's the nature of the beast.

Besides "The Time Element," did you produce any other early television plays for Rod?
No. I had a friend, Bobby Parish, who directed some of the early shows. Bobby introduced me. I said I had to get good writers to supplant the actors that I could no longer get, that *Playhouse 90* got. Because theirs was on Kinescope and mine was on film. So I needed good writers, so he introduced me to Rod and we seemed to hit it off, and Rod says, "Well, I don't have anything. Oh, I remember, there's something CBS shelved, but I don't know whether you'd like it or not." I said, "Well, do you mind if I try to look at it?" And he got me a copy, I bought it from CBS for $10,000, I remember. And that became "The Time Element."

But I don't see anything that should be put in a time capsule, on any of these things we do.

Well, *The Twilight Zone* has been shown for years, and it's something that's never going to go away.
Well, it's an ideal show for young people. It never was a big commercial hit, never in the top 10 or anything like that, but the college

Rod Serling between takes of his narration for the episode, "Once Upon a Time." A bit of a continuity flub — as it hadn't yet been established that the main character travels in time from the year 1890 to 1962, this opening narration scene should have taken place in the 1890 street.

kids liked it. The younger people liked it; older people shied away from it.

"The Time Element" almost ended *Desilu Playhouse*, because they kept sending out executives to tell me why I shouldn't do it, and they offered me $10,000, what I paid for the script, so that I wouldn't do the show. I went to Desi Arnaz and said, "You've got to back me up on this, because we're going to get this every week unless you do." I was executive producer for the studio, too, besides doing that. I'm a terribly fair man; if there wasn't

me, anybody could have done it, because the writing was always the key to that show.

You have to love the show you're on, or find the audience for the show.

What did you think of *Rod Serling's Night Gallery*?
Well, he was sort of outwritten by the time he finished *Twilight Zone*, so it's only an added nail in the coffin to me. I didn't see many of them, so it would be unfair for me to criticize it. I like black and white against color anyway; color is disruptive to the effect that you're stopping one illusion and creating another illusion, an unnecessary move.

Do you think Rod would have revived *Twilight Zone*?
I don't know. Unless he was in need of money, I don't know why the hell he would do it. He

had a nice lifestyle. I saw him one or two occasions later in life, and we were very cordial with each other, but whatever sense of friendship existed with him was not there.

When you do a lot of stuff, it fades into the background; at least, it has for me. The eye is always in the future, in creative work. Don't look back. If it's good, it's not bad to look back.

Carol Serling

Carol Serling is the wife of Rod Serling and a consultant for the Rod Serling Memorial Foundation.

What did you think of the show at the time of production?

I thought it was good, I enjoyed it. It's hard to put myself back in that time. I don't think that Rod ever felt it would have the lasting quality that it does. The shows were uneven. Some of them were great and some of them were not so great.

What do you think of this latest attempt to remake The Twilight Zone?

I'm frankly very angry at the fact that they've remade some of the old ones. Rod sold out all of his rights, so they can go off and do whatever they want to, but why do it? Usually a remake doesn't make it, and from the reviews that I've read, the camera work was nowhere where it had been in the original. Of course, it was in black and white, which was sort of the trademark of The Twilight Zone in those days.

Was Rod satisfied with the success of the original show?

I don't know. When you're involved with something like this, you keep working. And needless to say, the Nielsens were looked at

Serling performs his narration for "Static"; the one used in the final version.

every week. In the beginning, the ratings were not great — in fact, they were never huge. There was a wonderful, loyal following, but Rod was very busy with it. Particularly in the first three years, I think he was totally pleased with the production aspects of the show.

When he eventually sold the rights, he didn't think that much would happen in syndication?

In those days, there really wasn't any syndication, so no one was saying shows would be on for the next 50 years, because no one dreamed of that kind of technology. I don't think it was a major factor in those days, and CBS said, "We'll never recoup the costs of making the shows, and so here's x bucks, and please take a walk."

Rod Serling talks with a sound engineer as the rest of the crew set up what would become an alternate take of his narration for the taped episode, "Static."

Didn't Rod want to bring back The *Twilight Zone* in the early '70s?
That's not clear to me. He was involved in *Night Gallery* in those days, and he had some other thoughts about *Rod Serling's Wax Museum*, but not *Twilight Zone*, because he

wouldn't have had the rights to do it. He did plan to make a movie, but no more television.

How was the transition for Rod, going from the Golden Age of Television to doing this filmed series?
Well, Mike Wallace said, "You've given up on good television? Given up on doing anything important?" That may have been one of Rod's very first interviews. He was a bit nervous, but he defended himself then. You know, we've all heard you can do this and not be censored. I don't think the sponsors understood the

Serling and crew between takes of his on-camera narration.

Rod Serling makes his first on-camera *Twilight Zone* appearance during filming of his closing narration for "A World of His Own."

shows. He could pretty much say what he wanted to and he could comment on these universal themes and really get away with it.

He took on a lot, being executive producer, writer, and narrator for the show. How did he handle having such a long workday?

I was going to say he was a fast study, but he was also a fast writer. The first few years of *The Twilight Zone*, the ideas came thick and fast to him and he could sit down and dictate a half-hour story in a very short period of time. He wasn't a total hands-on producer; he was there when they were shooting some of the time but not all of the time, and he trusted who had been hired to do the work.

What was the experience like for him working at the MGM Studios on the *Twilight Zone* sets?

He loved the sets, and he loved the whole idea of being able to use the wonderful facilities at MGM. That's where some of the stories came

from, walking around the back lot. The first one — "Where Is Everybody?" — came from his walking around an empty set. He had a most fertile imagination.

Rod must have felt he had achieved quite a bit at that point, having been able to work with the backlog of MGM sets.

Back in the early '50s there was a tremendous conflict between the movie business and the television business. But by the time *Twilight Zone* came along they had accepted it, and of course, *Twilight Zone* was shot on film. So, I think MGM saw the writing on the wall and realized they had to open the studios to this great new medium.

What were his work habits like?

He'd get up very early in the morning and grab a cup of coffee, no breakfast. His office was right there at the house, a separate building, and

CAYUGA PRODUCTIONS, INC.

"THE TWILIGHT ZONE"

STUDIO: MGM
CULVER CITY, CALIFORNIA
UPTON 0-3311

OFFICE: 449 S. BEVERLY DRIVE
BEVERLY HILLS, CALIFORNIA
CRESTVIEW 4-8511

February 22, 1961

Dear Mrs. Slicer:

Your letter was forwarded to me, and I am very appreciative of all your kind words. It is always a real pleasure for me to hear from the viewers of our show especially when their letters are as nice as yours.

Thank you very much for your interest.

Cordially,

Rod Serling

RS:co

A letter to a *Twilight Zone* fan from the office of Cayuga Productions Inc.

he'd go out there and start work. Usually, maybe by 10 or 11 he'd pretty much finished the writing. In the beginning he typed on an old-fashioned typewriter, before the electric typewriter. As time went on, he started dictating, so his secretary would come in and transcribe the dictation. He'd take off for lunch, and during his *Twilight Zone* time, he would often go over to the studio and see what was going on over there. If he was really involved in something he'd work again at night. He used to work sitting in the sun by the pool, with his Dictaphone.

Rod obviously did some acting. Did he act out his characters on the Dictaphone?

Sometimes he did. He would pretend that he was

Serling visits the set during the filming of "Mr. Bevis."

Leisen looks on in wonder as actress Ida Lupino plays the part of movie queen Barbara Jean Trenton, in "The Sixteen-Millimeter Shrine."

A or B or C. Yes, if you listen to the Dictaphone tapes, you can hear a somewhat different voice sometimes.

Was there a frustrated actor in him then?
Probably. When he started the narration, that was something very new for him. He had written some scripts when he was in college and they produced those on a local radio station in Ohio, and he would often fill in if one of his college friends hadn't made the bus that day. He didn't really do a lot of acting. He was very nervous when he started doing the narrations for *The Twilight Zone*, and I think that's what caused that tight-lipped sort of grim delivery that he had. Later on, he really enjoyed being in front of the camera and he did some game shows and things like that. He did a little piece on Jack Benny and a piece on Danny Kaye and *Icabod and Me* — those were fun for him.

Director Mitchell Leisen goes over a scene with Lupino's co-stars, Martin Balsam and Jerome Cowan.

Jean Marsh, John Dehner, and Jack Warden take a break during production of "The Lonely." This was shot on location at Death Valley in 120-degree temperatures, which was extremely trying on the cast and crew.

Did he ask for your opinions on his writing or his ideas?

Always. Often the problem would be he'd bring in a page of an entire piece of work that he was doing; it was hard to take something out of context. But yes, I think I read everything he ever wrote. He took criticism fairly well. Sometimes he didn't want to hear it, but he adapted it. He said I was his toughest critic, and I think that's probably true.

The quality of *Twilight Zone* seemed to be well ahead of its time.

Perhaps. I think it was what he brought. I mean, it wasn't just a sci-fi show, it was so much more, and I think that's why it has this long life of never being off the air. It's been on

Veteran actor Jack Warden stars as James A. Corry in Serling's "The Lonely," the first episode produced after the series' pilot.

Cast and crew resting in the shade between shots.

Jean Marsh and Rod Serling take a lunch break back at Furnace Creek ranch pool.

the air someplace, somewhere, ever since the late '50s. Rod never considered himself the translator of the mystique, or a great science-fiction writer — he really wasn't. This particular genre gave him the chance to say for a time what he wanted to say. It was his particular hemisphere at that point. Later on he went on and did other things that had nothing to do with fantasy or any of those things. He just used this vehicle. Personally, he loved science-fiction stories and mystery, and his library was full of Poe and Lovecraft, but he never considered that he was a great sci-fi writer.

Did he really have a fascination with the supernatural?

Well, it was like a willing suspension of disbelief. He really, really wanted to believe that aliens had landed in Arizona. And he really, really wanted to believe some of the things Duke University was doing with ESP, and so on and so forth, but he really didn't.

Did you ever have a chance to visit the sets of *Twilight Zone* during filming, or at rehearsals?

Occasionally I did. Rod didn't want to make a big deal of it. I thought at that time it would be fun for my daughters to get a chance to be on the set and be in the show, but Rod never wanted to have that happen. That's too bad, because the girls hopefully wouldn't have gone into acting, but they would have understood it a little better. The family was not very closely involved with the shooting.

To the actors in the industry, working on *The Twilight Zone* was a prime opportunity.

I think that was true, and after a while it got a reputation. The advantage to an actor — or director, for that matter — was that they could come in and shoot this in a week, and it would be over and done with. It wasn't a commit-

Actor Jack Klugman stars as Joey Crown in "A Passage for Trumpet." This is his first of four *Twilight Zone* episodes; the only other actor with four starring roles in the series is Burgess Meredith.

Klugman, director Don Medford, and cameramen during the filming of a rooftop scene.

ment to a series of 30 shows, and I think they liked that. The anthology was a great place for actors to showcase themselves, and it's too bad we don't have anthology shows today. The networks are running scared. The Science Fiction Channel turned down a possible redo of *Night Gallery*, because they said they're afraid of anthology shows.

Did Rod have much input into casting characters?
Well, I think so if he wanted to. Again, he had a great deal of faith in the people that had been hired. I'm sure that they discussed the lead characters for all the shows, and it may be that Rod said, "No, let's not use him," or "Let's use him." He was fond of some of the actors, like Jack Warden, Jack Klugman, some of those people. I'm sure he said yes to Burgess

Meredith. Occasionally he wrote the show for somebody specific.

What was it like for Rod in the fourth and fifth seasons on the show?
Rod was less involved in those years. He came in to shoot his narrations and would often have to be on the set, but he was not as involved then. I think he tired of it.

How did he like teaching at Antioch?
In the beginning, the students kind of looked at him and said, "Hollywood fat cat, we don't need you around here." I think after a while they decided, "Well, maybe we'll listen to him," but they tore his stuff apart. Rod's teaching method was taking a film of his and having the kids critique it and discuss it. This was the '60s, and the kids really felt they needed to tear everything apart. But he also had an adult class, when he was teaching there in Ohio, and

A dimension of sound — Vaughn Taylor costars in Bradbury's "I Sing the Body Electric."

A portrait of Rod Serling early on in his career as a playwright.

he loved those students, he thought they were great. They seemed very serious and showed him the respect he hoped to have as a teacher.

Were there any stories he intended to have made into episodes but didn't get the chance?
No. That was not true on *Night Gallery* — a lot of them didn't get made. By and large, the scripts that he worked on were made.

Ray Bradbury only did one episode of *The Twilight Zone*. Was this because the studio didn't want two big names on the same project?
Not at all. Rod admired Bradbury; he thought he was absolutely fabulous. We actually went up to the Seattle fair, the families together, to make a presentation. I'm not sure what happened there with the personalities. Bradbury's things, as I understand it, were too expensive to shoot.

What were some of Rod's favorite *Twilight Zone* episodes? Even including the ones that weren't written by him?
Well, I think "Walking Distance," and "A Stop at Willoughby" — the return to the simple time of childhood. That was always a strong theme with him. I know he liked some of the Matheson pieces. I like stories like "The Odyssey of Flight 33"; I thought that was fun. And "The Eye of the Beholder," of course. The Cliff Robertson story, "A Hundred Yards Over the Rim." He liked a lot of the time-travel things. It's been said that some of the comedies are not great — I think some of them are kind of fun. There were some dogs in there, for sure. But *The Twilight Zone* holds up pretty well.

How would you like Rod to be remembered?

He said at one point he just wanted to be remembered as a writer. A person who strived to make television better. I mean, he never really gave up on it. He thought television had a commitment and tremendous potential to educate — not just entertain. Of course, you've got to entertain to get people to turn it on, but beyond that there have been some absolutely wonderful things that were done on television. I think he'd still be out there striving. So many of those early television writers said, "To hell with that, I'm not going to bother with this medium anymore." But Rod never gave up on it.

Robert Serling

Robert Serling is Rod's older brother and the critically acclaimed author of novels such as *The Left Seat*, *The President's Plane Is Missing*, and *Something's Alive on the Titanic*, as well as numerous nonfiction books on the airline industry. He was a technical advisor for the *Twilight Zone* episode, "The Odyssey of Flight 33," and worked as an aviation editor for United Press International.

What was it like being the brother of Rod Serling?

Rod was a good-looking son of a bitch, wasn't he? Geez, he looks like the *Reader's Digest* version of Cary Grant. I look more like Mickey Rooney. Are you ready for the revelation of the year? Rod didn't write any of the *Twilight Zone* scripts, I wrote all of them. He photographed better — that's why he got all the credit.

I could give you a little background first. I was seven years older than Rod. How the hell I'm still alive and he's dead I don't know. It's a matter of genes, I guess. Rod inherited my dad's genes, and on my dad's side of the family

A rare autograph from both of the Serling brothers; Rod wasn't the only brother with a sense of humor.

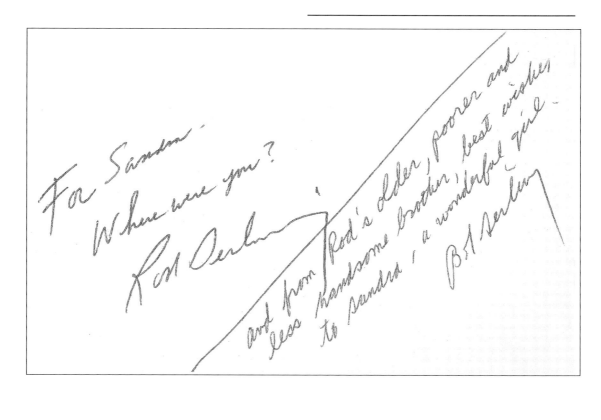

there wasn't a single male who lived to see 60. My mother's family — and I inherited hers — apparently had longevity. I had an uncle who was still chasing girls when he was 93, and he buried four wives. I'm 87 and I'm still active. I'm doing my 24th book. Anyways, I worked with Rod on one *Twilight Zone*, "The Odyssey of Flight 33," which was a story in itself. And I saw sides of him, of course, that nobody else saw — his self-deprecating sense of humor, and sometimes his insecurity.

What do you think separated *The Twilight Zone* from all the other television series?

The quality of the writing, and the fact that a lot of Rod's works were sermons disguised as science fiction. He had comments on social problems, and the way he handled it was a very subtle way of getting a message across. It was like giving you medicine and putting sugar coating on the pill. He was good at that. It's a funny thing, Rod was a liberal and I'm a kind of a moderate conservative, and the only fights we ever had were over politics. Until we went

A behind-the-scenes shot of Serling and director Mitchell Leisen going over the script of "Escape Clause."

A shot of Charles Bronson from Montgomery Pittman's third-season opener, "Two."

"Two" stars both Charles Bronson and Elizabeth Montgomery, as The Man and The Woman, in the story of two opposing survivors of a world war that learn to live together.

out to dinner with our respective wives one night and almost got into a fistfight. I don't remember what the subject was, but we shook hands and made up later, and agreed never ever to get into a political thing.

Did Rod ever talk to you about selling the rights to Twilight Zone to CBS?

No. I didn't even know it until much, much later. I think it was after his death that I found out about it. Carol, his widow, told me once she lost probably $4 million. But Carol also said it wasn't Rod's fault. His agent recommended it, his lawyer, his accountant, everyone was telling him, "Go ahead and do it, *Twilight Zone* is dead." And he got a pretty good penny for it, too. I don't remember what the dollar figure for the rights were, but I don't think Rod would have sold it if he had got some better advice.

You couldn't predict that *Twilight Zone* would go into syndication and that it would become almost a cult. Who could predict there would be a science-fiction channel that would have a *Twilight Zone* marathon, around July the fourth every year, 24 consecutive hours of *Twilight Zone*? Nobody could have foreseen that. One thing, it was black and white, and color was just around the corner. I probably would have sold the damned rights to it myself. Rod was a good businessman, he really was. He's taken a rap for selling *Twilight Zone* rights, but looking back in the context of the time, he was tired, the series had been on for five years, and nobody could have predicted the success of the syndicated show. Certainly not *I Love Lucy*, or *Twilight Zone*, or any of those.

Tell me a little bit about when you and Rod were kids.

You know, when we were kids we used to act.

Three years before Elizabeth Montgomery landed her broomstick as Samantha Stephens in *Bewitched*, she took a magical side route through *The Twilight Zone*.

I was seven years older, but even with that age spread we were fairly close when we were little kids. But we'd see a movie on a Saturday afternoon and then we'd come home and act it out. When we acted out westerns, we'd fill my father's whiskey shot glasses with ginger ale, down the hatch. I remember we saw *Dr. Jekyll and Mr. Hyde*, with Fredric March, in 1933. March won an Academy Award for it. That story has fascinated me ever since I read that, the short story it was taken from. We had bought a chemistry set and we picked some kind of concoction up where the bubbles and the steam and smoke rose from this mixture. And we'd drink it. I had a set of false teeth and I'd shake behind a couch and I'd come up with the fangs showing.

We had a lot of fun playing together. He loved acting from the time he was a kid. I didn't go in for drama; I went in for covering the news. Rod went in for drama. Both of us had an idea; both of us had career moves at a very early age.

Did he think he would pursue being an actor as a career?

I don't know. You have to remember, when he was in high school, I was a long ways away. He was still in high school when I went in the army after Pearl Harbor. I was in the army when he graduated high school and went in the paratroopers. We didn't see a hell of a lot of each other until after the war. I didn't discuss careers with him at that stage. I remember when I came home from college, I was kind of a — well, Rod called me "a phony intellectual." I was into symphony music, and it used to steam him to hear me play Tchaikovsky. As I say, we corresponded, but we didn't get close until after the war, because we didn't see that much of each other.

Biographers have mentioned that his nightmares based on war experiences helped inspire some story ideas.

I know it. He went to Antioch College, same as I did. Only I graduated long ago; he didn't go until after the war. I visited him out there in Yellow Springs, Ohio, once. And I took him and Carol to Springfield, which is nine miles away from Yellow Springs, where our college was. We went into a restaurant called the Wagon Wheel, I still remember, and Rod was drinking Southern Comfort. Well, he couldn't hold any kind of exotic drink. He could drink a lot of beer, but give him something with hard liquor and he was a basket case. Well, he got loaded on Southern Comfort and started having delusions of the Japanese coming into the restaurant after him. And we had to quiet him down, drive him back to campus, and I took him up to his dormitory room and stuck him

Here's a great shot looking down on the filming of a scene in "Two," when "woman" reacts to "man" by throwing a cleaver (Montgomery shown at half cleaver), a skillet, a bottle, and then another skillet. Eventually, man fights off woman and knocks her to the ground, providing a somewhat false start to this relationship.

in the shower and put him to bed. He didn't remember a thing the next day.

But I know he had nightmares about the war. And a lot of his *Twilight Zone* scripts and a lot of scripts he wrote for television, the dramas, reflected the experiences he had and what he saw. He could joke about it, he had the most self-deprecating sense of humor of anybody I knew, and I do too. We shared that.

He had some very intense experiences in the war, didn't he?

Oh, he did, yeah. One of the sleazy biographies written about him implied that somehow he got a Purple Heart that he hadn't earned. Which was total, absolute bullshit. You didn't get Purple Hearts by walking into a store and buying one. And I saw that wound, that shrapnel wound. I was visiting him once, and all of a sudden I looked down and there's blood streaming from his knee. The shrapnel wound had opened up after playing table tennis. And when I read the biography of his that implied that he hadn't really been wounded, holy crap!

How did you come about getting the job of writing the cockpit dialogue for the *Twilight Zone* episode "The Odyssey of Flight 33"?

I was visiting Rod in L.A. We went out to MGM, where they're filming *Twilight Zone*, and he picked up his mail, and in the mail was a brochure for American Airlines advertising a 707 cabin mock-up. American had used it for flight-attendant training, but they had built a new one for their new flight academy at Fort Worth. And the old one was up for sale or rent for a Hollywood studio. I don't know what the hell triggered something in Rod's mind, but he never looked at any of the mail except for that brochure. So help me god, he just stared at it. We go up to the car, it was a Lincoln Continental, and he wouldn't let me even look at it, let alone touch it, afraid that my eyeball would fall out and damage the paint. But he says, "You drive." Holy cow! I say, "Okay." So we're driving, he's still sitting in the white seat looking at the brochure, and all of a sudden he says, "Hey, suppose you were in a jet going across the Atlantic and you hit a freak tailwind, and you were going so fast, like 3,000 miles an hour ground speed, that you broke a time barrier. And when you came in over New York, you were in prehistoric times." I said, "A hell of an interesting concept, but it can't happen." He said, "Well, maybe you're right, I'll think about it some more."

I go back to Washington, D.C., to resume my job as aviation editor of UPI, and I get a call from him. "Remember the idea I had for a jet that goes back in time?" I said, "Yeah." "I need the cockpit dialogue on what would happen." I said, "You need what?" "They need to

Filming a shot in "The Big Tall Wish," when the opposing fighter, played by Charles Horvath, wins the bout with Ivan Dixon's Bolie Jackson.

read what happened in the cockpit if that would happen." "How the hell can I give you dialogue for something that can't happen?" And Rod says, "Well, give me, like, radio checkpoints. Or what would the crew be doing if something like that happened." So I said, "Okay." He says, "I need it by tomorrow." Rod always had to have something by yesterday. He was always in a hurry. That night I called a TWA captain I knew. He came over to the house and I told him the plot. Well, he brought his air maps with him and we looked at radio checkpoints and stuff. And discussed, you know, let's just suppose you hit that freak tailwind, and something like that happened, what would you be doing in the cockpit? What radio checkpoints would you be trying to get? Which ones would you be passing over so fast, that you couldn't get a fix on it? Well, he gave me a lot of the stuff and I sent it to Rod, and there was "The Odyssey of Flight 33."

Speaking of embarrassing moments, all that seems to be missing here is a bag of "Serling's Pretzel Rods of the Zone," sponsored by our good friends of "Cavender Is Coming."

Any cut scenes or dialogue from "Flight 33"?

No. I wish I could do it over again, because I found a technical error in there that was stupid and I'm not sure it was my fault. I don't remember putting it into the dialogue. It's when they come in over New York and they look down and they said, "Well, that's Manhattan Island, all right." This is after they saw the dinosaur. Well, in the age of the dinosaurs there wasn't any Manhattan Island. That whole damned topographical landscape changed millions of years ago. And I never caught that in the script. Anyways, it probably wouldn't have done me any good, because Rod fell in love with the idea of going back to the age of the dinosaurs. I think he told me that that one little five-second clip of the dinosaur cost him $2,500 to get that footage.

After "Flight 33," was there any talk of you writing a story or script for *Twilight Zone*?

No. My forte wasn't scripts or drama, mine was fiction and mostly nonfiction airline histories and books on air safety. I never had the gift for dramatic dialogue like he did.

The *Twilight Zone* had a very efficient production. Have you noticed any other flubs?

I wish I could have seen *Twilight Zone* in production. I would have had a permanent love affair with it. Sometimes I had wished he would have asked my help on a couple of scripts. One of the best ones, you know, "Nightmare at 20,000 Feet," had a terrible technical error in it. Nobody but a nut like me would have noticed it. The airplane in the movie was a Convair 240, a twin-engine airplane. It's very hard to tell, but I swear, it was a Convair. Well, in the script it talks about the flight engineer coming back to talk to William Shatner. Well, the Convair 240 was a two-man crew, they didn't have any flight engineers.

Did you ever have a chance to meet the main producer of *Twilight Zone*, Buck Houghton?

Yes, many times. He was a gentleman. I loved him. He was a terrific guy. He was the only *Twilight Zone* producer I ever met, and the only other person I ever met on *Twilight Zone* was one of the earlier casting directors, Pat Rose. What a gorgeous girl; I had a crush on her. She was beautiful.

She must have had a real talent for casting, because The *Twilight Zone* had some great people on there.

I don't care if she couldn't cast *King Kong*, she was gorgeous.

I think the thing about Buck was that his talent for production really matched Rod. It was a good balance.

I think they were the best of all the *Twilight*

Zone writer/producer teams; Buck and Rod worked together better than any of the others. And I'm not deprecating any of the others. But I think they were on the same wavelength. If Rod got out of line, Buck could rein him in and Rod could improve on stuff that Buck might have missed. But there was never any acrimony between them. They never fought over it, as far as I know. I talked with Buck many times and I know he was as angry as I am with the biographies about Rod.

Well, at least there's *The Twilight Zone Companion* and the PBS special, *Submitted for Your Approval*.

That was an excellent show. I hated the beginning. I thought it was hokey. The surgery and everything like that, I didn't think that was necessary. I thought it was the best thing ever done on television about Rod. They had one on the E! network that was horrible. They interviewed me on the show because I knew it was going to be a hatchet job, and then Carol asked me, "Please don't do it." I called them and told them I was willing to be a face on the cutting-room floor. I wanted to be on it, for one thing, because I knew it was going to be a sleazeball piece. I felt I was the only one who might tell the other side of the story because they weren't going to interview anybody else.

Was it difficult for Rod to live up to the award-winning plays like "Requiem," "Patterns," and "The Comedian"? He started off winning Emmys with these big plays, and then later created *Twilight Zone*, but in between, was he at all concerned about whether he could constantly deliver top-quality plays?

I think so. In some ways he was too self-deprecating about his own work. He was too apologetic. There were 156 *Twilight Zone* episodes. I think you'd have trouble picking out six that were real turkeys. The quality for

Out on location for "The 7th is Made Up of Phantoms," the stars, Ron Foster, Warren Oates, and Randy Boone go over the script.

an anthology show like that, where you had to come up with a different plot and a different cast every week, was incredible. Rod could get very defensive. I also think there was a tremendous amount of jealousy toward him in the industry. Among fellow writers and some producers, like Bert Granet, who wasn't the only one. I know Rod feuded with Ray Bradbury. Bradbury is a classic case of a writer becoming jealous of someone who became a sudden science-fiction guru on television, and Bradbury wasn't on television. He had a lot of jealousy toward my brother. Maybe that's standard operating procedure in Hollywood, to be jealous. I think Rod did too much apologizing to some of these guys who would unload on him. I'd feel like just going to battle with them.

During the train sequence, Inger Stevens looks on in complete terror of "The Hitch-Hiker."

The thing with Ray Bradbury is weird, because Rod had a lot of respect for Bradbury.

I know it. Rod was not jealous of anybody. I never heard him utter one word indicating that he was jealous toward another writer. I've even had people tell me he was jealous of me, because of *The President's Plane Is Missing*, taking off while Rod was right at the height of his own career. As if I had stolen some of his thunder. That is total bullshit. He was as proud of me as I was of him. I will say that without ever fearing any reputation. He was my brother and we loved each other, and I cried like a brother when he passed on.

It's hard to believe that he died when he was only 50 years old. You mentioned how he had inherited your father's heart condition. I guess it was a combination of that and all the cigarettes he smoked, and the high stress of being a big celebrity in Hollywood.

And you couldn't break him of that goddamned smoking. Four packs a day.

What kind of cigarettes did he smoke? Unfiltered ones?

It depended on who his sponsor was. At one time I think he smoked Camels, I think he smoked Marlboros. Chesterfield was a sponsor once.

How much of himself did he put into his work?

Quite a bit. A classic example was "The Velvet Alley" [on *Playhouse 90*]. Art Carney was in it and played a writer who changed agents. The one who had been his agent for years, when he went to Hollywood. That was autobiographical. The other one that he wrote that was autobiographical ["Exit from a Plane in Flight" on *Bob Hope Presents the Chrysler Theatre*], he's an actor who jumps, who was a paratrooper in the war, and he goes back to his old outfit and for publicity reasons, he jumps.

But Rod did the same thing, much to his wife's anger. When he turned 40. He goes out to Fort Bragg, where the old 11th Airborne was based, and went up and he jumped with the modern paratroopers. I've seen pictures.

He looks happy.

Yeah, he loved it. That was something about Rod, he hated to fly and yet he could jump out of a fucking airplane. I think his fear of flying dated back to the war. He was a great guy with airline people. Some airline guy wrote me once and says, "Your brother sent me a teletype message from one of their intercoms about selling Rod a ticket." They said he was the nicest VIP they had ever talked to, and he was. He loved airline people, like I did.

But he was afraid of flying.

Oh man, you go up in an airplane with him and this is "Nightmare at 20,000 Feet." I used to hate to fly with him. Carol told me he'd take a tranquilizer before a flight. There was a funny part of it — he flew all the time, and for Rod to go coach, I mean, that was like riding in the baggage compartment. He loved the good life.

How did becoming a celebrity affect him?

He loved it, it didn't go to his head, he was very gracious. If someone asked him for an autograph, he felt it was an honor to be asked. He felt that way all his life. He used to drive his wife crazy when they'd go into a restaurant and had trouble eating. Someone would recognize him and next thing you know he had 20 people around him at a table. He never, never tried to push anybody away, or "Go away, I'm busy," or "See me later." He always tried to accommodate people, and he was like that till the day he died. He was a sweet guy.

The only thing he did, as a celebrity — I thought he got a bum rap — he was one of the first celebrities to do commercials. And he took a beating on it. One of the biographers devoted pages to embarrassing moments, with television's Angry Young Man shilling for a tobacco company or something. I know why Rod did it. He did it for financial security for his family. He told me, "Bob, how else can I earn 15 grand and the use of a free Ford for one year? What's wrong with it?" Jodi, his oldest daughter, drove an Oldsmobile for years because Rod had done a commercial. Carol drove free cars for years because Rod did Ford commercials. Now you look at television and everybody including Captain Kirk, is doing them. My god, one-time candidate for president of the United States Bob Dole did commercials for Viagra. That's what Rod was criticized for then; everybody's doing it now!

I think that the criticism hurt him. I know why he did it, it was easy bucks. Writers by nature are insecure. And Rod, for all his success, was very insecure. I remember if he'd have a show on television, the next two days he'd look at the reviews. He'd have 55 rave reviews and one panning, and he'd sulk, moan, pout, and grieve over that one bad review, for the next week.

Rod told me once, "You know the problem with critics is that they're all frustrated writers, and it's easier to be cute and smart and funny if you're knocking somebody than if you're praising them."

What was Rod like when he was young?
He was effervescent, funny, a total, complete extrovert. His mouth never stopped, even when he was a little kid. A personality, you couldn't believe it. A hell of a horseback rider, believe it or not. And so was my dad; my dad was a show rider. He could pick up a handkerchief from the ground, riding a horse. And he used to own horses, Morgans. I was scared to death of horses. Rod rode from about the time he was five years old. I've seen pictures of him in his riding gear.

He was, in many ways, the apple of my father's eyes. More than I was. I was sort of Momma's boy. Rod was Dad's boy. I know my father loved both of us, but the tragedy in Dad's life was the same as in Rod's life — he died years too soon. He never lived to see Rod become successful. Because he died right before or right after VJ Day, he never knew Rod was going to be successful. But I'll tell you why I know how proud he'd been of Rod. When I was in UPI, I did a conjecture story — "Amelia Earhart Mystery Solved." If we could get into the Japanese naval files and find out if they really did murder her. It got played all over and a lot of people said Dad liked it, he got a smile out of it. When he died, my uncle took his wallet and there was a frayed clipping of that story, with my name on it. That's when I knew Dad loved me. That was a tragedy.

And I had inherited my mother's genes. She didn't live that long, but she did take care of herself. When Dad died, she developed high blood pressure; there weren't any drugs at the time that could lower it. I'm so goddamned lucky. I got high blood pressure few years ago, too, but by that time they had drugs. My blood pressure's lower than it was when I was a kid.

Rod inherited arteriosclerosis and he worsened it the way he lived. He was so intense, anyways, always under stress. Always hurry up, hurry up. . . .

He had a couple of heart attacks, he went in for open-heart surgery, and the surgery was successful, but then he had a heart attack?
He had a heart attack on the operating table.

Is it true that they tried to take a vein behind his leg?
Yeah, that's true. It crumbled. The surgeon told me later that he had the arteries of a 90-year-old man. He was 50 years old.

What was your relationship like with your brother?
When I was in college, we disliked each other intensely, and that's when he was in junior high. That was when the seven-year gap was the worst and the wildest. When the war came and we both went into the service, we closed ranks. And after the war, and he was just getting started, I was more protective of him. He never had to be protective of me because I was older and making my own life and career. But I remember sending him a few extra bucks to buy a corsage so he could take Carol to the senior prom. I remember every time I came to Ohio to visit, I'd always take him and Carol out to dinner. He'd always order the most expensive thing on the menu. Usually steak.

I still think Rod could have been a success at any form of writing if he had put his mind to it. His short stories he wrote — turning *Twilight Zone* scripts into short stories — I thought his writing for those were usually brilliant. But he never had the patience to do fiction, and he hated rewrites. Of course, we all hated rewrites, but sometimes it's necessary. I couldn't have agreed with some people who have written that Rod wouldn't have been a

ROD SERLING

1490 MONACO DRIVE

PACIFIC PALISADES, CALIFORNIA 90272

March 30, 1972

Mr.   Wingfield

Dear Mr. Wingfield,

Thank you for your good letter of March 16th.

Unfortunately I'm on my way out of the city with no plans to return before November of this year. My family and I maintain an eastern residence for about half of each year — and this period is upon us.

But I do thank you for your interest and I'm truly sorry I can't accommodate you.

Cordially,

Rod Serling

RS/ml

In a letter from Rod Serling, he mentions vacationing at Cayuga Lake, in upstate New York.

great novelist, that he was simply a dramatist. I think he was so goddamned talented, he could have written the New York telephone directory and made sense out of it.

What are your thoughts on all of these remakes of *The Twilight Zone*?
To tell you the truth, I'm not a very fair judge because I haven't watched it. I think I watched a couple, they weren't bad, but they weren't Rod. Now Carol is bitter because a few are Rod's stories; they just remade them.

Rod paved the way for a lot of those other TV shows, like *Outer Limits* and even *Star Trek*.
Yeah. Gene Roddenberry credited Rod with being the inspiration for *Star Trek*. Because *Star Trek* would very slyly take an issue of today and build a script around it, adapt it to the future. For example, the one where the inhabitants of this one planet, half of their faces were white and the other black, the one with Frank Gorshin in it. That was a commentary on blacks and whites. There were a lot of *Star Trek* episodes like that. Gene gave one of the speeches at the memorial they had in L.A. I borrowed some outtakes from *Star Trek* to show at an aviation writers' convention and Roddenberry, too, told me Rod inspired him to do the *Star Trek* series.

When was the last time you saw him?
The night before the operation. I went to his room, and they were shaving him and I just wished him luck. I had no idea it was going to happen. And that's the last time I saw him. We used to kid each other about being fellow hypochondriacs. I broke him up once — he was going to the doctor's and he asked me to go with him. He's so worried, I said, "What are you worried about?" He says, "Well, I've got two worries. I'm afraid of heart problems and I'm afraid of cancer. I'm quite sure I've got can-

cer of the heart." There's no such thing [laughs]. I broke up laughing, and he said, "It's not funny." I said, "Rod, if you have cancer of the heart, can I have your car after you're gone?" [laughs] What a great sense of humor he had.

How was it for him in his family life? Was it difficult for him being so busy?
I don't know, I honestly don't know. I think it was one thing that bothered his conscience that he wasn't there all the time for the girls. But there again, even though I was his brother, his family problems, or his difficulties, or his situations, were nothing he ever discussed. He was far more protective and concerned about my [life], domestic-wise, than he ever confided in me about his own. Rod really thought my second wife was a great lady, they got along very well. We used to play gin rummy together and they'd both cheat like hell, I used to watch them [laughs]. We played gin rummy in the hospital after his first or second heart attack. I remember walking into the hospital at Ithaca, and he burst into tears. I remember my wife went to the bed and put her arms around him. "It's going to be okay." And I just stood there with tears rolling down my face.

If there were anybody I would have wanted to meet, it would have been Rod.
Rod didn't have ego, he had pride, and there's a hell of a difference. He was proud of his fame. He was proud of his writing. Maybe he would have had a huge ego if he hadn't been so insecure to begin with.

I guess I miss him; I know Carol misses him. Carol has devoted her whole life to making a shrine out of his life. It's been hard on her, reading stuff about him, infidelities and all that. You know, she's said she never wanted to get married again. "You know why?" she says. I said, "No, why?" "Your brother was too hard an act to follow." Does that tell ya something?

Helen Foley

Helen Foley was Rod Serling's influential junior high school English teacher as well as the founder of the Rod Serling Memorial Foundation.

To a Serling fan, it's common knowledge that you were a teacher of Rod's while he attended West Junior High School. Do you recall the first memories or impressions you had of Rod?

My first impression of Rod: smart, witty, clever, energetic, cute (small and handsome), a leader, a convincing speaker, fun — a great sense of humor. Rod was in many assembly programs of which I was in charge. He was always great on the stage.

Rod was known for his charismatic character as a student. Did his likable personality help balance a connection between you both?

Rod was charismatic, all right. He had a smile and grin that enchanted all his teachers. We all wanted to pick him up and hug him. Especially when he returned from WWII in his paratrooper uniform and visited every one of his teachers — in junior high and central high. He liked his teachers *and* his schools *and* Binghamton.

Did Rod discuss his interests in becoming a paratrooper? And what do you think about when remembering Rod's service in the army, in WWII?

No, he did not discuss becoming a paratrooper with me. But he did with Gus Youngstrom, his high school history teacher. Rod was gung-ho to get into the war, quit school, and *go*. Gus advised him to finish high school first, and fortunately he did finish. My brother, Mike Foley, and Rod graduated together and went to war together — 18 years old.

ALL-CLUB RECIPE

By Rodman Serling

To describe the magnitude of the Parade of Clubs is no easy matter. To do so would take a vocabulary far exceeding that of this humble writer. The only way I could attempt it is to give it to you in the form of a receipe.

First, take a miniature World's Fair and add a Golden Gate Exposition. Mix well with a very liberal portion of fun, enjoyment and educational value, then deposit what you have in four massive rooms of West Junior and out comes the Parade of Clubs. Over 1300 pupils have had something to do with this gigantic undertaking, which is, incidentally, the largest of its kind ever attempted in West Junior's history. Four massive and immense rooms house the displays and exhibits. The beautiful auditorium, the cafeteria, the spacious swimming pool and the boys' big gym. Forty-one "Clubs on Parade," a pageant of color, beauty, enjoyment and many other available factors that can be witnessed at this magnificent school wide affair. The teachers and club advisors have done their part. Now it is up to us to be there with our parents and friends to boost "Clubs on Parade."

A young Rod Serling wrote for his middle school paper, *The West Junior Courier.*

When Rod's live television dramas such as "Patterns" and "Requiem for a Heavyweight" overwhelmingly launched him into the limelight of the industry, what thoughts did he share with you of these early successes?

Rod, of course, was pleased with his success, but modest, unassuming, charming, and glowing with pride. He, being self-effacing, *not once* discussed his success with me. He didn't

Helen Foley's memories of her past haunt her in "Nightmare as a Child," starring Janice Rule.

Terry Burnham plays the mysterious Markie. "Do you remember, Helen?"

need to. It was evident. In the '50s, after he had put the gold in the Golden Age of Television, he opened the door of my classroom and peeked in. The students had gone. That dazzling smile of his was just the same, and I hadn't seen Rod since he went off to win the war, except briefly in Binghamton when he worked for a local station. We hugged and hugged and talked for a long time.

What are your thoughts about what was happening with Rod at the time of creating this imaginative series?

I asked Rod to come and give a commencement address at school. He asked, "What will I talk about?" I replied, "Are you tough enough?" And what a speech it was. That elderly auditorium had never been so quiet! Rod was a commanding speaker. He never pulled punches. Rod's reference to *Twilight Zone* was brief — "Oh, it's one of those spin-the-air things. Maybe a little spooky, maybe a little goofy."

What was your reaction when you found out that Rod had named a main character in a *Twilight Zone* episode after you with teacher Helen Foley in "Nightmare as a Child"?

When "Nightmare as a Child" aired, I was at the Cortland Drama Festival with my drama club. When I arrived home late that night, I saw notes all over the house. My two sisters were thrilled with the program, but it was years before I saw it. When I did finally see it, I was pleased and proud. It was well-done and scary. I jumped and fluttered when I saw Janice Rule open the door and saw Shepperd Strudwick menacing through the door. The child that played Markie [Terry Burnham] was believable.

Rod's on-screen narrations introduced the public to his persona, and they're a lasting connection whenever one thinks of *The Twilight Zone*. What interests you in the show?

Everything in *Twilight Zone* interests me — the symbols, Rod's narrations, the music. But

Helen is threatened by Peter Sheldon, played by Shepperd Strudwick.

usually and especially, the moral at the end — where do we get that today?

In his later days, when Rod was having serious health issues, including a 30-year cigarette habit, why do you think he apparently didn't change his ways?
Rod, like most of us, probably had no idea that his time was up. He was an ardent smoker. I dropped him a letter when he was in the hospital in Ithaca — "What's the idea?" Back came a sassy reply — "No big deal."

How did Rod's death affect you?
Rod's death was not totally unexpected, since the local papers issued dark news on his condition. However, my sister Norma read about it in a Montreal paper (we were in Quebec on vacation in Montreal). She said, "I might as well tell you before you read it — Rod is dead." I simply stood still and looked out the window of our motel. I do not cry easily, but I did a lot of blinking. My grief is visceral. My guts ached for days.

Robert Keller

Robert Keller, an accomplished artist and the author of *House Proud*, was a close childhood friend of Rod Serling.

Could you tell us your first memories of Rod Serling?
If memory doesn't deceive me after 70 years, I think we met at the skating rink at Recreation Park in Binghamton, under the watchful eye of the bronze statue of George F. Johnson, the founder of the Endicott Johnson Shoe Company. I remember so well, there was a little girl named Mary who, if you skated up behind her and shouted her name, she would immediately fall down on the ice. For some reason Rod and I found this to be hilarious.

When you and Rod were growing up together as kids, did Rod ever mention what he wanted to be when he grew up? Did he know that he wanted to be a writer?
I've been asked this by the authors of some of the biographies of Rod, and my answer has usually been that, given the rather sinister and macabre fantasies of some of today's young people, ours were pretty mild. Whether these led Rod to envision a writing career, I don't really know. During summer, when school was out, we would often take our bicycles with a packed lunch and sally forth to a nearby cemetery, where we would sit in front of a marble mausoleum in the shape of a Greek temple and pretend we were Greek shepherds. I was learning to play a wind instrument called a recorder, and I would compose on-the-spot melodies I thought had ancient connotations. I always felt that there was a discrete limit to the perverse possibilities open to him.

On the set of "The Trouble With Templeton," Serling with actress Pippa Scott, demonstrating the dance routine she's going to do in the nightclub sequence.

Rod was very involved in high school activities, such as sports, drama, and writing for the school paper. How was he perceived by fellow students?

Rod had great charm, probably in retrospect foreshadowing his charismatic persona on television. Always a great smile for everyone. When he delivered meat for his father, mothers were quick to comment to others about his sunny personality. As editor of our school paper, *The Panorama*, his thoughts and words were of the help we could give to the war effort, especially with the Junior Red Cross, of which he was president at the time. I have copies of these because I was assistant art director, and there was generally great disappointment when I showed them to the [biography] authors, because they expected fantasy.

Once Rod began his early career as a television writer, did he stay in touch? When he visited Binghamton, what experiences of his work did he share with you?

Much of our contact was during two of our many high school reunions — the only two he was able to attend because of his untimely death. He was so loyal to all of his classmates, I can't help but believe that he would have attended all six. I often wonder if the fact of WWII impinging on our lives might have something to do with the apparent covenant we seem to share. When he did mention his work, there was very little negative conversation about personalities, but as time went on, the strain and stress of that would become apparent to me. He aged literally before my eyes.

Rod greatly contributed to shaping the infant medium of live television drama. What do you think of his work such as "Patterns," "The Comedian," "The Velvet Alley," and "Requiem for a Heavyweight"?

My two favorites of these are "Patterns" and "Requiem." I recently attended an off-line Broadway performance of "Requiem" and it held up so beautifully, so moving and sad and revealing the shadowy side of the fight game. Going way back to high school editorials, that so-called cosmic urge and sensitivity to others runs through as an ongoing thread in so many of his shows.

At the time of *Twilight Zone*'s original airing, do you know if Rod had any idea how popular the show would have become and of its impact on competing networks?

What probably clinched it was the inspired decision to let Rod host the shows. It is almost as if his persona and the content of the shows merged, and now it is hard to separate the "man" from the "medium."

Earl Hamner Jr.

Earl Hamner Jr. began his career as a television writer by penning the eight *Twilight Zone* episodes, "The Hunt," "A Piano in the House," "Jess-Belle," "Ring-a-Ding-Girl," "You Drive," "Black Leather Jackets," "Stopover in a Quiet Town," and "The Bewitchin' Pool." He went on to write screenplays for films, including *Where the Lilies Bloom* and *Charlotte's Web*, and created the television series *Falcon Crest* and *The Waltons*.

You're known for creating *The Waltons* and *Falcon Crest*, among other things. How did you get your start in writing?

I've written for magazines, I've written books, I've got a play at the moment I'm trying to sell. But *The Waltons* will be on my tombstone. And I am still a professional writer. I go to my office every day, I keep bankers' hours, I stop for lunch. And go back to Amanda Drive at the end of the day and say, "Honey, I'm home." And honey usually says, "Hi there," thank god.

Actually, I first became a published author when I was six years old. I had written a poem after Christmas, about my new red wagon, my new blue sweater, and pulling a family of puppies around in this new wagon, and the poem was called "My Dog Jack." My mother sent it to the *Richmond Times Dispatch* children's page, and they published it. So, at six years old I discovered the joys of being a published author, and also, that imagination is about 95 percent of the art of writing and 5 percent is talent, because I did not have a new wagon and I did not have a new blue sweater, nor did we have any puppies. I didn't sell anything else until I was about 23. I wrote some when I was a teenager, but I didn't know what I was doing. I kept a journal, but I didn't think of writing until I was in the army. I tried some short stories in college, but I was stationed in Paris during and after WWII, and I began writing seriously there.

So if your tombstone will refer to *The Waltons* as one of the most memorable pieces, as it were, what is your favorite thing you've ever written?

Maybe if *The Waltons* is first on my tombstone, right under it we can put *The Twilight Zone*. Because those were original pieces. Each one that I did, it was not an adaptation, it was totally my work, it was done when I was a much younger writer. Maybe more apt to be a little energetic, a little more in possession of the word, a little more in charge of my talent as a writer during those years, which was in the '50s. And so I'm quite proud of *The Twilight Zone*.

Speaking of *The Twilight Zone*, what was your first impression of Rod Serling?

My first impression of Rod was in 1949 when we met in New York. We were both there to

Pippa Scott and Brian Aherne during a nightclub scene in "The Trouble With Templeton."

accept awards for scripts we had written for a radio show called *Dr. Christian*. And that night that we met, we were there to be on a broadcast, and Rod had on sort of a zoot suit. He was already married to Carol. He was a highly energetic person, a person with a great deal of charisma. You noticed Rod. He was always a short, kind of, not a tall person. And like many people who are kind of short, he tends to overcome that. But Rod did it very successfully — you didn't think of him as a short man. He rose above being short. He was a likable person. He was warm. And I knew Rod in the context of a friend, not a close friend, because we for most of those years were business associates. But we were good friends.

I left a job in a radio television station in Cincinnati, Ohio. And when I left that job to write a book, I had been there long enough to make enough money to stop for a while. And Rod had just gotten out of Yellow Springs and came down and applied for the job that I vacated. And he got it. And so later in Hollywood, when we would run into each other at parties and awards events, he would always introduce me as the man who gave him his first job. Which was kind of a nice thing to do. And then when I came to Hollywood, he was the man who gave me my first job. So there were wheels within wheels.

Director Buzz Kulik and Dean Jagger appear to be discussing his role in "Static."

Do you think that Rod used the show as a way to address ongoing social issues, disguise them in fiction so it would be more palatable for both the audience and the network?

I think Rod was very clever in the way he turned issues into entertainment. But they were not just social issues. I think he was also concerned with all aspects of life — he wrote scripts about death, people dealing with death. He wrote scripts about people who liked to read. But also he strongly made statements about social injustice, and he was particularly fond of bringing the Nazis to their knees. And often these scripts would have an anti-Nazi flavor. And bless him for doing that. And I wish he were still here, because I don't think Nazism is quite dead, as we would like to see it.

The show was already pretty successful by the time you joined it in the third season. How did you feel about participating in a show with that kind of background?

My feeling joining *The Twilight Zone* was, first of all, one of great gratitude, because I had been looking for work in Hollywood for quite a long time and desperately needed money. So I could finally pay the rent. But, of course, I felt a great sense of pride even to be associated with Rod. And not only with Rod, but the very distinguished writers that also shared the writing chores with him. They also were superior directors. If you see some of those scripts today, they may seem limited in use of sets and makeup, but imagination took over. They may not be as technically perfect as one would want, but the imagination and the spirit, the life — the life, above all — was there.

It all starts with story, and so many projects today don't have it, the words aren't there. They may look great, but if the words aren't there, then the eye can forgive a lot, I think.

One of the things is that not only are the words not there, but the spirit that Rod was able to imbue in his writers in his directors. In his own deep belief in what he was doing. We all became imbued by his strength.

"The Hunt" was your first episode. How did you make that first sale?

Having met Rod briefly in 1949, I had kept up with his career, even though he stayed in Cincinnati and I had gone to New York and to Hollywood. I knew what he was up to, and had watched *The Twilight Zone*. But it didn't occur to me for quite a long time after I moved to California and was so poverty-stricken, that I could write for the show. I thought of a couple of ideas and one became "The Hunt." The other became "A Piano in the House." I wrote outlines and sent them over to Rod. And he sent a note back saying, "These are nice ideas, but our stories are chosen by committee and I have turned them over to the committee." So I thought it was a really nice brush-off, but I don't blame Rod. They must have been terrible stories and wrong for the show.

But almost a week went by and Buck Houghton called and said, "We like both of your stories and we would like to buy them, and we understand that you haven't written for television and you don't write film, so would you like to write them up like little plays?" And so I said, "I would like to write

them up, but like little television shows," which I did.

I'm quite proud of "The Hunt." I thought that Arthur Hunnicutt could have been cast better. Think what Will Gere would have done in that role. But in spite of limited acting, the story came across. And again, it combined a lot of my background: it had religious overtones, and I was raised in a very religious home and made to go to church every Sunday. It also had reverberated experiences going coon hunting when I was a boy. And a love of dogs, which was reflected in the story about the man who loves his dog. Maybe part of that story came from the fact that one night, my father, who loved his hunting dogs and kept a good many of them, had accidentally shot one of his dogs. And he looked and looked until dark and couldn't find it, and he still went back after dinner and looked for the dog again. And he finally found it and it was dead. But I think the emotional reaction to seeing my father's love for that dog reverberated in the fact that I wrote about a man who takes his dog to heaven.

What was the inspiration for your second episode, "A Piano in the House"?

I don't remember specifically, but I am a professional writer, and I think of a story, you know, I make my living writing. So I suspect I sat down and said, "Now I've got to think of another story." There was inspiration for "The Hunt." I can't recall any specific indication of inspiration for the second one. Except for adoration of Joan Hackett, the lady who played the wife. A gorgeous and talented and legendary lady who died much too young.

"Jess-Belle" was the only one-hour show you wrote for *The Twilight Zone*. Did the one-hour format give you opportunities that you didn't have in the half-hour form?

I didn't think of it as giving me more opportunities. I did think that I could do a big story, something, not just an anecdote, because I think many of the half-hour shows were really kind of expanded anecdotes, or short, short stories. Whereas the hour episode was more akin to a novella or a long short story. It gives you more scope, or the opportunity to explore, not tangential things, but depth in a character, or to develop more interesting effects. Which we had a lot of in "Jess-Belle."

I understand that you were under the gun to write that script from scratch in a week. Tell me how that happened.

Well, I wasn't put under the gun; I put my own self under the gun. Because Herb Hirschman, who was a wonderful director, he was producing and directing, called on a Friday and said, "I just had a script shot out from under me and I was wondering if you happened to have an hour-long script that you could adapt to *The Twilight Zone.*" And I said, "No, I don't." And he said, "Gee, that's a shame, I really need it — something by next Friday." And I said, "Well, I'll write you an original by next Friday." Again, arrogant, and just conceited and outrageous. And so Herb said, "Can you do that?" And I said, "Sure, I'll write an act today." And he said, "Well, you know, you write about those folks back home, and homespun down-to-earth stuff. Could you give me a story along those lines?" And I said, "Sure." Not knowing any better.

And so I thought of an idea over the weekend. It was loosely an idea that could easily have happened back in the Blue Ridge or the Appalachians. And having to do with a young woman who sells her soul to the devil for a young man's love. That's an old theme, and it's been explored a lot of times, but I didn't think that anyone had explored it in that particular background. And so I called Herb briefly on Sunday morning and told him what I wanted to do, and he said, "Go." And so I wrote an act each day and delivered it to him on Friday. Well, he didn't have time to change a word, so that was to my advantage. Not that he would have. And the next day, he called and said he liked the script and was going to buy it. The next call to Herb was to say that I had written in a panther, a cougar, a wildcat, and that the penalty for Jess-Belle's selling her soul was that at midnight she would be turned into a wildcat. And Herb said, "I'm up to my knees in wildcats over here, and they are all very mean creatures and can't easily be trained." However, one of the animal keepers brought in a black leopard instead of a wildcat. And I said I thought that would be wonderful, because this is *The Twilight Zone* and you can take those kinds of liberties. As it turned out, the black leopard was wonderful. And so is everybody on that show. From Anne Francis, who played Jess-Belle just beautifully, to James Best, who played the young man that she gave up her life for to love.

Laura Devon, James Best, and Anne Francis star in Earl Hamner Jr.'s folkish tale of black magic, "Jess-Belle."

You've mentioned that sometimes you felt that actors haven't been able to capture the Southern spirit of the characters, but these two seem to be right on the mark.

They were absolutely wonderful. And I don't know that Anne or Jim had ever been in the south. It's been a recurring problem with me. When I turned in my script for "The Home-coming," I wrote a two-page description of how to obtain Southern speech. But again, you see, I'm outrageously demanding of the people I work with.

Any fun stories or anecdotes that come to mind about the making of "Stopover in a Quiet Town"?

One of the nice things about working for *The Twilight Zone* is that, having watched it prior to coming to Hollywood, I was aware of the work of a lot of people who I came actually to know, or to work with. So it was quite a pleasure doing *The Twilight Zone* to have Nancy Malone play one of the characters in "Stopover in a Quiet Town," because I had admired Nancy's work for years on *Naked City*, which she did in New York. Wonderful actress, and she's still here in Hollywood.

Any favorite scenes or moments from the finished show?

I love the climax. Because I think I started with the climax of that show. I had that ending before I knew where I was going, how I was going to get there.

Maggie McNamara had the lead in "Ring-a-Ding Girl." How did you feel she compared with what you had in your mind's eye?

I thought she was superlative. At that time, I don't think I had met a Hollywood actress. I had seen them onstage and in my imagination and in films, but to write about a Hollywood actress was not something I was proficient in, so I didn't really know what I was doing. I was just writing a person. And when Maggie McNamara came in, dragging furs behind her, I thought, "Yeah, she's right." She was a very beautiful woman. And I thought she gave the quality that could have accounted for a woman of great glamour, and seeming not to have all that much substance at the same time, to give her life and to save the lives of people that she loved.

How did you feel about the casting on "You Drive"?

I thought the casting was wonderful. The gentleman, whose name is Edward Andrews, was perfect in the part. He was a little bit overly fastidious; he put you off just a little bit to the degree you could hate him for running over a small kid. And then you could sympathize with the car — the car was the hero of the piece — when you could see it plotting against this bad man. I thought the production was marvelous. I like the many turns and twists of the attempts of the car to bring the man to justice. Which was mostly my invention in the story, because I kept finding new devices to make the man attempt to rectify the bad thing he had done.

8-30-63   46

Maggie McNamara stars as actress Bunny Blake, in Hamner's underrated "Ring-a-Ding Girl."

"Black Leather Jackets" seems to be a precursor to biker films of the mid-to-late '60s.

Oh yes, they stole that idea from me. No, the only similarity I can find to real life of the guys in the leather jacket story were the fact that there were kids in my neighborhood — my son Scott, the Cooks' boy Steve, and the next-door neighbors the Hoblets' son Fred — all had minibikes. And they used to terrorize the neighborhood with their minibikes. There was an English lady, Pamela Goldstein, who lived next door who would get hoses out and throw water at them and shout, "Be gone!" As a matter of fact, I even call those characters Freddy, Scott, and Steve. And I understand a lot of people have felt that episode was rather faultily constructed, with a lot of holes in it. But still I had the fun of naming the characters after my son and his friends. I don't think they were especially pleased about it.

"The Bewitchin' Pool" paints a fairly sad picture of the growing phenomenon of divorce. Were there any personal stories that went into that, or just the general sense that that was an increasing social factor?
I guess I was raised in a very religious family. I had gone to church up until the army. And also I've had friends who've gone through very painful divorces, and I've seen what happened to the children. And I suppose that finally bubbled over into a story that said children suffer in a divorce. It's certainly not some earthshaking revelation, but I must have felt strongly enough about it that I dreamed up that story. And also, it reflected a certain comfort and love that women can give. And in creating the old lady who was able to comfort the children, I was able to balance the young couple who were incapable of giving love. I guess unconsciously I try to create a balance to the good and the bad, because my philosophy of life, if you could call it that, is that there is a balance of good and evil. And I always feel that I am one with all of humanity, so that there's good and evil in me because it exists within, both of those things exist within me. So endeth the lesson.

Mary Badham, who played Sport, was nominated for an Oscar for _To Kill a Mockingbird_. Did you feel that the kids, and she in particular, captured what you were looking for?
Yes, yes, yes. She was marvelous. I'm honored even to be associated in any way, even by that link, with _To Kill a Mockingbird_, which I think is the great American novel. And I felt especially drawn toward that work because Harper Lee wrote a beautiful recommendation for one of my books, which was reprinted on the book jacket, which I think accounted for it becoming a best-seller. The letter of recommendation was better than the book.

Did you watch much beyond the shows you were involved with?

Edward Andrews stars in Hamner's hit-and-run episode, "You Drive."

Oh, absolutely. I was a regular _Twilight Zone_ fan. And I watched every episode.

How would you like Rod to be remembered?
I think, as the father to _The Twilight Zone_, a remarkable achievement in an industry that is classic — classic being a work that has lasting message and expression and achievement. Toward the end of his life was a most heartbreaking experience for me, because I had heard on the radio that he had had a heart attack, that he was ill. And I did one of those things I wish we could all learn not to do, which was that every day I'd say, "I'll call Rod tomorrow, I'll call Rod tomorrow." And then I remember — I think it was a Saturday night

161

— the news came over the radio that he had died. And it was a horrible feeling that I had not called him to wish him well. And to thank him for what he had meant in my life.

What makes a good *Twilight Zone* episode?
I think this is something those people who did the second version never knew. *The Twilight Zone* is actually an expanded anecdote with a surprise ending that has something meaningful to say, usually a socially significant message. It also had that mysterious quality that sometimes comes through on television projects, that everything is right — the time is right, the music is right, all the ingredients are right there. I would also consider *M*A*S*H* a television classic. *The Mary Tyler Moore Show*. *The Honeymooners*, as a comedy. *I Love Lucy*. And *The Waltons*, without being self-serving, I do think, because it lasts.

Richard Matheson

Richard Matheson is a writer whose film credits include *The Incredible Shrinking Man*, *Duel*, *Somewhere in Time*, and *Stir of Echoes*, and whose television shows include *Star Trek*, *Night Stalker*, and *Night Gallery*. His first contributions to *Twilight Zone* were the two stories "Third from the Sun" and "And When the Sky Was Opened," followed by the original scripts "The Last Flight," "A World of Difference," "A World of His Own," "Nick of Time," "The Invaders," "Once Upon a Time," "Little Girl Lost," "Young Man's Fancy," "Mute," "Death Ship," "Steel," "Nightmare at 20,000 Feet," "Night Call," and "Spur of the Moment."

How did you first get involved with *The Twilight Zone*?
Chuck Beaumont and I were called in to see the pilot, I guess at CBS. We were the ones who outlasted the others, because we wrote that kind of story already, so we were ideal for *The Twilight Zone*. So it was familiar territory.

What would you say was your approach to storytelling on *The Twilight Zone*, in comparison to Serling's and Beaumont's?
Structurally, we all did the same thing, which was to start out with a little teaser that gets the viewer interested, and then have a little suspense item at the end of the first act, and then resolving it through the script, through the story, and then finishing it with a surprise ending, or at the very least, some kind of ironic observation regarding the story. Serling preferred doing message-type shows and Chuck Beaumont went for dark fantasy, and I went more for slightly ironic ideas that usually had a happy ending. They had some kind of ending that was ironic, but hopefully was not obvious during the show. There were a number of occa-

Director Allen Reisner, actor Dan Duryea, and Rod Serling behind the scenes of "Mr. Denton on Doomsday."

sions when we were able to get a real boffo ending like in that one with Agnes Moorehead, "The Invaders." That was, I hope, a totally unexpected ending.

What was the show's work environment like? And aside from your scripts, what personal involvement did you have in the series?

I had very little personal involvement with the series. I would go in to meet Rod Serling and Buck Houghton, who was a nice man and obviously knew the series, and later Bert Granet and the man who produced the hour-long shows, Herbert Hirschman. I would present them with an idea, and when I came up with one they liked, they gave me the go-ahead and I went home and wrote it. If rewriting was called for, I

Inside the set of the Busy Bee Café, William Shatner (Don Carter) questions The Mystic Seer fortune machine, while Patricia Breslin (Pat Carter) questions her husband's superstitious tendencies, in Richard Matheson's "Nick of Time."

met with them again and made agreed-upon alterations. Working with them was always pleasant and rewarding.

What was it like working with Rod Serling? What was he like personally and professionally?

I first met him when both Chuck and I went out to dinner with him, and later we were over at his house a number of times. He had a film club — all these top-notch people in the business would pick out a movie that they had wanted to see, and he had me over when they did *The Incredible Shrinking Man*.

I did very little work with Rod Serling other than story-idea submissions and possible rewrite meetings. He was always pleasant, always thoughtful, and, being a writer himself, very protective of my work as well as the work of the other writers on the show. It was good to be exposed to a writer/producer who had respect and kindness. Whatever his justification was, he did have it, and it encourages you to do the best you can. There were no problems, we never had a harsh word, and nothing was ever said like "This is a terrible script, I don't think we're going to use this one." I do not recall one line of my scripts ever being changed, except by Phyllis Kirk in "A World of His Own," and she didn't exactly change my lines but sort of did an approximation of them. Keenan Wynn and Mary La Roche read my lines exactly as written. Personally, Rod was good company and very generous in every way.

Did they put any restrictions to the types of storylines you could write about?

No, the only restriction I had was I couldn't use the word GOD. Rod could — he could have his characters say, "Dear god" or "Good god." I couldn't do that. They wouldn't allow me. So I don't know what I said. "Darn it," or "Rats!"

Were you happy with Serling's adaptations of your two stories, "Third from the Sun" and "Disappearing Act," which became "And When the Sky Was Opened"?

Well, "Third from the Sun" was all right because it was pretty close to the story, but the other one, Rod just did an entirely different story from the one I had. It wasn't just rewriting it, it was redoing it all the way from top to bottom. In my story — which had a wonderful ending, and I would have loved to have had that, that would have been a boffo ending — a writer is writing the whole thing in a soda-fountain shop, and he's alone and he's writing all this down while he sits at the counter, and he's able to describe everything so well. You get very used to him, and he starts talking about all these people who disappeared, houses that disappeared, and the last line of the story is, "I'm having a cup of coff—" And you know. Immediately you have a visual in your mind.

When *The Twilight Zone* originally aired, what did you think of the show at the time, and how do you feel about it today?

It was fun to write the shows, watch some of them being filmed, and seeing them on television. I thought the show very unique for its time, however, and to me, more interesting than the other shows of its ilk on television. I think it's lasted because it's in black and white. I was just reading this afternoon that CBS wanted them to do it in color, but Serling and Houghton refused. And they were so right, because this way it was film noir. The whole thing would have disappeared, because I don't think it would have worked at all in color.

Aside from your more popular *Twilight Zone* episodes, "Nightmare at 20,000 Feet" and "The Invaders," what are your thoughts about episodes such as "Nick of Time," "A World of His Own," and "Night Call"?

I loved "Nick of Time" because I thought that both Bill Shatner and the actress who played his wife — Pat Breslin — were wonderful. About a man who allowed superstition to dominate his thinking, and having that type of approach to his life, his business life, or any part of his life. And his wife finally talking him out of it, and him improving. Well, you have to assume there was some kind of fantasy for the machine to come up with an applicable answer to every question he had, a little beyond just accident. It played well, was involving and moving, and had a dandy snapper ending to chill the spine. A good *TZ*. "A World of His Own" is another favorite — outside of the comments I made about Phyllis Kirk who, I must add, did a fine job playing the role. I got

The Mystic Seer is actually The Swami napkin-holder fortune machine that flourished in diners across America in the 1950s. The property department worked with the Swami's creator to design a handful of unique Mystic Seer metal covers to use in place of the Swami covers. The devil's-head design was uniquely sculpted to follow the same look of a Halloween candy dispenser lid of the time.

an enormous kick out of being the only writer on the show to "wink out" Rod Serling at the end of the show. I don't know what made me come up with that idea, but I thought it was funny, and fortunately he had a great sense of humor and it was the last show of the season, so he could do it. He got a big kick out of it. His ego was strong enough — he didn't need to say, "Look, I don't want any fun made of my name," that kind of stuff.

Actresses Gladys Cooper and Nora Marlowe consult with director Jacques Tourneur while the crew (including director of photography Robert W. Pittack) prepares to film the next shot in "Night Call." Tourneur also directed numerous films such as *Cat People*, *Days of Glory*, and interestingly enough, *Nightfall*.

"Night Call" I like a lot. I talked them into hiring Jacques Tourneur, one of the finest directors in the business. He had a marvelous touch with both the visuals and the dramatics of the show. He was quiet and gentle and polite, and yet he got this marvelous look. Gladys Cooper was superb. An interesting sidelight: I was told that they couldn't hire Tourneur because he was a movie director and would take too long to shoot the piece. My recollection is that he had the shortest shooting schedule of any *Twilight Zone* — 28 hours. He was incredibly efficient. Like Hitchcock and David Lean, he knew what he wanted from every shot before he started shooting.

An Invader puppet made from foam rubber.

The Twilight Zone is popularly known for its twist endings, yet many episodes are sensitive, thought-provoking, and comedic. At the series' inception, was it Rod's intention that the storytelling approaches be varied?

I'm sure that Rod, being the consummate writer he was, did not think, for a moment, of making every *Twilight Zone* as though made with a cookie cutter. Their variety was perfectly in keeping with his creative awareness. What the story called for, we did. If the notion was serious, we wrote it that way. If it was comedic, we did it that way. Interestingly enough — I have said this before — the original submission for "A World of His Own" was very grim and serious indeed. They suggested making it a comedy, which I did gladly. A similar occurrence was on "The Invaders." My original story was not to their taste, so I turned it into a science-fiction approach. Many years later, the grim approach to the story — not that "The Invaders" is exactly comedy — became one of the stories on *Trilogy of Terror*, the Zuni doll chasing Karen Black all over her apartment.

"The Invaders" is one of your more popular episodes, and one of the best in the eyes of the fans. How does this episode hold up for you as its creator?

I didn't like the little critters that were chasing her around. They looked like little waddley toys you used to see men selling on street corners. That's what they looked like to me. The way I wrote it, you hardly saw them, there were just flashes of movement. I think it would have been much better. But Agnes Moorehead was good, and the director [Douglas Heyes] told me when she read the script, she said, "Where's my part?" Because actors and actresses, to them the job consists of dialogue or monologue, and it didn't have either one.

"A World of Difference" is another of your best episodes. What motivated you to write that script, and how did that episode turn out for you?

Every time I went on a set, my thought was always, "What if this turns into a real place and I can't get home because I don't know where my house is?" And that led to me coming up with

Howard Duff stars in Matheson's bizarre identity crisis episode, "A World of Difference."

Veteran actor Lee Marvin poses as his own broken-down robot boxer, Battling Maxo, and goes up against robot Maynard Flash, played by Chuck Hicks, in "Steel."

that story idea, and Howard Duff was very happy with it, and his wife, Ida Lupino, liked it. Ted Post directed that, a very good director. The woman who played the real nasty wife is Sean Penn's mother, Eileen Ryan. Her husband, Leo Penn, Sean Penn's father, directed the one *Star Trek* I wrote, "The Enemy Within."

Could you share some memories of visiting the sets while your episodes were being filmed?
Well, I spent the afternoon with Ralph Nelson and both Lee Marvin and Joe Mantell ["Steel"]. We went through it, and Lee Marvin really impressed me because he was acting out the story, even though we're on an empty set — no set pieces, no lighting, no music, no nothing, and he was acting out the part as if it were really taking place. And it wasn't just that he had a brilliant ability to do this kind of acting, it was that he lost himself in the role, he became the person I wrote about. It couldn't have been

done better. It's almost as if he'd read my brain when he read the script. It was all there.

What do you think about the attempts to remake The *Twilight Zone*?
I didn't care for *Twilight Zone: The Movie*. The only section I like was the one Joe Dante directed from my adaptation of Jerry Bixby's script ["It's a Good Life"]. I thought they blew "Nightmare at 20,000 Feet." Lithgow is a marvelous actor, as witness his portrayal in my *Amazing Stories* script "The Doll," but he was forced to start at 100 percent hysteria and work up from that — patently impossible. Bill Shatner's tightly contained performance suited the story much better. Although I wish they could have had the gremlin from the movie in the television segment. I thought it looked like a woolly bear. Intriguingly enough, the man inside that suit was Nick Cravat, Burt

Hicks wears the mask of Maynard Flash, created by makeup artist William Tuttle.

him, and I won't do the first draft." And it worked fine for us, but Froug was convinced that Chuck was just carrying me. So we didn't get along. Every once in a while you meet a producer that you simply just do not like, and he doesn't like you, and you don't know why exactly, but it happens.

Your film contributions are quite memorable. What interests you in fantasy and horror?
Nothing interests me in horror. I hope that I have never written horror, but terror, which is a different kettle of fish. Horror is visceral, makes you feel nauseous. Terror needles the mind. I prefer terror — although now I don't write in that genre either. Fantasy can cover many areas. To me, *What Dreams May Come* is not a fantasy, since I believe in what I wrote about, as witness the 100 research books I list at the end of the novel. At the moment, I am not sure what subject I will write about. I am drawn toward metaphysics, and have done two books in that area.

Lancaster's old acrobat associate. Made-up properly, he would have looked exactly like the gremlin I described in my novelette. With no makeup, maybe just enhance the black around his eyes, and a little toying with his appearance, he would have been perfect.

Why was your story, "The Doll," not used in the *Twilight Zone* series?
Well, by the time I submitted that, I had producer William Froug. When Chuck and I were doing some detective show and Froug was producing it, Chuck should have straightened him out. But he got the idea that because I had made an arrangement with Chuck, I didn't like driving into town, so I said, "You go in and front for us and tell him what you have to tell

George Clayton Johnson

George Clayton Johnson wrote stories that became "The Four of Us Are Dying," "Execution," "The Prime Mover," and "Ninety Years Without Slumbering," as well as the scripts for "A Penny for Your Thoughts," "A Game of Pool," "Nothing in the Dark," and "Kick the Can." He wrote the premiere episode of *Star Trek,* and the films *Ocean's Eleven* and *Logan's Run.*

Here's a question you've probably been asked hundreds of times. When did you first realize you wanted to become a writer?
I took a course in a local college on the short story, and I wanted to write a short story. But I decided with the help of a friend to write

Actor Martin Landau prepares for a scene as Hotaling, the bully in "Mr. Denton on Doomsday."

Ocean's Eleven in the form of a sort of a novel, that turned into a screenplay, that ended up being sold to Peter Lawford and through him, to Frank Sinatra and ultimately became a big movie. I think even when I was 10 or 11 or 12, when the papers would say, "Well, a noted writer has said so-and-so, so-and-so," I'd wonder, "Who is this noted writer? Why does he have such special class that he can get in the newspapers and be quoted and things like that?" I felt very knowledgeable about writing and I envied writers, I wanted to be one, I knew that's where the chewy center was. But I don't think I ever really believed that it was possible for me until I began to try to do it.

What were the early struggles of becoming a freelance writer like for you? Did you ever want to quit?

Yes, many times, but I couldn't. I had quit my job. I had cast our fates to the wind. I had to wait — from the time *Ocean's Eleven* was sold, till the time it appeared on the screen — six years. And during those six years, for about five of them, I spent my time digging dry wells. I found myself writing short stories, and often rewriting them under the encouragement of friends or people I could get to read them, and sending them out and getting them sent back with messages that told me nothing. And it was very discouraging, because I just sort of became a beatnik. I let it all slide. I took to heart the idea of "Tune in, turn on, and drop out." And I did, to a large extent, thinking it sort of, oh, Jack Kerouac-ish, sort of avant-garde. And I suppose I was really part of the societal avant-garde in my growing attitudes toward society, and trying to find ways to reflect these ideas in fiction. I, of course, came across the work of Richard Matheson, Charles Beaumont, and Ray Bradbury, and a whole host of other writers.

But before you knew them, when you were just reading their writing, they're people who you're either inspired by or influenced by, and then when they become your friends, you realize they're just people.

Ray Bradbury has never become "just people" to me. In some bizarre way, he has that magnetic core of energy that has him always looking over the next hill, even when you're looking into his eyes. He's a remarkable man. He's served as my mentor, and as my friend, and as my inspiration. He's read my stories, he's commented upon them, he's praised them. He's just a loving person in my life, and so are many of the others that I've named. Because the first thing I did, when I finally was able to meet one of this group, was to get to know and meet them all, find occasions to do so, travel a distance to meet, or go where one of them would be.

Director Walter E. Grauman on the set of "Miniature."

What were your first impressions of Rod Serling?

Well, of course I was awed, since he was the greatest author from the East Coast who had won all the Emmy Awards, who was celebrated, who was briefly the president of the Academy of Motion Picture Arts and Sciences. Who had all of the connections, who had been on television, had been interviewed by people all over the place — he was big news. And I was unknown; I lay in the shadow of Ray Bradbury and Charles Beaumont. My access to many things was simply because I was that writer who was a friend of theirs, and then so many doors would open for me. And so this was one of those doors that semi-opened for me and I, of course, was intimidated completely. I didn't want to say the wrong thing or do the wrong thing; I didn't want to try and be too bold, or I didn't want to be too timid. I wanted to be totally respectful. Of course, this whole attitude baffled him

and intimidated him, because I was that guy who was a friend of Ray Bradbury's, Charles Beaumont's.

So, here we were, and every time we met we were super-polite to each other, like gunfighters, you know, each one watching the other one's hands. Me, sort of tongue-tied, a little afraid to assert myself or to try to take the floor, always waiting to sort of be a counterpuncher and reflect back what I was hearing, trying to find a way to break into this business. So it wasn't really a fair contest between us at first, because I was just totally awed that I would even be in the presence of such a man. And so it was like I had penetrated almost to the very center of things, from the outside, over a very brief period of time, by getting to know and to work with Rod Serling. If he raised his voice in a room, I'd shut up to see what he had to say.

And his *Twilight Zone* series became a phenomenon.

Yeah, it was a phenomenon, but it was a borderline success while it was going on, while it was being made. It slowly grew to be a phenomenon, by virtue of its merit, but in the beginning it was still competing with shows like *One Step Beyond*, and then years later, *The Outer Limits*. Things like that started to come, but in the beginning, it sort of held its own, and it was a very literate thing. I was very glad to be associated with it, because it had a lot of intellectual appeal and prestige, because Rod was one of the really great adaptors. I would watch how he would work, and later on I would see short stories by people like Marvin Petal or Manly Wade Wellman or John Collier, and the words would just jump off the page, all because Rod had this ability to take something literary and transform it into something visual. He had an eye for what you call "photogenic fiction."

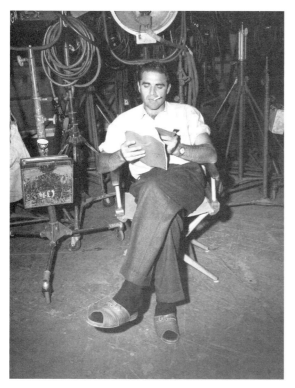

Actor Steve Cochran takes a break and reads through his script from "What You Need."

Matheson, he says, "What about the *Lusitania*?" Rod says, "What's that?" "Well, you know how it's the greatest liner of all time and it went down with all hands, everybody died, a real, real bad disaster?" And Rod says, "Yes," and he says, "Well, do it with a spaceship. Now we're in a spaceship, the spaceship is in space, and suddenly there is a collision with an asteroid. My god, it's the *Lusitania*." And of course Rod says, "Yes! Yes!" because he was eager to buy almost anything that would run an hour. And I was sitting there running through all these ideas I dreamed up for *The Twilight Zone*, all neatly tailored to be a half-hour long. Trying to think of something offhand that would appeal to him as a premise for an hour, because I could have gotten an assignment to do one of them if I'd just spoken up that evening with a premise that sounded half-logical.

The hour episodes, in many fans' opinions, don't work quite as well as the half-hour.

I felt that it was a slower pace and they were using up more time, killing time, and that they were basically half-hour stories stretched, or they were somehow compressible into a half-hour if you really would work at it. Like that one that Robert Duvall did of Charles Beaumont's, about the miniature house with the little women in it and this poor guy in the museum looking at all this stuff inside the glass case ["Miniature"]. They could have handled that in a half-hour. It certainly was stretched out just because that was the new requirement. But everyone there knew that's exactly what we were doing, that little one-act play. Only do it to make it look sort of semi-artificial, because you had the back lot of MGM to work on, and so there was no real great attempt to try and make things look as they exactly looked. If that set could have appeared to be a bank, then that set was a bank.

Did you get to know Rod personally?

Well, we had a number of talks together on various occasions, and I went to several parties that he was at. I saw him at the studio, I had a couple of story conferences with him. I had lunch with him in a place in Santa Monica called The Bat Rack, along with Richard Matheson and Charles Beaumont, where we were trying to figure out what to do now that they had made up their minds to do *The Twilight Zone* as an hour show, and on videotape, or, in a new media — you know, electronic media. We all had trepidations trying to wonder how to take this format, really make it work in any way in an hour form.

I remember one particular thing. Richard

Crewmen observe actors Ernest Truex and Steve Cochran during filming of an apartment scene from "What You Need."

I'm curious to hear any anecdotes about your meetings with Rod.

Well, there is one sad thing that has come up in my mind again and again, and that is that I had a meeting at one of the large agencies — IFA, I think it was — and while I was sitting in the lobby, Rod comes out slowly, and so I get an opportunity to brace myself and we meet each other fairly politely. And he starts to light

up a cigarette and he says to me, "Well, what do you think about that *Liar's Club* thing?" And then when I showed a little bafflement about just exactly what he meant, he said, "Do you think I should be doing that?" *Liar's Club* was a very strange television show that was hosted by Rod Serling [in 1969], probably as a gift to someone who wanted him to do it. But anyway he liked doing it, and his job was to introduce some outlandish object and give it to four contestants who were stars, or television and movie people, and they would try to each tell a different story about what this implement was used for, to determine which one was the best liar. And it was okay in a sort of

Director Alvin Ganzer looks on as Cochran (Fred Renard) runs through the bullying of Truex (Pedott).

mournfully slow, slightly boring way with a laugh track, and poor Rod sort of serving as bookends. I should have told him what I believed, which was that he was much too important to be wasting even a minute doing something like this, but instead I said, "There comes a time in a person's life when they want to run off and join the circus. You can deny it and stay at home if you want to, but everybody's entitled to do it, Rod. To go and follow

their heart and —" "Okay, okay, the circus, let's go out to the circus." Little did I know that within a year or two he would be gone.

The moralistic things that he wrote about human nature seem to have been a part of him.

He was a very common man basically inside of himself. He could identify with a tailor much easier than he could with a banker. He had it in him.

Let me ask you some questions about *The Twilight Zone*. What were your thoughts about the show at the time, and how do you feel about it today?

Well, pretty much the same. I had a reverence for it. It was one of the very few places on television where I felt myself capable of getting excited enough to actually spend the time to write a television script.

There are photos of you on the set of "Nothing in the Dark." Did you visit any other sets of _The Twilight Zone_?

Yes, I went to watch them shoot all of my episodes. I was allowed on the set freely, I got to meet the actors. In fact, I've got publicity photos of me taken with the actors. I went to them and I studied them and I watched with some fascination, because I would not really know what I was looking for when I would write "close shot," or "tight shot," or "tilt shot." Then I would watch somebody set it up and I'd see where they'd place the camera, and I couldn't imagine how they were going to get from here to there. Only then I'd realize they're going to swivel the camera, they're going to point it here and they're going to put it here — oh, now I'm beginning to see it. And then after a while, the whole geometry of it becomes clear, and then I see the actors brought into the scene, and then I see the way the camera knows just when it's looking at them closely, for that tight shot. And when you look at it, the guy has caught what was in the darned script, but he's caught it in a way that moves, and in a way where he's imbedded in the action and it's not up on a stage happening in front of him. Of course, they had that marvelous cinematographer, [Clemens] that was the hero of this show.

So you met a lot of the actors who were playing your characters and were able to see your characters come to life, firsthand.

It's awesome when you start to see that it really works. Her saying this to him, and him turning away that way. When you watch it, you can feel — you _know_ — the emotion of it. Often times there are prickles up your spine or up your arm when a certain effect that you

Jonathan Winters stars as billiards champion Fats Brown in "A Game of Pool."

had hoped for really works, because the actors got it and knew just how to do it.

And you were able to feel that without the soundtrack.

Yeah, and I've seen lines of dialogue taken out of a script, and when I asked why, directors like Lamont Johnson would say to me, "The actors can do it without the words, you just watch. Watch this, he doesn't have to say those words, he doesn't have to do those words, and she'll get it and so will the audience."

Could you elaborate a little bit about each of the stories you did for the show? Anything behind the scenes?

I wrote "All of Us Are Dying," a short story that Rod Serling bought that he retitled "The Four of Us Are Dying," and he wrote a marvelous script for it. The same thing happened with a story called "Execution." When I originally wrote it, I called it "The Hanging of Jason Black." Rod changed the man's name to Joe Caswell, and the title to "Execution." The third story I sold him was called "Sea Change," but then I had to buy it back because of censorship problems [the cutting off of a man's hand]. The fourth story was "A Penny for Your Thoughts," in which Dick York plays the part of a mild bank clerk who discovers one strange morning that he has the ability to read people's minds, and he can tell what everyone is thinking. And he finds that very disturbing. Rather than feeling like it's a great gift, he feels that it's almost a curse looking into what the people around him are thinking.

And then I went on from that point to write "A Game of Pool," which had Jonathan Winters and Jack Klugman. Now Jonathan really took me away with his ability to be a dramatic actor and to drop all of the shtick that made him world-famous as a comic. I didn't believe it could be done when I had heard that he had been cast in the role. I thought Jack Klugman, perfect, but I thought, "Why couldn't they have gotten even Jackie Gleason?" But when I saw the show, of course I was absolutely thrilled, and what grand luck it was to have him playing a role in one of the pieces I had written.

I went on to write "Nothing in the Dark," which had Robert Redford and Gladys Cooper in it. It's a very, very touching story, and in my view, the best one. Next to maybe "A Penny for Your Thoughts," because a comedy is very, very hard to do. I'm curious to see if "Penny for Your Thoughts" has very great legs. I know that "Kick the Can" does.

Were you happy with Charles Beaumont's script based on your story, "Prime Mover"?
Oh, loved it, loved it. In fact, I missed a lot of the Writers Guild Awards — my wife and others went, and Charles Beaumont had *Twilight*

Seen here with members of a men's club is actor Franchot Tone, starring as aristocrat Archie Taylor in Serling's episode, "The Silence."

Zone on that evening, and it was this particular episode, and I was at that awards dinner because my movie *Ocean's Eleven* had been nominated by the Writers Guild for the best screenplay of the year, along with *North by Northwest* and a couple of other big-name films, including *Psycho*. *North by Northwest* won it, but while it was winning it, instead of being at my table where I could rush up to the stage, I was in the bar with Charles Beaumont, trying to catch a glimpse of how this thing turned out and how these guys were doing it. So, we could watch Chuck's adaptation of my story.

"Kick the Can" is comparable in sentiment to "Walking Distance."
I get that feeling from people, that if they were to put together their top dozen *Twilight Zone*

175

Jonathan Harris costars as Taylor's lawyer, George Alfred, in what turns out to be an episode with a double twist ending.

episodes, "Kick the Can" might very well be in there, because it is one of those sentimental ones. So is "Nothing in the Dark" — if you watch it properly, it will really bring tears to your eyes. I consider that pure gold when that can happen, because I consider the dimension of the heart as the deepest dimension; that's what a writer should strive for in trying to affect the emotions. I mean, not just to terrify him, that's easy, but to make him feel pity, another thing altogether.

Besides your story "Sea Change," were there any other *Twilight Zone* stories that did not get produced?

There is one half-hour teleplay that William F. Nolan and I wrote together, as a sort of a speculative adventure. It was submitted to Rod Serling almost days before they closed the show down. Rod had bought this script,

because they had a couple more to finish shooting, but the thing was pretty much over. The only real problem was this script took place aboard an airplane and they had already done that this season — something like three airplane stories — and this they thought would overload it. So they put it on the back burner and while it was sitting there, the show died. The story is called "Dream Flight." And it's a story of a young woman who wakes from a terrible dream, in which she's in an airplane, and they're crashing, and she's really unnerved by the dream partly because she's got to go to the airport and get onboard an airplane and fly someplace. And with such a dream, she is really disturbed. Then she starts seeing things that are just like what was in the dream. And she begins to get more and more frightened as she gets pressed deeper and deeper into this situation, into where she appeals to her seatmate, who is disturbed by what's happening. And she tells him what has happened, and then the story is really quite a nice little love story, about how these two people have sort of achieved a really fine rapport in such a way as to break the spell of the dream. Anyway, I think it would have been a splendid movie for the show, if something to do with the end of the series hadn't intervened.

What are your thoughts about all of these remakes — *Twilight Zone: The Movie* and the two new *Twilight Zone* series?

See, Buck and I talked about the new *Twilight Zone* and he was amazed even from the very beginning, because they opened the show up to members of the Writers Guild, and they were encouraged so that they ended up with a bunch of scripts, and then they started to wade through the scripts, and it was clear to them that none of these guys got it.

Part of the uniqueness of it is the fact that it was shot in black-and-white, and was therefore able to be lit by people who were accustomed to dealing in a situation where the camera was more sensitive to light, and you could work in much darker places with the camera than you could with the videotape machine. The videotape machine, you've got to flood everything with light to illuminate it, and when you don't do that, it looks like it's got a film between you, or smoke between you and the actors, even when they're in medium shots. Also, what is so important to a good story, and why so many of mine were turned down in the early days, was because no matter how startlingly brilliant or interesting a situation may be, it ought to have an ending. If it doesn't, it just leaves you hanging. And if it's just a fragment, you wonder what it was, why you saw it, and all those other things that are answered by a good strong ending. So when I look at *Amazing Stories*, I never see any endings there. Or if I do, it'd be because they were based on a very strong short story and somebody understood the importance of it.

I'll tell you one thing that does give me hope for the future: almost everyone I meet has a half-hour *Twilight Zone*–type script that they've written, with that tilted quality that takes you out of the mundane and into something exceptional. I think that one day, some intrepid producer will advertise for *Twilight Zone* scripts, original scripts, for a remake of *The Twilight Zone*, and I wouldn't be surprised how many good pieces of writing would come out of the woodwork already prepared.

One last question. How would you like Rod Serling to be remembered?

I would like to see him remembered as a man who succeeded at his goal. I think too many people think of him as a man who at the end, lost his direction, and therefore never really

Actor Jonathan Harris is best known for his role as Dr. Zachary Smith from the Irwin Allen series, *Lost in Space*.

returned to his roots of the big stories, and the things that they were expecting of him never came about because he wasted all of his time writing *The Twilight Zone*. That's a mistake in their thinking. If they look at *The Twilight Zone* as one thing, it's one long story with lots of different kinds of chapters in it. And you look at the monumental size of the thing and it compares with any great work, from the Holy Bible almost, to the *Iliad* and the *Odyssey*, or any of those great books. Rod never came to really appreciate who he was, or what he had done. So I would like to have him remembered as a man who made his mark on society, made his statement, was completely successful at it, and that none of those people laid a glove on him.

Fritz Weaver

Fritz Weaver starred in "Third from the Sun," as William Sturka, and in "The Obsolete Man," as the Chancellor.

What was your first experience with *The Twilight Zone*?

I was in New York, and my agent called me and said, "They want you to do a *Twilight Zone*," and I said, "Do a what?" Because I hadn't heard of it — I had been on the stage for about nine years. So I went out to do this "Third from the Sun" program, and it was my first film, in fact. And I had to learn the hard way; I had assumed it was all the same. I mean, acting is acting, right? It didn't turn out that way. It turned out that what you did on the master shot, you had to repeat on every subsequent shot, the close-ups. Well, I chose rationally, to smoke a cigarette, and so when we finished I had been acting up a storm, blowing out smoke and talking animatedly with my hands. And they said, "That was great. Okay, let's move on to the medium shot," and I said, "What medium shot?" And so the script girl came over and kept saying, "No, you lit the cigarette on *this* word, and then you blew out the smoke on *that* word," and it drove me absolutely crazy. I couldn't repeat what I had done because I wasn't aware of what I had done. So, we did several takes like that, and finally they decided 'Let's scrub, let's start all over again, let's scrub the cigarette entirely.' So Eddie Andrews, who was in that, sidles over to me and says in that sly way of his, "Why do you think Gary Cooper keeps his hands in his pockets?" So I had learned my lesson, I learned the lesson that if you're going to smoke, you'd better be damned sure when and where you're going to do it. And so that was my baptism by fire. But I loved the episode, with that great, surprise ending.

Fritz Weaver stars as the Chancellor of the State in Serling's powerful episode, "The Obsolete Man."

Did *Twilight Zone* have a uniqueness that you hadn't dealt with before?

That was the main thing. I mean, first of all, I met Rod Serling, and you know he was in on the set, not often, but he would come in, and what surprised me most about him was that he was like a big kid. He was enjoying himself so much. He was jumping and we'd rehearse something and if he liked something, he'd say, "Oh! That's great! Keep it in, keep it in!" And it was that enthusiasm that made you realize it was going to be a wonderful series. I saw him several times, talked to him on the set, and my impression was that he was having fun, because he came to Hollywood with some heavy luggage as an important playwright and I think he found something that he really thought was fun. So he would say, "Ah, not so much social commentary," but the odd thing was that he got all that into the series anyway. "Third from the Sun" was all about the possible nuclear thing, and "The Obsolete Man"

Joseph Elic, playing the Subaltern who then becomes the Chancellor's replacement, looks on as the crowd of followers pulls the Chancellor down the long table in preparation to tear him apart.

A closer shot of Weaver being dragged down the long table.

was the human condition. It's odd, because at that time I was thinking back on it, and we talked about it a great deal, the phrase "planned obsolescence" had begun to come into the language. It had to do with the fact that you made your product so it would wear out, and then you would replace it and that would keep the economy going. Planned obsolescence was considered a very good thing. But Rod picked up on that and said, "Well, what if that was applied to people?" And he really ran with that idea and he loved it.

While filming "The Obsolete Man," did you stop and think about how intense that story was?
Oh boy, did I ever! It was like fascism in the highest degree, and we knew it. Of course, we had a wonderful director, Elliot Silverstein, and he was a madman but with crazy good

ideas, and it was he who talked the MGM brass into turning the whole studio into that vast room. You know, broke down all the sections and segments; it was like an airplane hangar when you went in there in the morning. And he had these big ideas — it was sort of like El Greco paintings, with towers that went straight up into the darkness there, and there was the leader. And a long table down which he'd drag the obsolete ones. It was terrific.

Rod was just having the time of his life. That was my impression of him. He felt like, "Well, I don't have to do all these important plays now, I can just relax and have fun with this." And he did, he ran with it. It's funny, but I said we didn't know it was the Golden Age, but we knew it was something unique. We knew this was unlike most series that you went out there for. And later, I realized to my regret that most of the stuff is just cookie-cut stuff, you know, no real imagination at work.

The cameraman follows the movements of the crowd during a pivotal scene at the end of the episode.

Did the cast have rehearsal time?
You would have a rehearsal to show the camera what was going on with the geography of the place, and then you'd go back while they lit. You had about a week to get this done, or it may have been a couple of days longer. That was good in a way, because it left a lot of room for spontaneity and that's what Rod liked very much.

Did you have any memorable moments working with Burgess Meredith?
I was in awe of Burgess because he was a big stage star, and film as well. We were all staying, as every New York actor did in those days, at the Montecito Hotel, out in Hollywood, and Elliot was there too. And so we would get together afterward and we'd drive home together, and Burgess would tell stories, and it was just a terrific thing. And Elliot would drive us to the studio, so we got pretty close on that one. I loved working with

While taking a break, Meredith goes over his own handwritten notes for his part in "The Obsolete Man."

Burgess, he was very good. He got impatient with me one time on "The Obsolete Man," because I had lost my voice screaming the day before, and my voice had dropped a full octave. He said, "Well, you can't do that with that —" I said, "I'm trying my damnedest." He said, "You can't do it with the voice, you've got to do it with —" And I said, "I'm using what voice I have," and he finally understood what it was, it was a physical problem. But he was great, and I can remember Elliot jumping up and down when Burgess and I did the first long scene together and he came running up and he said, "Would you like some coffee? I'll fill it with gold! It was wonderful!" Burgess specialized in those strange and rather eccentric roles and loved "The Obsolete Man." I loved working with him — I thought he was great. We would sit with him in the MGM commissary, and the reigning stars of that era would come over to the table, and you got to meet them all, and it was great fun.

Boy, that must have been something.
Yeah, the MGM commissary, everybody ate in there. It got to the point when finally only the crew were in there, but Marlon Brando was sitting at the next table and he'd known Burgess, and I guess Burgess didn't know he was there, and Marlon very mischievously took his knife and inserted it between the third and fourth rib of Burgess Meredith, and he jumped up in the air and said, "What the hell!?" Yeah, Burgess had worked on *Teahouse of the August Moon* onstage, and Marlon did the movie of it. So they got to know each other.

Were you able to work in any of your own ideas for your characters, or were the scripts followed exactly?
Well, there were moments in "The Obsolete Man" where you would think of something, some small piece of business even, and turn away and then suddenly turn back, and if Rod would see that, he'd say, "Oh, that's great! Keep that in." And Elliot was also like that, he wanted to really improvise the whole thing. Although Rod was never a stickler for "I want this, all of my words in the right order," you said them in the right order anyway because

Larry Gates stars in "The Shelter."

they were good. There was a great sense of a fresh flow of feelings as you did a scene more and more times, and so you were improvising in a way. Physically, you'd improvise.

Any anecdotes about "Third from the Sun"?
What I remember was the fear we all were under in those days, about the nuclear threat. It was in the air! We all thought it was going to happen. I did a movie called *Fail-Safe* somewhere in that period. I think they first discovered the Soviets had put missiles into Cuba, and there were daily broadcasts about what should you do when you get the warning signal, and what children should do, and it was very much in the air.

There's around a half-dozen *Twilight Zone* episodes that are concerned with the nuclear age and the fear.

Well, you see, Rod came from that school of playwrights in New York who were very much into social commentary, and theirs were plays of social significance, and they were all very talented. But this is what I mean about Rod coming to this thing — I think he saw a way to do it in a more entertaining way. He's quite a man.

What were your impressions of him as a person?

Well, I got the impression that he was nervous, but full of mischief. I can remember hearing him laugh. He's full of mischief, but he was very shy, too, when you first met him. Then you got more aware of him and, as he was around more, he warmed up. And he was delighted with the whole production side of it, delighted to be on the set and watched the guys working, he loved all that. And he watched the rehearsals and he was pleased.

Was he there for both of your episodes?

Yes, he showed up for both of them, one or two times at least. I do remember his enthusiasm; I remember that as a cardinal thing I remember about him. He really loved what was going on. Rod would come in, he'd almost start rubbing his hands: "Okay, let's do this one now. Let's get to work now." So it was fresh, and he'd probably just finished writing it.

So what do you think makes a good *Twilight Zone*?

Well, mystery is one thing, mysteriousness and the circumstances. Something odd about this man sitting there at the counter drinking his coffee. And it's very stimulating to the imagination, because you wonder what's about to happen. Most of the time you didn't know what the outcome would be — as an audience, I mean. And I think Rod enjoyed fooling people. He was like a magician, or like an entertainer, anyway. I remember his laugh. I can't remember the jokes but I remember this kind of shrill laugh that would come out of him.

But one of the reasons why it's called the Golden Age was because television didn't know where it was going. It was a new medium and it wasn't geared to the maximum audience. I mean, the very fact that they would go after Rod Serling, nowadays he'd be just a figure off-camera somewhere, in his little abattoir in the studio turning out plays. Writers, you know, are no longer very welcome on the set.

It is a shame, because the thing is "It's ours now, and thanks very much for this sketch you've given us." Yeah, that's right. And in that era, they didn't know yet where the medium was going, so they brought in people from New York, and good people, who were just as intrigued by the possibilities as they were. Oh, we had such great times in those days.

Elliot Silverstein

Elliot Silverstein directed the *Twilight Zone* episodes "The Obsolete Man," "The Passersby," "The Trade-Ins," and "Spur of the Moment." He also directed television shows such as *Route 66*, *Naked City*, and *Tales from the Crypt*, as well as many films, including *A Man Called Horse*.

Do you have any behind-the-scenes memories of working on "The Obsolete Man"?

"The Obsolete Man" had a kind of importance outside of itself, in that I had a big fight with the editor at that time. And the reason for the fight was that this was a kind of Kafka-like scene, in which a man was to be destroyed by

The new Chancellor relishes in his power of the state.

A frightening shot where the crowd prepares to tear the obsolete Chancellor apart.

a group of black-shirted Kafka figures in a Kafka-like trial. I had a whole ring of black-shirted figures surrounding this man, and when the time came to execute him, I had them start to make this kind of massing growl while they were standing still. And they were slowing moving forward, and this sound grew with intensity that suddenly burst as they just attacked him. Well, the editor said he didn't want to cut it that way. I said, "What do you mean you don't want to cut it that way?" He said, "Well, they're not moving." I said, "That's exactly right. They're standing there. You're waiting for them to move, wondering why they're not moving." "Well, I want them to move." And I said, "Well, I don't want them to move and I'm the director. Please cut it that way." "I don't want to." And there was a big argument over that, in which Buck Houghton, who was the supreme of producers, had to keep me from throttling this guy.

And that led to a compromise, which every time I see any part of that piece, it still disturbs me today.

Did you run into any other troubles directing any of your *Twilight Zone* episodes?

I did one with Diana Hyland, about a woman being chased by a black figure on a horse ["Spur of the Moment"]. And the lesson I learned on that one was to never ask an actor if he or she could ride a horse. Because it was very specific — this woman is being chased on horseback. "Diana, can you ride a horse?" "Yes, absolutely," is the stock answer an actor will give. And much to my frustration and shock, when the time came to get her up on the horse, with the camera running alongside, she didn't even know what side of the horse to get up on and we had to fake the whole thing.

I think every director has to be a multilin-

Joseph Schildkraut (of "The Trade-Ins") takes a break during the filming of "Death's-Head Revisited."

guist, because there are actors who will come to you from a school of acting that requires a lot of introspection and motivation, and there are others who work right off the top. You have to be able to speak their language; they don't have the time to learn your language. They don't know anything about your language. You have to get the job done with them, so you have to deal with them on the level that they can understand.

One of the problems, and I suppose I'm kind of fascinated with the nuts and bolts of the job, is you have to often deal with pretty unique problems. There was a case of another *Twilight Zone* I did, with Joseph Schildkraut, called "The Trade-Ins." His wife died right in the middle of it and he was shattered, and the moral conflicts there are enormous. In the humane sense, you want to say, "All right,

let's wrap and go home." As a matter of fact, I asked him, "Do you want to stop? I'll certainly call Buck and stop." Joseph Schildkraut came from a great European acting family, and he said, "No. I've taken the assignment. This must be finished before I have time to grieve." And between takes he was crying like a baby, and I had to kind of comfort him — how you comfort somebody in a situation like that, it's almost impossible — and he came back on the set.

What made *Twilight Zone* different from other shows of the time?

The fact that two people who were supremely competent guided the material to the point where it went to the stage, and that was Rod Serling or one of his compatriots, and Buck Houghton. Buck Houghton was a producer in the preferred sense of the word. That is, he knew what he knew and he assumed that you knew what you knew, and he didn't get his fingers into at least my pot. Scripts were prepared properly and on time. I can't recall him saying no to anything, as long as there was a rational explanation for why we wanted it, and rarely was one of those demanded. Buck was a first-class producer, and I think that made much of a difference. Directors could direct and not have to write or rewrite, or reconceive or argue, or beg or plead or do any of the things that directors had to do to get some kind of realization of the vision of the material.

It's true that the script is the foundation for all efforts, and it's very tough to face a blank page. But it's also tough to build a superstructure on top of that foundation when there's great pressure and great anxiety on the part of almost everyone around you. So with a producer like Buck, who set the ship on a course through calm seas, one could really do the best work in what was a three-day schedule.

William Reynolds

William Reynolds starred in "The Purple Testament," as Lieutenant Fitzgerald.

I've read about the tragic plane crash that occurred when "The Purple Testament" was first scheduled to air. Could you tell me about that?

"The Purple Testament" was originally scheduled to show on February 12. At the time, I had been working at MGM on a television pilot called *The Islanders*, in the next season at ABC, in 1960. I was down in Jamaica doing some background shots for some run-throughs and things like that, and we were trying to get back. The director of this series, as well as the direc-

tor of *The Twilight Zone*, was Dick Bare. And Dick and I were trying to get back to Puerto Rico in order to see the show that night. The plane crashed, and they didn't know whether anybody was alive. As a matter of fact, the cameraman, George Schmidt, was killed when he bled to death, and it was really a very bloody and messy type of thing. But I had postponed my leaving, because my son was born on January 30. They had heard about the plane crash, Rod Serling and Buck Houghton, and postponed the airing of the episode; it was about a macabre scene of my seeing my own

Dean Stockwell stars as Lieutenant Katell/Lieutenant Yamuri in "A Quality of Mercy."

Actors Dick York and William Reynolds with Rod Serling during his visit to the set.

death, which probably wouldn't have been thrilling for my wife with a 12-day-old child.

Anyway, Serling stepped in and they cancelled the broadcast for that night. This is the kind of sensitivity I don't think that you would find in most circumstances. I have forever been grateful to him. I have a very high opinion of this gentleman.

Strange circumstances, it was scheduled to shoot sometime in December. Somebody already was scheduled and I was a replacement. I think it was Dean Stockwell who was originally scheduled to play Fitzgerald. Stockwell had already done another episode that was similar to it, where he played in the military ["A Quality of Mercy"]. It was three days before shooting. I don't think Rod or Buck knew much about me, and I walked into the office and after we said, "Hello, how are you?" he just looked, and after just a few minutes he said, "Fine. Welcome aboard, I'm glad you're doing the part." And whatever it was he saw in

me was an instant judgment. And we started shooting two or three days later.

Did you have any rehearsal time?
No, we had nothing, no rehearsal. I worked pretty hard, obviously, on the words, but the character wasn't a reach. Looking back on the character now, I probably could have, or should have, made it more interesting, or could have found ways to make it more interesting, but his dialogue was so precise there was no reach, I didn't have to accommodate anything.

The Twilight Zone is based in story, and when they say it's Rod Serling, they mean it's out of Rod Serling's imagination and the actors are able to contribute to the thing, but it's the story. I hadn't seen a really good movie, much less a great movie, that doesn't have those characteristics quite right, the cult of the personality. I would say Rod was the most honest and straightforward [person], and I think those

186

I guess I could work now if I wanted to, but I'm kind of a tweener — I'm an old leading man who didn't really do too many character things. I really don't have a character presentation. I could play doctors and stuff, but the business is so much rejection now, you meet for everything — it doesn't make any difference what it is, you know, two or three lines. I'd really like to work every fourth or fifth day. There used to be a feeling for performers that had paid their dues and you were treated with a kind of respect, but now that's not part of the game.

What was director Richard Bare like?

He was a crazy man, a nice man, and a very accomplished director. He'd do stuff faster and did several other *Twilight Zone* episodes, deservedly so, because he was an excellent director.

Anything else that sticks in your mind from working on the series?

The only thing I was aware of was Rod smoked more than I did, and I was a chain-smoker. I can still see him chain-smoking, he was terrible — not nervous really, very laid-back. Well, you step out and light a cigarette and it's kind of a release, the energy and focus, so then you can refocus and do it, and it really was a thing that can serve that for most people.

As quickly as *The Twilight Zone* happened, it's still got legs, it's still one of the highlights. If people ask you what you did, you say, "Well, I did a *Twilight Zone*." You know, there weren't a lot of egos there, no prima donnas. These were his words, his stories, and his ideas. You can go on a show, any show, and you can sit on the set for half an hour, and you know who's in charge, who's the big cheese, who's gonna make the noise. And I think you could have walked on the set and there was no ego. The director, of course, was obviously giving orders, because he's setting

Rod Serling enlisted in the US Army 11th Airborne Paratroopers Division in World War II, and served from January 1943 through January 1946. He was in combat in the Pacific, and while in the Philippines, was wounded by shrapnel in the knee. He received numerous decorations, including the prestigious Purple Heart and Bronze Star medals and was discharged with the rank of Technician 5th grade, the equivalent rank of Corporal.

people who were associated with that kind of function, in that capacity, they tried to project what Rod Serling was trying to do.

Had you been contacted by the producer, Buck Houghton?

It might have been Buck. They called my agent and they wanted to see me for this thing and so I went in and, as I say, I had been working on the lot, on *The Islanders*, which was being shot at MGM, and that was sold for the upcoming season.

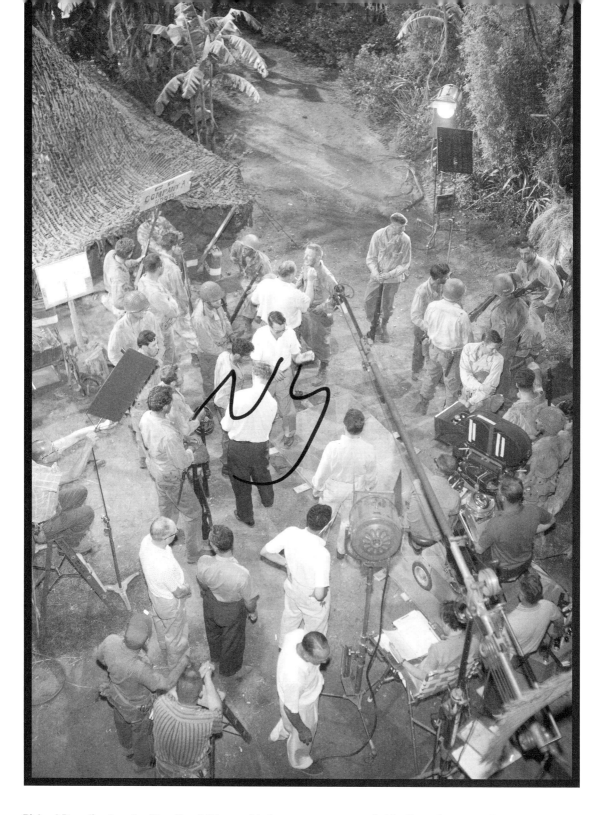

Richard Bare directs actor Marc Cavell (Freeman) between scenes surrounded by the entire cast and crew.

Director Richard Bare works with the crew during scenes in the jungle set. Seen on the right is actor William Phillips.

up camera angles and stuff like that. Dick was such a low-level guy, I don't recall ever having any difficulty.

What an enjoyable experience! The more I think about it the more I like it. But I do remember a scene I wasn't comfortable with. It was the scene after the hospital sequence where the young private died. I did it anyway, and it wasn't bad, but I could have done it better, or found a hook that could have made it more effective.

Bert Granet commented that he thought Rod was a frustrated actor.

Well, I don't know how frustrated he was, he was very good. There was much more collegiality in those days. You used to go on other people's sets and see how people worked. But *The Twilight Zone* came at the end of that era. The people who worked in the industry of the time were still veterans of this kind of thing, and like I say, there were no egos, unlike today. I don't know whether Rod could have functioned in today's industrial age. A lot of camaraderie back then. We all knew each other, they were my friends.

Today, they let the actors be so self-indulgent, they have too much power. They want to optimize what they can do, but that doesn't make for a tight ship. There's got to be some type of principal point of view at work, and *The Twilight Zone* was Rod's, and it wasn't the point of view of whoever's got the clout and whoever's got the money for the moment.

Paul Comi

Paul Comi starred in "People Are Alike All Over," as Warren Marcusson, in "The Odyssey of Flight 33," as First Officer Craig, and in "The Parallel," as the psychiatrist.

Did your work on *The Twilight Zone* have a uniqueness that you hadn't dealt with on other television shows?

In its own way, it was really a very professional and quality-driven show, and you really felt very proud of doing it. Most actors knew of Rod's reputation and ability from some of the other things that he had done, and so it was kind of a coup, in a way, to be included in that. That became more of a reality in the ensuing years, as the series went on and it was earning its following at the time. Other friends who were actors were in it, and I did three of them, and there's not too many of us that did multiples. When you look back, even though these people were working actors at the time, a lot of them hadn't achieved the real status they would eventually have, but they still were respected at the time. So a lot of the actors that performed on that felt that it was a prestigious show.

You worked on the show in its first and fourth seasons. The first season it was still a little bit of an unknown entity, while by the fourth season it was very popular. Can you talk about any differences between the two?

Well, the first season we did "People Are Alike All Over," with Roddy McDowall and Susan Oliver. It was the first time that I had worked with Roddy, and it was a wonderful thing. Mitch Leisen, who directed it, had been a scenic designer for Cecil B. DeMille, and so it was one of those things where it was not simply doing a film — we found ourselves getting involved socially. Later on, Mitch brought us all over to his studio, and he catered a dinner. And I was there with my wife, Roddy was there, Susan was there. And he talked about films he had done before. So my memories of

Paul Comi and Roddy McDowall star in "People Are Alike All Over."

190

that show were pretty much related subjectively to specifically Roddy, working with Roddy, because later on, we did do *Conquest of the Planet of the Apes* together. And that kind of etched it in my mind.

As opposed to when we did "The Odyssey of Flight 33," which was interesting because Rod himself really took an interest in that show. Unlike when we did the "People" show, we rehearsed for two days almost like a play, and Justus Addis, who directed it, wanted us to get acclimated to the cockpit, wanted it to be very natural. And Rod seemed to have an interest in this — his brother was a pilot or something like that. And I've had people who were associated with flying tell me it was the most realistic dialogue they had ever heard in a movie. And they had an advisor on the show, and so the idea of rehearsing, getting acclimated to the show, getting the ensemble work going, was a totally different experience than when I worked with Mitch on the first one.

Then I did the hour show "The Parallel," which was really not that satisfying of an experience. Because I think they themselves sensed that this format was not the proper format for the formula Rod had worked out. In fact, even people who have tried to replicate and do *Twilight Zone*, they've never really understood fully what he discovered and the formula he had. Those are really my specific memories of those two shows, because those are the two that remain with me. "The Parallel" is still a vague memory.

Well, Rod introduced us to an element that we very, very well know is possible. And I think maybe some of the experiences coming through WWII, and having experienced what the world experienced at that time, gave him an understanding that as an artist, he wanted to convey. And it's interesting, some people say we are more cynical today. But I think it's a cynicism born out of the awareness of what people like

Rod at that time had the understanding of. But the world — the rest of us — was very naive. And so I think that my understanding of that type of material may have opened up a window intellectually for me. But to that point, I probably hadn't thought too much about those types of things.

Is there anything you specifically brought to the role that was either a performance element or something you take ownership of?

Well, I felt that again, because Roddy's part seemed to be less physical and so forth, I had to project. I was the one who was bringing stability and strength to the beginning. I would be the guiding light. I would encourage him and try to help him get past his fear and concern. So that was basically my action, as far as what I was playing on. And the fact that when I was wounded and dying, I wanted to see what was happening out there. I just wanted to see. I knew I was going to die, and basically I wanted to play my desire, the urgency of wanting to get past this man who was almost hysterical in his fear of what could be out there. So those were basically the two qualities I played.

What was the Mars set like for "People"?

They used a backdrop on that. I remember seeing the setup for it — they used a cyclorama behind to get that depth. Most of the stuff was confined to the soundstage. All the stages at MGM are the old stages, and so they're fairly standard, full-length soundstages, so when you open them up you can really get a lot of room in there. When you go on the stage, they're usually cluttered with other stuff not necessarily related to what you're doing. Or it might be a number of different scenes, and that's why you get the feeling that it's not as big. The Mars set didn't have too many scenes. We had the opening sequence, where we were behind the wire fence at the airport, looking up into the sky and waiting to go, for the launch that was taking place. That was shot in a little section, and I mean just a little section of wire fencing, so you could cut right into that. Then, the set after the crash was again a small set, and then after that, you had the exterior stuff where you had the smashed capsule, and where he comes out of it, and where they're all standing, but there was a depth shot when you looked reverse, back of the people. They had the cyclorama behind them, so you're looking off almost into infinity, you got the feeling of spaciousness.

Did you enjoy working with director Mitchell Leisen?

Mitch Leisen was a fascinating guy, because he was one of those directors from the old school, who relied upon his casting correctly. He knew when he cast he was going to get the quality and performance that he wanted. Mitch seemed to have a great respect for actors. Being a scenic designer, and that was his background, he was looking at it pictorially, and expecting the actors to provide what he cast them for. So I really don't remember that he had to tell me too much and what I had to do; most of my stuff was when I was hurt, and I was mortally wounded and just playing through the pain, and trying to want to see what I'm dying for — I've got to see. And for the most part, I felt that it was friendly, and probably fortunate for me, because I don't know how I would've dealt with a tough director at that point in my career. So again, I feel that many times I was lucky, and it was later on that I began to realize *how* lucky.

What was it like working with director Justus Addiss on "The Odyssey of Flight 33"?

Working with Justus was very much different, he was very specific. He was almost a theater

Actress Ida Lupino and director Mitchell Leisen during a break on "The Sixteen-Millimeter Shrine."

director, and knew how to relate to his actors. And this is why he put a premium on having a day of rehearsal; he knew as a theater man that he could get performances by analyzing and getting into the gut of the thing right from the beginning. And it proved to be the case. No one was searching for character or what the moment of the scene was all about. By the time we were shooting, we knew it cold.

Did your Airborne experience help you in that role as a first officer?

Well, probably not too much. Except that I know that my instinct would have been to find a parachute and get out of there. But I don't know that it did too much. The fact that we had an advisor on the set, he was very helpful specifically with those of us who had very

192

clear bits of action to do. As we were descending, for example, when Anderson said, "All right, we're gonna take it down, we're gonna take a look around." The apprehension of how we didn't know if we were going to crash into another plane because we had lost contact. And they told us how the first officer had to reach up and make these various moves that will assist in having the plane in its descent. So we had a clear understanding of our actual movements. It wasn't like the many times in these shows where you're just creating movements and praying to God that it was real. But in this instance, we knew everything we did in that cockpit was authentic. So we felt comfortable with it.

It looks like they used a real training cockpit for the set of "The Odyssey of Flight 33."

I don't know if they used an actual portion of a plane or not, but I do know the cockpit that we worked in. I don't know if this was an actual cockpit that they had cut in such a way that they had the ability to film in and out. I have a feeling that when you look at the cuts, the angles of the shots, they're usually shooting from almost a window on the side where they're shooting across from John and myself, where we're looking out — the direct on — and then the individual shots are close in of the long shot. I remember us climbing up into something, and so I have a feeling that this was a portion of an actual plane. Of course, we always worked in the cockpit, and I know in parts where the stewardess came back, she came through that door in the cockpit, and I can't remember when we're looking back, it may very well be that they had the whole portion of the plane in one spot. It could have been the whole piece, because whenever you saw the two stewardesses in that little bay that they're working in, I don't think that when she opened the door you see us.

Paul Comi stars as First Officer Craig, in "The Odyssey of Flight 33."

There's a shot in that show with the stop-motion dinosaur that was reportedly the most expensive shot of the series, a whopping $2,500. How do you think that worked for that show, and what was your reaction seeing it worked in?

We never saw it until the actual episode. We had to imagine as we looked out there when they brought us all over. And I had that line where I said something like, "Skipper, check something for me, look." And everybody comes over and we're all supposed to be reacting to seeing this dinosaur. Well, I don't know how many of us had ever seen a picture of a dinosaur at that time, even the conjecture of dinosaurs. This was too soon for kids to be excited about them. When I first viewed it, the dinosaur was a little bit jarring. It worked, but the point is that it was the state of the art of

193

the time. The budget was so low — when they made that insert there, and I'm looking at it from Craig's viewpoint, because I'm sitting there and thinking, "We're literally flying at treetop level," which would have been a little bit too close, to have a jet that low. At that point, you see the dinosaur at tree level, you see the reactions of the crew, and when it comes back from a commercial break, the jet is in high altitude.

So when I saw the thing, I was really much more fascinated by it in later years. Because in retrospect, we have the advantage of seeing how something is done digitally and so forth on computers, and this looks very primitive when you look at it today. But there's no question of its impact for its time.

You had a supporting role in the fourth-season episode, "The Parallel." How did that compare to your previous episodes?

It's really hard for me to remember that show. It almost came as a surprise to me when I was looking at *The Twilight Zone Companion* a number of years ago, and I couldn't remember the name of the episode, and there it was: "The Parallel." And I never did meet the fella playing the lead [Steve Forrest]. So it was a strange, strange thing. I think I did it in one day. So whatever I worked on for the psychiatrist, it had very little to do with the script.

Why do you think *The Twilight Zone* still captures an audience after all these years?

Well, the quality of writing. And you look at the people who were cast in many of these things, and you look at the careers that they encompass, and you realize at that time a lot of these people were entering the industry, too. At the same time they had veterans like Mickey Rooney and so forth. Guys like Jack Klugman were people coming into the industry when a lot of stars would not do television. So they

Jack Klugman and the uncredited twin actresses from the theater's ticket booth sequence in "A Passage for Trumpet."

had the opportunity, and we also had the opportunity because of this, to work with some of the really finest writers that the industry had. When you look back at those times and the writers they had, even pedestrian material had a certain life to it, because the writing was good and because of the enthusiasm and innovation of a lot of the actors. Robert Redford and Bobby Duvall, people like that, it was an exciting time. We didn't know it at the time, but we just did it. And, of course, Rod's talent speaks for itself.

Looking at the series, do you have a favorite episode?

Yes. I like the things that Jack Klugman did. Especially the trumpet-playing episode. I just loved the script and I loved him in it. Some of the shows really were very, very memorable. When I think of Gladys Cooper and Robert Redford in an episode that was based on so little, or the Agnes Moorehead one where, you know, you just almost focused on the performance of this woman. I'm more taken really by the acting, what some people did with some of the roles. And Shatner, I thought, never acted as well as he did in "Nightmare at 20,000 Feet." I bought into that part, he was just wonderful. I just really had to respect what he did with that. So I thought that was one of those scripts that really worked.

You were talking about the fact that people have tried over the years to redo *The Twilight Zone*, and you mentioned "the formula." What was the formula?
Well, I know some of the things that it wasn't. It wasn't science fiction. It wasn't horror. I think it was some of the elements of the human existence and the human experience that, when you really begin to look into it, is the potential of what lies behind some of those things with the imagination such as [Rod] had. Offer insight into situations that you just don't get. People who have tried to do it, they suddenly set it in a formula: "Well, what can I do? How can I bring in a monster? How can I scare people?"

That wasn't him, if I can be so presumptuous as even to define what Rod does, or did. He chose to infuse his insights into human relations and the human existence. Rod was infinitely a storyteller, a person who told it through character, through circumstance. But whatever it was, it's what genius and talent is. He was able to do it and put it all together, and express it in his form. And others tried to copy it and they didn't do it.

I feel I was very fortunate to have been in the business at that time, and to have participated in some types of shows that I was fortunate enough to get into. And certainly his shows — I just feel blessed to have been a part of it.

Robert Sorrells

Robert Sorrells starred in "The Mighty Casey" as Casey.

"The Mighty Casey" is a good episode of *The Twilight Zone*, and one of the better comedy ones. How do you feel about that?
That was such a big deal in my life, because then, as now, even when it was brand-new, everyone knew this was a prestige show, and of course every actor wanted to be on that show. I got the part so easily, I probably got it over a

Robert Sorrells plays Casey, the Hoboken Zephyrs' robot pitcher, in "The Mighty Casey."

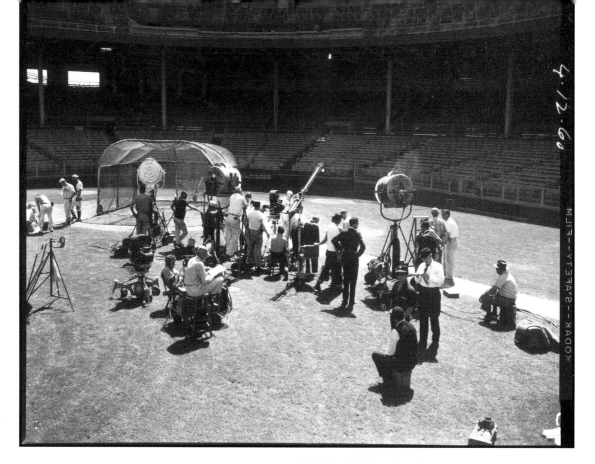

Out on location at the Hollywood Baseball Park, the crew films a scene with actors Jack Warden and Abraham Sofaer.

couple of cocktails with Rod and John Frankenheimer: "Hey, I know a guy, you know, he's a great big guy and he's very innocent-looking like a robot, maybe you can look at him." I think it was something like that. That's my internal scenario. I was called in, and first I had to go see a gal named Ethel Winant, who was casting, and then I had to meet Mr. Serling on a subsequent day. And Rod, he just took a look at me and he said, "Well, I don't want you looking like Tony Perkins out there," and I said, "Well, I've played some ball, you know," which was true, but I never pitched in my life, which I failed to mention [laughs].

Rod says, "Okay, you're hired," pretty much. I only knew it was confirmed the next day.

Cameramen film shots of Sorrells pitching the ball.

So I had to learn to pitch that ball! And so I went to Larry Parnell, he used to pitch in the minors and played first base. And he taught me

196

to warm up — the looks, the stance — and he worked with me for days, and I got it down pretty good. I had no accuracy, no speed, but I could look like I did. I got back the day after we were shooting, and only found out then that the guy had to be a lefty! I think Rod Serling was thinking about Sandy Koufax when he wrote that thing. I said, "I can't do that, Rod, what about just reversing the name Hoboken Zephyrs on the jerseys and then turning the film around?" And he said, "Well, what are we gonna do with the outfield?" I said, "Oh, gosh." So, at any rate, I went back to Larry, I learned to wind up and tried to not embarrass myself, but they still had to get a body double for the long shots. It looked a little awkward if you know what's going on, but if you don't know what's going on, maybe it'll pass.

That was pretty exciting, all that put together. You know, you could just see how it went for me. I just fell off the cabbage truck, yeah: "Which way's Hollywood?" And I'm going just to get the part initially and to then be devastated by, "Hey, left-handed," after I had worked my tail off.

But he was known for showing up to help, in case an actor needed something changed in a line, and he could do that on the spot.
You know, when you have a very decent part in a really good show, you don't really socialize or look around too much, except in talking to the script consultant, maybe the director of photography. And you're in your dressing room studying quite a bit. But yeah, I'm sure I saw him, Mr. Serling, there at least a few times.

We shot "The Mighty Casey" twice. We shot it with Paul Douglas instead of Jack Warden. Paul was ill when we were shooting. As far as everyone was concerned, including CBS, that was in the can! And the word that I got, and I think it's true, is that CBS wanted to release it with Paul Douglas. And Rod Serling, to pro-

Seen here with Sorrells are actors Abraham Sofaer (Dr. Stillman), and Paul Douglas, who originally played the part of manager Mouth McGarry. Douglas had been feeling ill during the shoot (it wasn't known at the time he was suffering from an incipient coronary), and sadly passed away 15 days afterwards. Instead of scrapping the episode, Serling reportedly paid $27,000 out of his own pocket for a reshoot of scenes involving McGarry, with Jack Warden playing the part and Robert Parrish directing.

tect Paul's memory, if you will, took out his own wallet and refinanced the reshoot. And when I got rehired for the reshoot, which was about half of it, it gave me so much confidence, because I said, "Well, I don't think I'm doing that big a performance, but I must be doing something right if they still want me to do it again." That gave me an immense amount of self-confidence. But it took an awful long time to be released. They shot it in '59, and they showed it in June of '60.

Does anything else about that shoot stand out for you?

Gosh, the only thing I remember is being an almost-scared-to-death young boy, you know: "God, I hope they don't hurt me, I hope they don't fire me, I hope I can get through this." Because I was just trying my wings, just being in front of the cameras, having been giving it away for seven years down in Long Beach. And just to get paid for acting, and that whole experience of being in front of the cameras, it was so intense. From my subjective perspective, it was hard for me to really get a view of what was actually happening. I think it was certainly a high point in my life, and Rod Serling was a hero to me. He was my guru, if you will, my showbiz guru.

I think Rod Serling was misused by people, by the networks. It's always been my view, personally, the more creative a person is, the more they need a good agent, the more they need protection by other people. The easier it is for the guys with the three-piece suits and the computers to knock him over. I think Rod was certainly victimized almost.

Mouth McGarry and Dr. Stillman observe robot pitcher, Casey. Warden also starred in the episode "The Lonely."

Any memorable moments working with your costars Jack Warden and Abraham Sofaer?

Well, Jack Warden, in my opinion, is like a typical New Yorker, if there is such a thing. He could be a cab driver, to be tough enough to survive in New York. Something that was very embarrassing to me: we had a brief dialogue where he said, "'Yeah, I don't want you to be nervous out there, Casey," and Casey says, "Nervous?" and he says, "Yeah, it's something . . . something . . . in the ninth, and Joe DiMaggio is on the plate." And I said, "Well, that wouldn't worry me, I don't know anyone named Joe DiMaggio." But I said, "Joe DiM*ah*ggio" and he said, "Joe DiM*a*ggio." And I've always cringed about that. Being a *robot*, I should have repeated him, and said, "Joe DiMaggio." It's something that I missed it; I blew it.

Warden, director Alvin Ganzer, and cameramen during filming of a scene in the dugout.

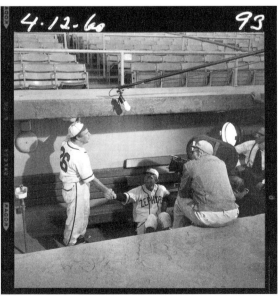

The camera crew ready takes of Casey pitching; note the crewman on the left holding an "EFFECT" cue.

Sorrells, Ganzer, a cameraman, and Sofaer observe Warden at work.

One of those little things, though. . . .

Yeah, but to him, that was like the worst thing I could have done in life. You know, personally, to respond in that way. I was really innocent, just a little stupid. But I don't think Jack respected me too much. I was new and I was naive, but he equated that with something I don't think it quite was. I probably wasn't as tough as he was then. He had a lot of chutzpah, moxie, and I didn't have any of that stuff.

But, the part of Casey was undoubtedly much better than I had initially thought, because they keep showing it. And they did hire me twice. You know, regarding those scripts, I think most writers have a whole file full of unsold or unfinished short stories, and I think that once *The Twilight Zone* got cooking, Rod Serling took out some of those and dusted them off, and made them into teleplays. Which any writer would do.

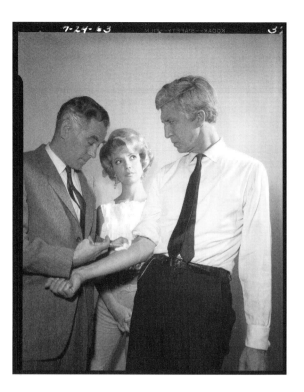

Actors Walter Brooke, Ruta Lee, and Patrick O'Neal star in "A Short Drink From a Certain Fountain." This is one of the four half-hour episodes not included in the initial syndication run.

Ruta Lee

Ruta Lee starred in "A Short Drink From a Certain Fountain," as Flora Gordon.

What was it like being part of *The Twilight Zone*, as a performer and coming to the set?

Well, at the time it was one of the hot guest spots to be on. And *Twilight Zone* was kind of way up there in the weekly series, it was the prestige piece, and they had prestige directors and prestige actors certainly, so being invited to do it was great. I did the show, and it was to this day one of the best roles I've ever played. Only because she was such a divine bitch, and so sweetly nasty and a pleasure to play, so it really worked very well. And, of course, Rod Serling was a friend. He became a friend shortly after that, we had mutual friends, and friends in common, and we'd see each other socially here, there, and everywhere, and it was always one of the favorites for him, too, this episode called "A Short Drink From a Certain Fountain." Rod was always a dear lovely man with his perennial cigarette, which of course, I loved the look of, but not the results of.

This is a show that has been playing continuously for nearly 50 years. Why do you think other shows have come and gone, but *Twilight Zone* still holds an audience today?

I think because it piques your imagination. It tickles your sense of the weird and adventurous, and the stories are timeless, they will go on forever, because they deal with the strange and the unknown. And I think we all like to be captivated by the unknown. We're all a little bit afraid of it — be it death, be it space travel, be it microbes — we're all just a little frightened of anything we don't know, and these stories certainly captured them in a very identifiable way. That's what I love so about Rod's writing, and the people he chose to use as writers. They grabbed each and every one of us and said, "This could be you, this could be you." And it's still doing it. It could be you.

Rod seemed to explore morality and social interests as well, by calculating a fantastic realm. What you do think about how that was handled?
Oh, what a lovely way, instead of a preacher banging it out on Sunday morning, where you maybe wanted to sleep through it. You got your lesson in right and wrong. In a beautiful and a little bit subliminal way, it came to you, and I love it, I wish we had more of it. I wish we had more lessons in morality and how you are going to wind up paying for misdeeds one way or another.

What appealed to you about the story of "A Short Drink From a Certain Fountain"?
It appealed to me because, being a young hot little chickie-poo, I was faced with that same sort of thing. There were always "sugar daddies" that were around, and it was kind of fun because I've always been a Miss Goody Two-Shoes. I may not have played it, but I have always been highly moral and am still to this day. And it was fun to let loose and play a girl who was there just for the money, and just for the good times, and just for what she could get out of it, and to have her get such a punch in the gut and nose in the end of it was just so wonderful, and it gave me a chance to do some very nice work.

After a scene, the crew complimented Ruta Lee by calling her the next Carole Lombard.

How did you get that part?
I can't remember. I think I simply got a call from the casting director, and the script was sent out. I didn't have to go in and read for it, I know that. And one of the nicest things in the world happened to me on that. You know we actors love applause — we like the check at the end of the week, too — but I think we like the applause and the recognition for good work better than anything. After one of the scenes, the grips and the lighting guys who were up in the catwalks leaning down watching the scene, and the cable pullers and everything else, stopped, applauded, and said, "We had a consensus of opinion, and we've all decided that you're the next Carole Lombard." And what a compliment that was, because Carole Lombard

was the best dame who ever came along. She knew how to swap bawdy stories with the boys, she knew how to be a performer, she knew how to be there on time, and be professional and do her work. So I said, "Thank you, gentlemen, and thank you, god, for the privilege."

Can you tell me about working with director Bernard Girard?

Barney Girard is one hell of a director. Gentle, easy, wild sense of humor, a feel for the natural and, in this case, the unnatural. And he was very conscious of making everybody look good, to make him or her look like they're doing their very best. And I loved him.

Barney Girard didn't give me any special direction, and he gave me rope. He let me do things. When the script said, "She dances," he let me just go and do whatever. He said, "Remember who you are, you're impatient with your life, that you've gotten yourself into something, you're bored, you're cute, you're hot, you want to get out there." But he just gave me rope to do whatever, which was very nice. And to have pleased Barney Girard made me very happy.

Do you remember anything specific to your character that you brought to the role that differed from the script?

What I brought to it was my ability to dance, and my ability to use my body very freely and very easily. And when I say, "use my body," I mean as an actress, whether it was handling a drink or stumbling or doing whatever, I brought that to it. I brought the experience, as an actress, of imagining what it would be to be trapped by my own choosing in a marriage with a much older man, which I can't imagine is good unless you really love the man. In this case, there was very little love. There was love for the looker, but not the individual that

brought the money to the table. I'd like to play it again.

Do you have a favorite episode?

Sure I have a favorite episode — it's mine. And of course mine wasn't in syndication for a long time. I think there were either three or four shows that were withheld for some reason. And so during the festivals of the running of *Twilight Zone*, I didn't appear, and then finally after several years they pulled them out, and thank god I'm in there. And I love watching it every single time. Above all, to please Rod Serling — that, my dear, is one of the greatest toasts anybody could get.

Cliff Robertson

Cliff Robertson starred in "A Hundred Yards Over the Rim," as Christian Horn, and in "The Dummy," as Jerry Etherson.

Evans Evans (Mary Lou in "A Hundred Yards Over The Rim"): "All I can remember about that episode were my tight blue jeans and what a pleasure it was to work with Cliff Robertson."

What did you think of *Twilight Zone* when it first aired, and what do you think of the show today?

I thought then that it was cutting edge, ahead of its time, and I think the same thing today. They didn't have a lot of the technology, of course, but in a way they had to revert and resort to the words. Storytelling, not gimmicks. Shtick affects shtick.

What was it like working at the MGM Studios, on the *Twilight Zone* sets in particular?

Well, it was good. There was one called "A Hundred Yards Over the Rim," and I had done my research, because it was about a family going westward on a covered wagon, and they become discouraged because they hit this desert, and a boy was sick. The leader, the character I played, was determined to continue on, and they want to turn back, back from Ohio or something. So, I did my research, and I think what was so interesting to me was these people were poor, the clothes they wore were always those black wool things, which is all right in the winter, but god forbid you hit a desert. So I thought that was kind of even, that that would add to the terrible odds against them — the heat, they didn't have the right clothes. So I went to the wardrobe and I picked these clothes, and then I picked a stovepipe hat, because I was looking at it visually with my directorial eye, and I thought, visually, if he walks a hundred more yards over the rim, and he said, "Just let me look over this rim," this would be a very effective shot of this guy in the ill-fitting, black, hot trousers, and with this hat. I thought that made a very effective shot.

Anyway, I went to the wardrobe and I picked my outfit, and then I got the producer and he said, "Oh no, you can't use that hat!" I said, "Why not? It keeps the sun off his head." He told me they wanted to dress me like a banana safari outfit. I said, "Wait a minute, they were people that weren't prepared, and if they were, they didn't have the money." So the producer and I disagreed, and the producer finally called Rod and Rod said, "He's right!" And I always remember that —

Cliff Robertson stars as settler Christian Horn in Serling's "A Hundred Yards Over the Rim." The desert scenes were filmed on location near Lone Pine, California, and to save money on the budget, this episode was filmed along with "The Rip Van Winkle Caper."

he supported me. The producer had only hit a blind spot there. Buck was a good guy. But it's like going to war without bullets. You've got to have something in there to not only achieve some kind of even questionable victory, you've got to do something to protect yourself. So the more information you know about the character and about the play and about the relationships — it's not that you're being artsy-craftsy, it means you're being responsible.

You filmed normal days, morning and midday?

It was a regular day shoot on "The Dummy." But in "A Hundred Yards Over the Rim," we

Actress Miranda Jones costars with Cliff Robertson in "A Hundred Yards Over the Rim."

went up to Lone Pine. I fly my glider over that now, I'm a commercial pilot and could be doing it for a living, if I had to. I've been doing that for 35 years, and I also love soaring. I have a glider I keep up in Mendon, Nevada, on the eastern slope of the Sierras, where we get this mysterious, what I call "Rod Serling wave." That's the wave that is invisible but fascinating.

What was it like coming into that show during its second and third seasons, when it already had some momentum to it?

It was a delight. Rod Serling went to the same college as I did, quite a bit before I did, and he lectured in the summertime, but I knew enough about him to trust him. And I also liked his words, and I liked his personality. He liked actors; he didn't come in with this attitude that actors are all children. He treated actors as adults. That was reassuring, and the people that did the show, his staff, were efficient, but they were very good. And so I was delighted.

When did you meet Rod Serling, and what was your first impression of him?

I had the highest regard for Rod. I talked with him on the phone before I ever met him personally. When I met him personally, face-to-face, it was very friendly and he knew I'd gone to Antioch, which probably helped. But he also seemed to like the fact that I was stage-trained. He liked actors that had come from New York — one of the reasons, I suspect, was because he felt they were not just a pretty face, a haggard face. He liked the theater, and I always had a feeling that he maybe harbored an unadmitted desire to write for the theater, but maybe wasn't quite ready for that quantum leap. That's nothing more than a guess.

We talked on the phone, we were always going to do more, but then he died. He liked my work and I sure loved his. He was so supportive on that thing on "A Hundred Yards Over the Rim." He said, "I do appreciate an actor who takes his work so seriously that he does his research and homework." Anyway, great guy. I just thought he was terrific, a man way ahead of his time, obviously.

What was your impression of that script when you read it?

Well, I was fascinated, as it's a story of early 1800s migration from the east coast to the west — in this case, a wagon train. And I knew that was a tough thing, because I had ancestors who had been on wagon trains, so I knew it took a lot of courage, a lot of grit. So I did a lot of reading about that migration, east to west in those days, and one of the obvious things was they were, for the most part, very poor. They came in those wagons with everything they had, and it wasn't much. And the clothes they had were the clothes they had on their back, and that was a trigger for me. Because the character has gone over the mountains, he's gone a ways in the desert, and the people are tired and his son is sick. And there is every reason to do a 180 and go back, and all the people want to go back.

Tell me about working with director Buzz Kulik.

Buzz was a very amiable guy. So amiable that I sometimes thought that he must've once been an actor. Because he seemed to understand.

Most of the shows were shot on the lot, but as you've mentioned, this one actually went out on location to the desert. How tough of a challenge was that?

Hotter than hell. But I was glad. Because it helped again — it helped me realize how desperate this man had to be, and all these people had to be. And it helped me get into the character, if you will. So I may have been a little discomforted with the heat and the sand and all that, but, hey man, it just helped that character and I embraced it with great alacrity.

Do you have a favorite moment or scene in the episode?

I must tell you in all honesty, and this is not modesty, I've done *Spider-Man* as my 60th starring film, and I've done god knows how many television shows. But the dead truth is I have never been satisfied. It's a degree of dissatisfaction — I'm less dissatisfied with some things than others, so there's nothing in "A Hundred Yards Over the Rim" that I'm particularly struck or impressed or amazed by. As you get older and more mellow, you gradually come to the realization that, although you're not satisfied, you recognize maybe you've done about as much as you can do, given the limitations of the script, of the production, of the actors. You can only do so much. As my late grandmother used to say, you cannot get blood out of a turnip.

"The Dummy," which was also written by Rod, was directed by Abner Biberman. What was it like working with him?

Abner was a delightful man. He had been an actor, and I think he'd also been blacklisted at one time. He was pretty much of a political activist, I guess, maybe in his earlier days. Bright, very persuasive, and at the same time he'd listen to the actor. That's why I think he'd

Actor Cliff Robertson poses with the ventriloquist dummy made from his likeness, in the frightening episode, "The Dummy." The dummy of Robertson was created by William Tuttle, and based on caricature sketches commissioned from artist Frank Campbell.

A candid shot of Robertson, Willy, and a crewman on the set of "The Dummy."

---

been an actor. I have a tendency to do that — whenever a director is particularly compliant, I have a tendency to automatically affix in my tired brain, "Well, he had to be an actor." How else would he know the problem?

Did you do the voice of Willy? Was that you?
Yeah, that was me.

On "The Dummy," what was Frank Sutton like to work with?
Frank was a delight. He was good, he had studied, he worked in New York. When you came out to do these shows, when it was a movie or television show, you were delighted to see on the set actors that you knew from New York. There was a kind of an invisible

ensemble really — chances are they were good, certainly experienced in plays off Broadway, and the Actors Studio whatever — so there was a degree of comfort. On the other hand, you come out here from New York, and you've got your chip on your shoulder, you're so full of yourself. You come on the set and you see your bunch of Hollywood types, with your pretty faces male and female, you have a tendency to kind of get a little chip on your shoulder. But many times they were just young people trying to do the same thing you've been doing — make a living. But we had a tendency to be a little bit [points up his nose] up about being a New York actor, and many times we weren't that good at all.

During the final sequence, the cameras had a tilted angle on virtually every shot in that chase, which makes for a very eerie sequence. Do you remember anything about filming that sequence and whether that presented any challenges technically?
When I saw Abner doing that, I was delighted. I felt, "Yes, this is right." I didn't feel like some artist who was being self-indulged, I felt, "Hey this is great, it's a wild, wild scene and I think he did a hell of a job." You know, you hear grumbling sometimes in those days of a guy who had the courage to do that. You'd hear some old gruff voice somewhere saying, "What the hell is he doing, what's he trying to do, who's he trying to put on?" And in many cases these guys were on the cutting edge, and maybe some of the big movie directors looked at some of those shows, those relatively small shows, and picked up on some of the things they were doing and used them in their big films. They may not have admitted it to themselves, but it had an influence.

Why do you think this show is so timeless and has found new generations to watch it?
This is a generation fascinated by sci-fi, high

tech, fantasy. This is not a kitchen-sink generation. Some of the wonderful things that Paddy Chayefsky and those wonderful writers wrote are not in vogue right now, but it doesn't in any way diminish the quality of their words, it just means they are going through this thing now of hi-fi and crazy stuff. My daughter said to me one day, "Daddy, let me get this straight. You fly a twin-engine airplane all by yourself across these United States and you cannot work my stereo?" And I said, "You know, you're right, because I don't really give a damn about your stereo."

It always struck me that Rod found a good way of using fantasy and drama to talk about other, more important, real issues that if he dealt with overtly audiences wouldn't be absorbed or entertained.
Very good point. He had his own agenda and it was relevant to today. He had a wonderful way of bouncing it off of these surrealistic things, but somewhere or another it permeated our brain. We were left with a feeling of, even though this is sci-fi or whatever, it was relevant. And I think he was a moralist in that sense. He was a great man, and we lost a great man, and those were great times. And I'm delighted it's being shown all the time somewhere around the world. Not only for the actors, although we don't get any money from it, but the ideas. If those good ideas — even though they're subtitled maybe in certain countries — if some of Rod Serling's ideas are percolating and distilling themselves down to people who are examining it and saying, "This is true, this is true, this is true."

Shelley Berman

Shelley Berman starred in "The Mind and the Matter," as Archibald Beechcroft.

Actor/comedian Shelley Berman seems to be doing an impression of Rod Serling, posed alongside rubber-latex masks of himself from the comedy episode, "The Mind and the Matter."

What were your first impressions of Rod Serling?
All my impressions, first and always, of Rod Serling were of admiration. First of all, he was such a sweetheart of a guy, a gentleman. You didn't know how such a really relaxed laid-back type of guy like that could think of the things he thought of, and be able to discipline himself to put it down. He was quite a decent man. He loved to sit out there and write by his pool. That was his big thing, he had a world-class tan and he was happy with that, he was a nice-looking guy.

Did you have an opportunity to work on anything else of his?
No, just that, but of course, nobody knew at the time. When we got an opportunity to be featured in one of his works, we didn't know that it was forever. Nobody dreamed that it

As actor Shelley Berman stands by, director of photography George T. Clemens and a cameraman prepare the next shot for one of the subway scenes.

Rod Serling poses for a candid shot during the filming of "The Eye of the Beholder."

would continue, that a following would result, that a kind of cult group would take up this piece of work, all of his works. I still love to see Agnes Moorehead in that marvelous thing where she had to fight off the "invaders." She is such a glorious actress who, even without dialogue, just was magnificent. I loved one with Burgess Meredith where all he wants is to read — the irony is so terrible! Those of us who have seen these things are pretty much thrilled to witness them; we enjoy seeing them again and again. You didn't know when you did this that you would be honored to be a part of that milieu, and people would say, "Hey, I saw you on television last night, you're part of that *Twilight Zone*."

Along with your colleagues, that must have been a good gig to get.

Oh yeah, for sure! Everybody wanted it — a supporting player, a starring player; you were dying to have that. But you didn't know how important it was, it's eternal. I swear, after we're all gone, people will be looking at this show. You can revisit and revisit, and you don't tire.

I've seen every episode so many times, and it never ceases to amaze me how I can always catch something that I haven't before.

When you were working on the episode, "The Mind and the Matter," do you know if any other episodes were being filmed or rehearsed at the same time, in the studio?

No, we did one show at a time. He may have been sitting at home writing the next one, but he was at the shoot all the time. You always knew he was going to be around. Little changes would be made and he would watch rehearsals, and he would be involved. He was on set a lot, yet you had to know he was busy, still creating what was going to be happening in the future. He made little writing changes in our script; they just couldn't figure out the

The crew rigged the camera to move with Berman and alongside the subway train, thus giving the illusion that the train was moving into the station.

best way to have this sudden change, the sudden transition where he has now done the incantation or whatever, and suddenly the world has changed for him. We had a bit of a big rocking affair, a kind of an explosive earthquake affair with lights blinking, and they tried that, they tried something else. And my memory on that particular thing was that we spent most of the day trying to make that change — how does Beechcroft get into that other world? They tried it three or four different ways, shot it a couple of times, and they had to set up the set in order to do that. They finally settled on how they were going to do it and we went on, but Rod was very much involved in that.

Did he make any changes to dialogue for you?
Well, he rewrote here and there, it was not major rewriting. And it was Buzz Kulik, a marvelous man, who directed this, who was in conference with him frequently, so they could come up with the best possible way. You know, in those days, we simply didn't have the special-effects capability that we have today. For example, the masks. I had to go in there

209

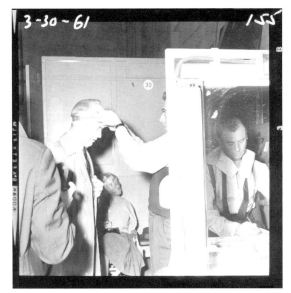

A makeup artist fits actors with rubber-latex masks of Shelley Berman.

Berman is surrounded by a group of Archibald Beechcrofts.

and sit there while they made a life mask on my face. I sat there for a couple of hours with plaster of paris put on me, and today they make a rubber mask and that's it, it's amazing. But there I sat and breathed through a straw and had my eyes covered, so I wouldn't get that crap in my eyes. Afterward, they had the mold and poured rubber masks, and the interesting thing is that there is an increase in the size of the face because you've now applied something and now you're going to apply something else, so you have the increase of the face that you can't avoid. So there were a lot of big-faced Shelley Bermans walking around in there. Like in the subway station, all of those people piling in, I was looking at about 50 people wearing Shelley Berman masks. Very interesting, because when I finally get to see the show on the air, I said, "My god, look at all those people wearing Shelley Berman

masks. I don't know if they really look like me at all, they just look like people with my face on them." It was okay, it did the job, and the viewers, as always, cooperate. They fill in. They understood what was happening, because the viewer, the spectator, invariably supplies what is needed; film artistry can rely upon it. Yet today, we have such abilities and such capacity for special effects that the viewer isn't obliged to do anything.

Had you ever been considered for other *Twilight Zone* parts?

No, just the one. It was written for me and I'm very honored by it. That was it, but that's enough, it really is enough. One time and people can relate to it. Whenever the marathons happen, people see it and say, "My god, you were on that thing I saw." Hey, that's just super! It shows every time and is quite a thing for me. I don't get any money [laughs]. They could show it maybe 1,000 times and I'd get 12 cents if anybody sent me anything. There was some other show that I get three cents on. Percentages have to go out.

Were there any script changes during filming?
Well, I didn't have any changes, but I did say to Rod after the first or second day of shooting, "You know, this guy hates all kinds of people, and now they've all turned into him. His face is there, he's all the people, but you don't have a scene in which there's a woman." And the very next day there was a script change, and I was in the elevator and I was a woman. And I was standing next to a guy who looked like me, and it was me. I'm not sure what the line was, but as we're in the elevator riding, I said something like, "Would you watch your hands, you dirty little man." And it got us an extraordinary reaction. It was a funny moment. And Rod was very happy with it. So was I. It was just beautiful.

Tell me about working with Buzz Kulik.
It was so easy. It was really so easy. You never thought you were being directed. You thought you were being carried and taken care of. You always felt at ease with him. You didn't feel like somebody saying, "Well, you go here, you sit here, and you do that." However it came to you, you knew where you were going to sit, you knew what you were going to do. Because the writing was so good. Rod was a marvelous writer. You always knew how to interpret; you always knew what you were going to do, how you were going to do it. We had a special effect, and that is when this magical moment comes of changing everything in the world. It was supposed to be a big shake-up of the world. So the set shook and the camera shook and I flew. And they had to do it again, and the set shook and the camera shook and I flew.

Director Buzz Kulik sets up a elevator scene with Berman and a group of Beechcrofts.

Kulik directs Berman for the earthquake shot.

ACTORS TELEVISION MOTION PICTURE MINIMUM THREE-DAY CONTRACT
Continuous Employment—Three-day Basis—Three-day Salary—Three-day Minimum Employment

THIS AGREEMENT made __March 28__, 19_61_ between CAYUGA PRODUCTIONS, INC.
a corporation, hereinafter called "Producer," and __JACK GRINNAGE__, hereinafter called "Player,"

WITNESSETH:

1. *Photoplay; Role and Guarantee.* Producer hereby engages Payer to render service as such in the role of "HENRY",

in a photoplay produced primarily for exhibition over free television, the working title of which is now "THE MIND & THE MATTER"

Player accepts such engagement upon the terms herein specified. Producer guarantees that it will furnish Player not less than_____

_____days employment. (If this blank is not filled, the guarantee shall be three days.)

2. *Salary and Advances.* The Producer will pay to the Player, and the Player agrees to accept for three (3) days (and pro rata for each additional day beyond three (3) days) compensation as follows:

Three-day salary   ($ 600.00   )
*Advance for television re-runs   ($)
*Advance for theatrical use   ($)

Three-day Total (including advances)   ($ 600.00   )

3. Producer shall have the unlimited right throughout the world to re-run the film on television and exhibit the film theatrically.

4. If the motion picture is re-run on television in the United States or Canada and contains any of the results and proceeds of the Player's services, the Player will be paid the amounts entered in the blanks in this paragraph plus an amount equal to one-third (⅓rd) thereof for each day of employment in excess of three (3) days and if the blanks are not filled the Player will be paid the minimum additional compensation prescribed therefor by the 1960 Screen Actors Guild Television Agreement below mentioned, and the amount, if any, designated in Paragraph 2 as an advance for re-runs shall be applied against the additional compensation for re-runs payable under this Paragraph 4.

2nd run	3rd run	4th run	5th run	6th and all succeeding runs

5. If the motion picture is exhibited theatrically anywhere in the world and contains any of the results and proceeds of the Player's

services, the Player will be paid $_____ plus an amount equal to one-third thereof for each day of employment in excess of three (3) days (but in any event the total shall not be less than the minimum required by the 1960 Screen Actors Guild Television Agreement). If this blank is not filled in, the Player will be paid the minimum additional compensation to which he would be entitled under such Television Agreement, and the amount, if any, designated in Paragraph 2 as an advance for theatrical use shall be applied against the additional compensation for the theatrical use payable under this Paragraph 5.

6. *Term.* The term of employment hereunder shall begin on __March 28, 1961__ on or about **_____
and shall continue thereafter until the completion of the photography and recordation of said role.

7. *Basic Contract.* Reference is made to the 1960 Screen Actors Guild Television Agreement and to the applicable provisions set forth in such Agreement. Player's employment shall include performance in non commercial openings, closings, bridges, etc., and no added compensation shall be payable to Player so long as such are used in the role(s) and episode(s) covered hereunder and in which Player appears; for other use, Player shall be paid the added minimum compensation, if any, required under the provisions of the Screen Actors Guild agreements with Producer. Player's employment shall be upon the terms, conditions and exceptions of said schedule applicable to the rate of salary and guarantee specified in Paragraphs 1 and 2 hereof.***

8. *Player's Address.* All notices which the Producer is required or may desire to give to the Player may be given either by mailing the same addressed to the Player at __6125 Glen Oaks Ave.   L.A. 27__, California, or such notice may be given to the Player personally, either orally or in writing.

9. *Player's Telephone.* The Player must keep the Producer's casting office or the assistant director of said photoplay advised as to where the Player may be reached by telephone without unreasonable delay.

The current telephone number of the Player is __HO. 3-5007__

10. *Motion Picture Relief Fund.* The Player (does) (does not) hereby authorize the Producer to deduct from the compensation and advance hereinabove specified an amount equal to 1% of each installment of compensation and advances due the Player hereunder and payable during the employment, and to pay the amount so deducted to the Motion Picture Relief Fund of America, Inc.

11. *Furnishing of Wardrobe.* The Player agrees to furnish all modern wardrobe and wearing apparel reasonably necessary for the portrayal of said role; it being agreed, however, that should so-called "character" or "period" costumes be required, the Producer shall supply the same.

12. *Next Starting Date.* The starting date of Player's next engagement is _____

IN WITNESS WHEREOF, the parties have executed this agreement on the day and year first above written.

CAYUGA PRODUCTIONS, INC.

__Jack Grinnage__   By __Buck Houghton__
Player   Producer

(The Player may not waive any provision of the foregoing contract without the written consent of Screen Actors Guild, Inc.)
*No advance for re-runs or theatrical use may be made unless the weekly salary prescribed above is at least $1,500.
**The "on or about clause" may only be used when the contract is delivered to the Player at least seven (7) days before the starting date.
***Producer shall own all rights in and to the results and proceeds of Player's services hereunder which the 1960 Television Agreement or Theatrical Agreement permits Producer to acquire; respecting all others rights thereto without limitation, Player grants same to Producer subject to Producer's obtaining requisite consent or waiver from Screen Actors Guild.

Enterprise Printers & Stationers • HOllywood 5-2540   27

Actor Jack Grinnage's signed contract for his part as Henry in "The Mind and the Matter," also signed by producer Buck Houghton.

And Buzz wasn't happy with it, and we did it again. Till finally I thought maybe I'm going to die here, and we're never going to shoot this and I'm going to be shaken to death, and everything is going to end, and my life would end here.

Jean Carson

Jean Carson starred in "A Most Unusual Camera," as Paula Diedrich.

What did you think of *The Twilight Zone* while it was in production and what do you think about the show today?

I don't think any of us expected it to be on the minds of people this much later. I was thrilled because I thought Rod Serling had a wonderful eye for proper casting, and I know that he liked to use people who he had seen working on Broadway before. He used a lot of people who he knew had true theater experience rather than just screen experience. He came to see me in a play out in Los Angeles that I had done when I had first come out to the coast, and he came backstage, which of course thrilled me, and said that he had something in mind for me that he was writing ["A Most Unusual Camera"] and that he knew I would be right for, and of course that was quite thrilling. It took a little bit of time to get that particular show done, because CBS continuity didn't accept the ending. In the story, Fred Clark and I were con artists and thieves, and we would steal from antique stores, and we just happened to have stolen this most unusual camera from a pawnshop.

You mentioned how CBS continuity weren't accepting the various endings?

Actress Donna Douglas seen in character for her role in "The Eye of the Beholder."

Well, they wanted the characters to be punished more for all the money that we'd stolen and that we made from going to the races.

Did they shoot any of the alternate endings?

No, they didn't shoot any of the other endings. Serling was so prepared with his scripts once they were ready to do, and I don't remember any cuts, changes, or anything during our reading or rehearsals before we actually shot. Naturally, we didn't shoot with an audience, that wasn't the type of show that would have an audience. They finally accepted the ending where we all fall out of the hotel window [laughs]. I would get a call now and then, from the casting woman or from Rod, saying that they still hadn't been able to get the ending passed. I believe it was more than a year before he had finally done that ending, the way we died. *The Twilight Zone Companion* thought the ending was very arbitrary.

It's a fun episode and the fans like it. People ask how the very last guy fell out of the window, and my answer is that he was shocked to see himself down there, dead in the photo, and he fainted and fell out the window.

Exactly! Because he counted the bodies, and then there were "*four*"!?

Do you remember working with the director of the episode, John Rich?

Yes, but I'm not going to say much [laughs]. I don't think he liked women too much. It's all right, it's just that I was the only woman in the cast, and he was kind of rough on me, I felt. He said to me once, "Can't you hear?" He was the only director I ever worked with — Broadway, live television, television, film — who treated me like that.

After you had done that episode, were you ever contacted to do another?

Oh no, that was it. Nobody talked to me about another one, and of course if you're not invited to do more than one episode in something, you worry about it a little bit. I noticed in rewatching a lot of the shows that if an actor did a strong character, they didn't usually repeat him. Now, Burgess Meredith did two or three, I think.

He did four *Twilight Zone* episodes.

He was probably one of Rod's favorite actors. Then, of course, a lot of other people's favorite actor, and he fit into an awful lot of those scripts. Now, in my case, when you do a character like that, what else are you going to do with them, you know what I mean? I was kind of dumb and whiny, I would say, "Oh, palpitations!" She was always sort of whiny. "Oh, Chester. Poor Chester. Poor Woodward. Oh, well, life must go on." Or something like that. I know that at the same time we were shooting our

episode, Agnes Moorehead was just beginning to rehearse one, and I remember going over to their rehearsal room and listening to some of the show.

Did working on *Twilight Zone* differ in any way to working on other shows you had been doing, like *The Andy Griffith Show*?

I was very impressed with the fact that it was so well prepared, and so many of them aren't when you go in for a guest shot. So many of them are not prepared that well, and it was just uneventful from that standpoint. We didn't have a hassle about changing this and changing that, and in those days we wore our own clothes. If you notice the neckline, you'll notice net[ting] that has been sewn into the dress, because at that time, in the '60s, they were very fussy about too much bosom showing [laughs]. I believe they did that with two dresses of mine that were low in the front.

So, did you get to know Rod Serling outside of the *Twilight Zone* work?

I remember seeing Rod at a party up in Malibu. I think we talked about the show, because by that time the show had been done, and that was about it. He was very nice, just charming. He was very little, you know — like five-foot-five. I remember not looking up at him.

And was he happy with the episode?

Oh, yes! He said it was one of his very favorites. I think that the *Twilight Zone* fans are a far more sophisticated audience, a more intellectual group of people. You know, the fans of *The Andy Griffith Show* are more like teachers, policemen, laborers . . . But listen, without the fans, I would be nothing right now. *The Twilight Zone* and *Andy Griffith* are the only two things I'll be known for.

Anne Francis

Anne Francis starred as Marsha White in "The After Hours," and in the title role of "Jess-Belle."

You worked on the show in the first season, and then again in the fourth season. Was there a change between that time? Can you describe what it was like for you being on the set?
Well, as far as the work, no, I don't recall any big change from the first season to the last. Of course, the last one I did was an hour show, so it took a little longer with rehearsal and all.

But it was always a very professional show, and the folks who worked on it were just pros from the top to the bottom, just wonderful, wonderful people. I enjoyed it tremendously. It was a wonderful experience for the actors, we had time to rehearse, and there were no surprises. We started rehearsal on a Monday

**During a break on the shoot for "The After Hours,"
Rod Serling sits for a candid shot with Anne Francis . . .
*or is it Marsha?***

ber of interesting characters, whereas on "The After Hours," it was a study of the growth of fear of the complete unknown, and the other was a story story.

When you were working on this show, did you have a sense that the quality was such that it was going to stay around for 50 years, whereas so many other shows had their run and were pretty much forgotten?

Well, *Twilight Zone* is a timeless show. Because it's dealing with so many dimensions, the hidden aspects of ourselves, as well as the material. It played with the fact that — Ah, I'm trying to find the right words . . . the wonderful switch of mind. See that's what it is, *Twilight Zone* is very difficult to pinpoint, because it's dealing with so much of ourselves that we can't see.

It's hard to define, that's why we love it. I love all of the *Twilight Zone* shows, because you're not dealing with what we can feel and touch as the worldly. It plays with our senses; it plays with our imagination.

Do you have a favorite episode?

There was one with the outer space ship, and as I recall, the people in the ship were tiny, and this was with Agnes Moorehead. And she was this big creature with the broom going after this small ship, and all of these frightened characters. That's where they are playing with the mind. I mean, sometimes we consider ourselves like ants on this planet, but for the most part, man and womankind are strutting around being bigger than the next guy, and yet when you look at it from way up here, it's kind of funny looking at all of these little critters down here, posturing and trying to be of great importance, Agnes Moorehead can come along with a broom and knock you out. It's twisting the general reality, as we know it. And that's such fun to me.

and usually shot on a Friday, so we had three days to completely rehearse scene after scene.

When I did "The After Hours," the whole soundstage was that department store, and there was an eerie feeling when we were working on that show, because of the immensity of that stage, and the lighting and the darkness beyond. Ah, I still get the chills sometimes. But it was a lot of fun working on that particular project. And the last one, the hour show, that was completely different. That was written by Earl Hamner, and it was a story of a back-hills country hillbilly gal who wanted desperately to hook this young man. But that show was different in the respect that there were a num-

Do you think the show had a social and moral voice, using drama and fantasy to talk about issues that might have been difficult to deal with in a more direct manner?

I never really thought *Twilight Zone*, as they say today, had an "agenda." The main idea was to make us think, to make us step into the realm of our imagination. It helped us to stretch our thinking and look at what we look at normally and be able to see it a little askew, rather than straight on. It was always playing with what we would imagine the outcome would be. It was always surprising us, always sneaking up with something else that we didn't expect.

Describe your first meeting, and your impression of Rod Serling.

Well, the first meeting was on set. He just was a delightfully charming, kind human being. Good sense of humor, very gentle. Just very, very, very bright. You could see the sparks going on, but a gentleman above all other things, with an incredible imagination. And great respect — great respect for everyone around him. Great respect for his actors, great respect for his producers, his directors. I was going to say you have a feeling of family, but it was more than that, it was camaraderie. A general reciprocal respect for each other.

What was your first impression when you read Serling's script for "The After Hours," and how did you feel about the show?

I loved it. My first impression was what fun it was going to be to play that role. The humor in the beginning. The spaciness of each little step that took place, sort of just a little bit off-center until the horror begins for this young woman who has absolutely no memory at all of who she is or why she's on the ninth floor. The progression of the character was a lot of fun.

Do you remember how you landed that role?

I was called to come play it. In those days, the producers and directors pretty much knew who they wanted. Today they could call in 500 people to read the role. It was different then.

In "The After Hours," what was it like working with director Douglas Heyes?

Love Doug Heyes. Worked so well with him. He just stepped back and let it happen. He created the wonderful images, the darkness beyond where we were. There was always the feeling of being in another realm when I was doing it. When I was doing the part, there were a few lights and there's darkness beyond. I had to be able to imagine all of these strange things in the darkness that seem to be following her, and her not being able to get down to the root of what all of this was, until the very end.

Have you got a favorite moment or scene in the show that comes to mind?

Ah, I think when Doug decided to do that shot of her final desperation — not final desperation, but the impending desperateness behind the rippled glass on that door. I thought that was quite brilliant of him. To see the distortion of her shadow when she said, "Somebody? Anybody?" And then the final turning event of just crumpling completely, and her fear, and pain.

What was it like working with Buzz Kulik in "Jess-Belle"?

Buzz was excellent. I remember more of the characters working with Jeanette Nolan and Jimmy Best. Buzz guided us, moved us through, but again, he let us be who we were as those characters. I don't recall his particularly leaning on any of us for a certain interpretation. Again, you know, we're working with an Earl Hamner script, and Earl is a wonderful writer. So the

Francis plays a sultry brunette country girl, in Earl Hamner Jr's tale of black magic, "Jess-Belle."

writer's intent was there, on the page, and it was for us to take it in through osmosis, become these characters for Earl. I'm delighted he was so pleased with it. He really enjoyed that show.

Did you get the feeling that there was a difference between that and doing the half-hour?

You can do a lot more developing of characters in an hour. However, "The After Hours" was basically one theme — a haunted woman finally facing reality. This one, we were able to indulge more in the different characters. Like Jeanette Nolan as the witch was wonderful,

and she had her great scenes. And Jimmy as the innocent young man who is tormented really with these two women — the darkness of Jess-Belle and the spell of Jess-Belle, and the other woman, the sweet woman that really should be his love. But every time Jess-Belle was around, her spirit invaded him. There was more time to play with these emotions and characters, and to sit back and see how all of them were tormented in their own way. Except for the witch. I've told Earl I want to play the witch in his musical version. And he said, "No, I want you to do Jess-Belle." But I'd think it would be such fun to play the witch. With all the little potions, and wear the wonderful crazy nose and put the warts on and the wild hair. Anyway, the hour show gave time for all of these characters to emerge for the audience to enjoy. But probably everybody knew that Jess-Belle would eventually come to no good end.

James Best

James Best starred in "The Grave," as Johnny Rob, in "The Last Rites of Jeff Myrtlebank" as the title character, and in "Jess-Belle," as Billy-Ben Turner.

Twilight Zone was already fairly successful by the time you appeared in the third season. What was it like coming onto a show that was already a phenomenon?

Well, I was very lucky, because I was under contract with Universal Studios for two years, and after I got out of there I got up with Gene Autry and his series. So I was working constantly.

Twilight Zone was a class act. I did an awful lot of westerns and everything, you see, and they shot in 15 minutes for 45 cents. And you did all your own stunts — fistfights and everything — until you're ready to get killed, and then they double you perhaps. But *Twilight Zone* was a whole different thing: they had the real professional writers, they had the real actors who had trained and had the experience needed to really give a beautiful performance. That's why it was successful. This day and age, of course, the industry is

After giving instructions on how to do a fight scene, Montgomery Pittman, the writer and director of "The Last Rites of Jeff Myrtlebank," observes actor James Best throwing a punch at actor Lance Fuller.

full of personalities, and if you're over 30, you're not on the cutting edge and have no knowledge of the business.

Did you watch the show much as a viewer?

Of course, I was a fan of *Twilight Zone*. As I say, it was a class show. It was very interesting and different. What I loved about it, it didn't rely on naughty words or body parts or sparks flying off of people's chests, it was more realistic. They had a wonderful imagination. It was a very intriguing show and so well done, because you had the best actors in Hollywood — later on they all became superstars, or a very large percentage of them.

Actors Strother Martin, James Best, Ellen Willard, and Lee Van Cleef, with some of the crew during a cemetery scene in "The Grave."

In a scene that passes through a graveyard, Gunman Connie Miller, played by Lee Marvin, is wagered to visit the site of outlaw Pinto Sykes.

Did you get a chance to meet Rod Serling on the set of your episodes?

I met him briefly. He came down to the set. He was very much interested in what was going on. Unfortunately, I didn't do one of his scripts — it was written by Monty Pittman — "The Grave," which I was fortunate enough to do with Lee Marvin and Strother Martin and Lee Van Cleef and a wonderful cast. It was a ghost story I had told Monty Pittman. I was born in Kentucky, and adopted and raised in southern Indiana across from rural Kentucky, and for entertainment in those days, we told stories. And ghost stories, of course, were very intriguing. I think later on that was my fascination with *The Twilight Zone* — they, to me, were elaborate ghost stories, very interesting stories that were a little beyond the average imagination. So when I told Monty Pittman the story, he wrote it into

a western and called me up and I was in it, and very flattered to be so.

When you told it to him, was it with the idea that it could be a show?

Oh, no. I had no idea he was going to make it into a western. I was quite surprised when he called me, and I read the script and said, "Oh, this looks familiar." Well, he told me then, "I based this on the story you told me." He was a nice man.

With the character of Johnny Rob that you played in "The Grave," do you remember any special James Best additions that you brought?

I played Johnny Rob as a sort of sniveling loudmouth coward, and I like to believe I'm anything but that. And I'm hoping it took a certain amount of talent to portray that, you know. Because in those days, I can truly say I wasn't afraid of anything that walked, talked, or dug holes.

You have some really fabulous costars in that episode — Lee Marvin, Strother Martin, Lee Van Cleef. Any comments about working with them in "The Grave?

Well, I worked with both Lee Van Cleef and Lee Marvin before. Lee Marvin was a practical joker as I was, too; we'd get bored on the set. I remember we pretended we were fighting between filming once, and needless to say, there were quite a few coronaries when they saw us playing like we were fighting. But Lee loved to have a nip now and then. And he got himself into trouble for a while, but he was always there, he knew his dialogue, and Lee was always exciting to watch.

Strother Martin was one of the most insecure actors, and one of the finest actors I've ever worked with. But he's always insecure, and he'd come and say, "Did that look all right? Was that all right?" And I'd say, "Strother, it was marvelous."

Do you have any favorite moments or scenes from "The Last Rites of Jeff Myrtlebank"?

I'll tell you one that wasn't my favorite was them closing me into a casket, and I took a pencil and put it into the lid, and said, "Don't close it all the way down." And they'd leave that little pencil in there. I guess I was afraid of getting closed in that coffin. Working with Anne Francis in "Jess-Belle" was a pleasure. Because I've played so many mean guys and heavies and getting killed and stuff, so I didn't have too many chances having romantic scenes with beautiful ladies like Anne Francis. I really enjoyed that, certainly.

In retrospect, was there anything with Jeff Myrtlebank that you would have done differently?

No, because I think as an actor, and I've taught

Actors Strother Martin (Mothershed) and James Best (Johnny Rob) visit the graveyard the following morning, when Miller never returned.

Connie Miller (Lee Marvin) makes it to the gravesite of Pinto Sykes.

A cameraman captures a fight scene between James Best and Lance Fuller in "The Last Rites of Jeff Myrtlebank."

Sherry Jackson stars as Best's love interest, Comfort Gatewood, in "The Last Rites of Jeff Myrtlebank." Jackson is seen here with her father, director and writer Montgomery Pittman.

acting for about 30, 35 years, motion-picture technique. When I do a performance, I don't really judge myself. If I have fun doing the part, if I really enjoy doing the part, modesty be damned. If I have fun doing the part, I feel that I did it correctly. Not saying that if I had another take or two takes or three takes, that it would improve. In my case, I don't think that's true, I think I'm better in the first shot. First time out of the box, you've got the energy, it's like throwing a punch, you know. You throw a real good one and deck him in the first punch, you've won. If you have to hit him four or five times, he's gonna get up and maybe kick you around. Same thing with acting.

"Jess-Belle" was one of the one-hour shows. How was that different than working on the half-hours? Did you feel you had more time for the character?

It didn't matter to me. I didn't care if it was five minutes or five hours, it's acting. I know my dialogue, I get in front of the cameras, I expect the other actors to know theirs. We do the best shot we can, and most takes don't last longer then 15 or 20 seconds. And the editor puts it together and makes you look like a hero. But the cameraman, you hope that they can follow your actions if you give them false starts and so forth. I certainly hope I've improved over the years, become a better actor than even in *The Twilight Zone*, if they considered me a good actor. Perhaps I was certainly adequate at that time, at that age. I hope that I'm better now that I'm at this age.

Tell me about working with Buzz Kulik.

Buzz Kulik was one of the better, fine directors around. He was an actor's director. There are a lot of bad actors out there who are mechanics. But then you have wonderful directors, like Buzz Kulik, and a whole raft of certain people that really talk to you as a human being rather than a piece of acting material. That

they just push you in front of the camera and say, "Just say the line, don't worry about it." I've had a lot of those. So you sometimes remember certain directors, and he certainly has to be one of them that was very favorably thought of in my opinion.

Are there any fun stories or anecdotes about making that episode?

Other that when Anne Francis turns into the panther and they put the panther on the roof, and I walk out and light my pipe and the panther is over my head. And the keeper of the panther said, "Don't move." And I found out later that they had not really tied that panther off to the extent they should have, and the panther normally, he said, jumps on their prey from the top. So I suggested a long chain, which they didn't use, but they did use enough cable. I think I was safe. At least, I hoped I was.

Any favorite moments in the finished show?

Oh sure, kissing Anne Francis was fantastic.

Dennis Weaver

Dennis Weaver starred in "Shadow Play," as Adam Grant. This was his last *Twilight Zone* interview.

What did you think of *Twilight Zone* at the time of production?

Well, I thought it was terrific. I loved *Twilight Zone* in those days. It was a real groundbreaking effort on the part of Rod Serling, and it was innovative.

What were your impressions of Rod Serling?

[Laughs] I wish I could answer that from my own experience, but I never had a chance to actually meet him while he was on the set

Seen with costar Jack Hyde, is a candid shot of actor Dennis Weaver, staring as Adam Grant in "Shadow Play."

Dennis Weaver observes Serling discussing his opening narration with director John Brahm.

doing his narration. It was one of those weird things that I thought, "Boy, I'm going to have the opportunity of seeing this creative genius, and actually talking to him and getting some impressions, and some thoughts of his about the industry and all that sort of thing." And it just never happened.

What stands out most for you in the making of your episode, "Shadow Play"?
Well, what excited me about the script was dealing with the dream concept, that life is a dream. That's also very much part of Eastern philosophy, that we're living in a dream, and they compare it to a lot of our dreams at night. When we dream at night, it's totally real to us — nobody can tell us it's not real until we wake up. And then we say, "Oh, that was a dream, that wasn't reality at all." But when we're living through it, dreaming it, it is terribly real, and sometimes it can be absolutely frightening.

Characters can change very quickly and it's just an incredible experience, but we feel that it's real. That's the point, and that was the point of this "Shadow Play." Which I felt dealt with that subject matter very interestingly.

What do you think makes a good *Twilight Zone*?
First of all, the writing. It always goes back to the writing. In other words, you have to have a good concept of some subject matter that is not common to everyday life as we understand it, but dealing with things that are in the *Twilight Zone*. That's what made it unique, and that's what created such an appeal that it had for so many people.

I don't think anyone turned down working on *Twilight Zone*.
They jumped at the chance. I was very excited that they offered me a part on *Twilight Zone*. Those were the days, I guess, that I'm sure it

As seen in the opening shot, a distraught Adam Grant faces his terrifying recurring dream of being executed.

was during the time I was on *Gunsmoke*, and I had such a recognizable kind of character on *Gunsmoke*, that it gave me an opportunity to play something totally away from that, and that was one of the things that excited me about that opportunity.

What do you think of the original *Twilight Zone* series today?

Well, I still think it's a lot of food for thought. "Shadow Play," for instance, has got to make a lot of people think, a lot to question life and that sort of thing, and that was one of the motivating forces behind *Twilight Zone* — to make people think past what they normally do in their daily routine.

How was it working with costars Harry Townes and Wright King?

Well, of course, Harry Townes was a very popular television actor in those days. Wright King was a very dear friend of mine, we had a very close relationship family to family. He had three boys who were practically the same age of my three boys. As a matter of fact, I directed a *Gunsmoke* once that required six kids, and I used his three and my three. It was a fun thing to do. So it was nice to see Wright again on television.

I certainly enjoyed doing "Shadow Play." It was a feather in my cap at the time. You know, most of the actors on *Twilight Zone* are not with us anymore.

In "Shadow Play," Harry Townes stars as District Attorney Henry Ritchie. Townes also starred in the episode, "The Four of Us Are Dying," as well as in Serling's *Playhouse 90*, "The Rank and File."

Adam Grant ponders the many illogical details of his dreamlike world.

How would you compare working in live television and then doing filmed television?

Well, in many ways it was a relief to do filmed television, because I got my beginning in television, my roots were in New York when television was totally live. What you did at the moment, the audience saw at the very same time, there was no delay. You know, if you blew a line you just covered up, and there were a lot of carpenters walking through sets, a lot of dead bodies getting up and walking away, and it was a pretty exciting time. And you had to really be on your toes, you had to rehearse tremendously. We did a lot of time rehearsing, so it was like a stage play, the same kind of immediate contact with the audience. So, getting on filmed television, where you have a retake or two, or three, or five, was kind of a blessing in a way. You'd say to the director, "I think I can give you something a little better than that, if you give me another take." We had the rehearsal of the scene, and the blocking of the scene the day we shot it.

There's nothing like the old pictures.

Yeah, you go back and you see the very first television series about Superman, it's so laughable because, you know, today they do *Spider-Man* and all of these wonderful special effects, and they couldn't possibly do that in the infancy of television — it wasn't available to a director. So they tried the best they could, and in this day and age, if you see it, it's very funny.

What was it like working at the MGM studio, on that back lot that was just so immense.

Well, Universal had a big back lot also; we shot most of *McCloud* on the back lot of Universal. You know, in those days, the whole studio, the whole atmosphere, was family. It's so different than it is now. You had people who made decisions at the top, and they were made on the lot, they were made at the studio.

You could go to a producer or somebody and mention that there was a certain kind of film that you'd like to do, and they wouldn't just dismiss it.

Wright King

Wright King starred in "Shadow Play," as Paul Carson, and in "Of Late I Think of Cliffordville," as Hecate.

What were your impressions of Rod Serling?

Rod Serling was an exciting man. I knew him, I can't think exactly where, early on somewhere in New York, and the last time I saw him was in Los Angeles, in the airport, and he always remembered you. We talked just briefly — he was going his way, I was going mine — but he was just a wonderful, always-up kind of guy, always interested and interesting. He was vital, very substantial, and a very attractive kind of guy. I'm always amazed when they say he was short — well, he was, but you didn't get that; he was a very straight guy, very straightforward.

What do you think of the show today?

Today, I'm so happily surprised. There are so many things I did, and so many phases, and *The Twilight Zone* is right up there. It was done with segments that are going to bend your mind and it's done concisely. That was good writing and it was directed well, and it went well. In those days, I was spoiled, I worked with a lot of good writers.

There was a guy named John Brahm, he was a very famous director. He directed the movie *Fury*, which got him a lot of notoriety. He was a nice guy. He wanted me to be drunk in "Shadow Play," and I'd never played drunk before, and I had to show up at Harry Townes and Anne Barton's house drunk. I had never played drunk onstage before, and that was a little bit of a problem for me. I tried out a couple of things, and John said, "What you're doing is just right," and it worked out. On "Of Late I Think of Cliffordville," I played this young guy Hecate, and you had to know that he was the guy, later on, that was an older man. And the director, David Rich, wanted some handle on that, so he gave me a nervous kind of thing where I pulled at my ear, and so I was doing that in both scenes. I think I would have done that differently — I had some kind of an idea that was different than that.

I remember that tall gal that was in "Cliffordville," Julie Newmar, I didn't have scenes with her in that. She's really quite good in it. Albert Salmi was a weird guy — a good guy and a good actor who took a lot of chances. I remember he had a collection of

Actors Wright King and Harry Townes star with Dennis Weaver in "Shadow Play."

Julie Newmar has her devil horns applied by a makeup artist for "Of Late I Think of Cliffordville."

William Tuttle proudly holds the masks he created of Battling Maxo and Maynard Flash for the episode, "Steel."

canes. I liked him — he was really nice. And John Anderson was in that, he was a very good friend. Harry Townes was a very close friend, too.

The makeup for the aged version of your character Hecate worked out fairly well. How was it to see an elderly version of yourself?

I remember William Tuttle was a very famous makeup guy. He had made up all the different people, and he was still there and he did my makeup, made me an older man, for "Cliffordville." And what they do is put a plastic cap on over your hair — I had thick hair — and then he colored it the same color as my face, he made the guy kind of bald. I had a homburg hat on, as I recall, kind of on the back of my head, and I looked like my dad! Somebody said, "That's what you're going to look like when you're old." I was going from a fairly young-looking guy, the character I was playing, to this, and it was a big thing to me. And William was really nice to talk to. He had done all kinds of things. He's like any of these guys. They're the oldest guys, the ones that have been around in the old studios who were just fantastic, and had a lot of great stories to tell you. So he left the bald makeup on, and I went home and scared the hell out of my wife! That was good.

James Sheldon

James Sheldon directed *Twilight Zone* episodes "The Whole Truth," "A Penny for Your Thoughts," "Long Distance Call," "It's a Good Life," "Still Valley," and "I Sing the Body Electric." He also directed numerous other television shows, including *My Three Sons*, *The Waltons*, and *The Equalizer*.

Having directed several *Twilight Zone* episodes, do you have any favorites?

My favorite episode was "It's a Good Life," with Billy Mumy, where he turns people into things, and another one with Mumy called "Long Distance Call," where his grandmother had died, and she had given him a toy telephone and he talked with her on the phone.

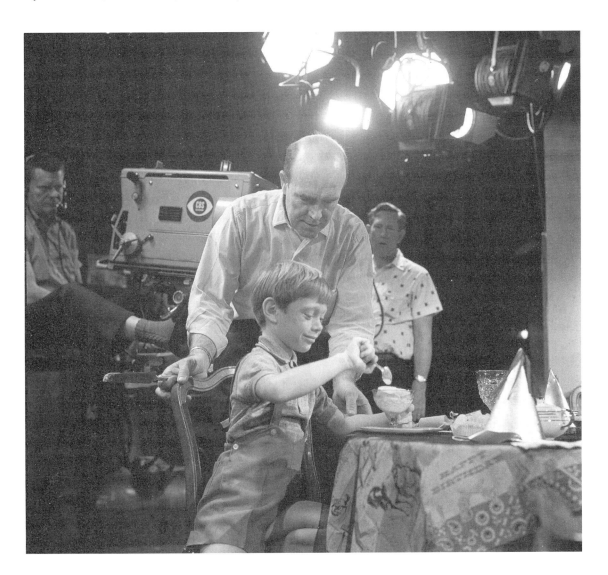

Cameramen await taping the next scene of "Long Distance Call," while James Sheldon directs a young Bill Mumy. This was the sixth and final videotaped episode in production.

I can tell you a story about how I almost closed down all of MGM. Little Billy Mumy and I had worked together before, and it was 6 P.M. and he had to leave — kids had to only work certain hours and that was Billy's time — and I needed one more shot. And illegally I went to his mother, who was a lovely lady, and I said, "Could I get just one more shot?" And I did, and it worked fine, but the next day the producers and the studio executive and everybody were on my back, because if anybody had found out about that, I would have been in trouble. So I never did that again.

What can you tell me about working on the few taped episodes in comparison to the majority of episodes done on film?

It was a show that was really better on film, but CBS co-owned it with Rod, and they had these big studio facilities at Television City, and they wanted to do them on tape to utilize the facilities. So we did six shows on tape; the two that I did were the one with Billy with the telephone and another with Jack Carson where he couldn't tell a lie ["The Whole Truth"]. But I think that after they saw the six shows on tape, they realized that having George Clemens and the camera crew, you could do much more in the vein of *The Twilight Zone* in film. George Clemens was a great cinematographer and a delightful guy to work with.

Did your work on *The Twilight Zone* have a uniqueness that your other shows lacked?

The Twilight Zone wasn't just a job. It was fun. It tested your imagination all the time, and the tools that you worked with, because of people like Buck Houghton and the unsung hero Jim Lister [casting director], who really brought all these actors forward for us, and the whole crew. You just knew you were on a good show. It had good scripts, and that's

what really made it work. These guys were such good writers, and it was always a pleasure to go there, and we always had good casts and all of the good directors.

One of the most exciting things about *The Twilight Zone* is that every week you'd have something completely different. Not only was it a completely different storyline, but they were completely different in style, because Charles Beaumont wrote one kind of thing, George Clayton Johnson wrote another kind of thing, Ray Bradbury another. It wasn't like doing another episode of *The Fugitive* or some other show, which had similarity. This not only had new casts, but the whole concept was always different. One week it might be a comedy, another week it's frozen people, or you're on a foreign world or another planet. So it was exciting, as it was for the audience, but for a director, that was fun.

Bill Mumy

Bill Mumy starred in "Long Distance Call," as Billy Bayles, in "It's a Good Life," as Anthony Fremont, and in "In Praise of Pip," as Pip Phillips.

Did you have a chance to meet Rod Serling while he was doing his narrations or when he was visiting the sets?

I remember him being around quite a bit. I remember him doing the narration for "It's a Good Life," because we were out on that exterior set and it was the same day when we were filming the "Gopher, you be dead" thing. So, I was there for that, and he was on the set on "Long Distance Call" a lot because they were rewriting that ending. My memories of Mr. Serling were basically that when he was around, everybody was relaxed, as

opposed to when a lot of producer/creator–type people come around on a set, and people get really uptight. I remember his presence being very relaxing, and I also remember him cracking jokes and being light. You think of him as being this stolid character in a way, or at least it seems that that was his image. But he wasn't the least like that — he was light and funny and very cool. Also, remember, when you have a television series that goes multi-seasons, when you've got a hit series, or a popular series, your actors can tend to get fabulous or difficult — not so much in that era as in the last couple of decades, but

Billy Mumy stars as the series' number one most-powerful character, Anthony Fremont, in the chilling episode, "It's a Good Life." Mumy reprised his role as Anthony in the revised episode of *The Twilight Zone* (2002), "It's Still a Good Life."

nonetheless personalities, celebrities, they can be obnoxious. But because there was no regular recurring cast, he was, in essence, the star of the show.

Mumy stars as innocent Billy Bayles in his first of three episodes, "Long Distance Call."

Grandma pretends to talk with Billy through his toy telephone, a game that proves to become a twisted reality.

What do you think makes a good *Twilight Zone*?

Wow, it's a hard question. First of all, I think all of them are good. I think most of them are great, and I think a lot of them are exceptional. A lot of elements go into that, although 90 percent of the great ones, you just have to say that Rod Serling is what makes a great *Twilight Zone*. It's like when you ask what makes a great Beatles song — I mean, it's the combination of the Beatles. If you say what makes a great Bob Dylan song, it's Bob Dylan. And it's Rod Serling. Which is why I've always felt that all of the *Twilight Zone* projects that have been called *The Twilight Zone*, since he passed away, should not have been called *The Twilight Zone*.

The writing of *The Twilight Zone* is number one. The shows were largely in a fantasy or science-fiction arena, but the themes of the shows were very socially applicable to what was going on at the time. The fact that you're in an arena where your emotion and your imagination can run free makes it easier for people to just kind of suspend disbelief and get into it. I loved the *Twilight Zone* scripts, because they gave me the opportunity to do unusual things . . . fantasy things. I wanted to be an actor, as a child, because of watching Guy Williams as Zorro and George Reeves as Superman. It was fantasy, sci-fi, adventure stuff that I wanted to do. *The Twilight Zone* was close to that.

I also think, quite honestly, that black-and-white is a perfect medium for this kind of television or this kind of film. I remember when we were doing the sequel, "It's Still a Good Life," a couple of years ago, and Ira Behr and I both really wanted to do it in black-and-white. We really wanted to do it that way, and there was no way at all. You can see the very, very beginning is a fade from black-and-white into color, which was as far as we could get with it.

So let me ask you, you worked with director James Sheldon on "Long Distance Call" and "It's a Good Life." Do you remember much about working with him and what he was like?

I remember him as being a really, really pleasant guy. I remember running into him at Disneyland, he had a couple of daughters that were close to my age. I was really young when I did those shows, but I know that I went in there reasonably prepared, even though I was a little kid; it's not like I showed up not knowing my lines or anything. I know they were pretty happy with what I chose to do and there wasn't a whole lot of any crisis or anything like, "What are we going to do with this kid? How are we going to make him work?" It went reasonably smoothly. I know that on "It's a Good Life" we worked together on making the eyes really big when I was using Anthony's powers, and I can remember Mr. Sheldon kind of working that stuff out with me. And I remember working with Cloris Leachman, because I had already worked with her before on a *Loretta Young Show* when she played my mom in an hour drama. On "It's a Good Life" she helped me focus. I can remember goofing around off-camera, when I was doing off-camera dialogue for her, and her just kind of letting me know very nicely and very professionally that when you're doing off-camera, you've got to do it as well as you were doing it on-camera. And that was an early but big lesson learned. I just remember James Sheldon not being stressed, and believe me, a lot of directors, especially television directors, can be really stressed.

Sheldon mentioned something about how one of the shoots went over your time limit, in regards to child labor laws. Do you remember that at all?

No. I never heard about that at all. Well, certainly I wasn't looking at my watch wanting to go home. I can remember every day on *Lost in Space* was like that, because I was generally heavy in all of those shows, and there is the time limit, and I can remember the teacher social worker saying to the assistant director, "You're going to lose Billy at six o'clock, and it's five minutes to six." And I can remember I was always like, "Oh come on! Who cares! Let's get the shot." I'm sure my mother would have said, "Oh, who cares?" I don't mean overwork the poor kid, but if you've got a shot to get and you need an extra ten minutes, it's not the end of the world.

Anthony Fremont is literally *the* most powerful character in the series, if you think about it. He predates the Q, from *Star Trek: Next Generation*. Tell me a little about the role, how you prepared, and what place Anthony holds for you?

Anthony Fremont was the ultimate mutant. He could do anything. He was totally in control of everyone and everything. He took absolutely no bullshit from anyone. I just loved playing him. Oh, I knew it was pretty cool to be able to read everyone's minds. It's pretty cool to wish people into whatever you want to wish them into. I can remember using, or *pretending* to use, Anthony's powers all of the time when I was little, going to and from the studio with my mom, to like, make the traffic lights green. I'm sure a lot of other actors will say this — you learn from characters that you get to play, because obviously you've internalized these words and things, but I've kept a lot of Anthony inside with me over the years [laughs]. It's probably the second most popular character I've ever played. Not to diminish or say it's a better character than Will Robinson, but it's probably not as popular. I've had 40 years of people coming up to me and going, "Oh, it's good you did that. Don't wish me into the cornfield, man." Who wouldn't have wanted to play Anthony when you were a kid? I mean, it's the ultimate character, and I loved returning to it in the sequel, and with my daughter. I really wanted to do a whole spin-off series, just the Fremonts.

So you worked with Ira Behr to come up with the story for the sequel?

Yeah, we did. Ira couldn't have been nicer about the whole thing. When he got the gig of producing *The Twilight Zone* [2002], he asked me, "Do you think I should do *The Twilight Zone*?" And I said, "Dude, you have to do it so you can protect it." And that was his reason for doing it. He kind of knew it was a damned if you do, damned if you don't gig, because he knew you can't be *The Twilight Zone* without Rod Serling. Yet he knew that if he didn't say yes to the job, they were going to get someone else, and he wanted to be as much of a protector of the original concept and what Rod Serling would have wanted as possible. So I admired his guts and tenacity, and I really appreciated him doing it.

We were talking and having dinner one night when he first got the gig, and I said to him, "Wouldn't it be cool to see what Anthony Fremont was up to now? Not a redo. Just like, 40 years later, what happened to Anthony Fremont? What happened to Peaksville?" And he thought that would be very cool. We tossed around a handful of other concepts, and I ended up writing the story for one of the earlier episodes, and then I get a call from Ira and he says, "The network wants to do your idea." And I said, "What idea?" He says, "They want to do a sequel to 'It's a Good Life.'" I said, "What?! You're kidding." He said, "Yeah, and they want to do it for sweeps week, and they want to do it right away." I really liked the idea of doing the sequel, but I didn't want to do it, or agree to do it, if there wasn't a really good story in place. I told that to Ira and he said to me, "Look, I'll make you a deal. You're on board. Tell them you're going to do it. If

you don't think the script would be given a thumbs-up by Rod Serling, we'll can the whole thing, I won't cast anyone else as you. I promise that I would never let anyone else do it, and if you don't think it's good, we won't do it." Which was pretty damned generous of him; it's not like he's talking to George Clooney.

So I agreed, and I wrote a treatment and he wrote a treatment, and we exchanged them. And quite honestly, I have to say, his treatment was much better [laughs]. His treatment included Liliana [Mumy's daughter] as my daughter with the power and everything. Working together with Liliana like that was just fantastic. I thought she was just great in it, and I would have loved to have done a whole series: *On the Road With the Fremonts*.

Getting back to the original series, how was it working with Jack Klugman on "In Praise of Pip"? Do you have any memories of working with him?

Oh, absolutely! He was wonderful, a very passionate actor and really into it. First of all, I'm really proud to be a part of the first American teleplay that addressed American casualties in Vietnam. It was a bold show, and I salute Rod Serling for writing it. As you know, we filmed a lot of that episode outside, out at this old creepy amusement park. Anyway, there was a scene where Jack Klugman grabs Pip and swings him around, and kisses him and everything. And, you know, look, I'd been working for quite a few years at that point in time, with a lot of very talented people, and everybody knew what they were doing. But he was such a gentleman, he came up to both of my parents who were there on location at this pier, and he came up to my mom and my dad, introduced himself to my parents, and said, "Look, I just want you to know in this next scene that we're going to shoot, I'm really going to kiss your son. I'm going to really grab him and kiss him and hug him, and really go for it. And I want-

Jack Klugman, as seen in the episode, "A Passage for Trumpet."

Seen here is the cast of "Long Distance Call," Patricia Smith, Lili Darvas, Bill Mumy, and Philip Abbott, during the filming of a scene where Grandma pronounces her love for her grandson, Billy.

ed to say hello first and let you know I'm going to do that." And they thought that was so sweet of him. It was unnecessary for him to do that, but I always remembered that. I saw him a few times over the last ten years, and it was just great — we reminisced a little about Pip and *Twilight Zone* and how proud we were to have that in our catalog, so to speak.

I've always dug the scene inside the House of Mirrors.

That was creepy. I remember that reasonably well, because it was *the* House of Mirrors at Pacific Ocean Park. It was a really long shot to set it up with the cameras and the reflections of the lights and everything. It was a pain in the ass to shoot that scene. On one hand, the character I'm playing is basically a ghost, who had to have that ghostlike expression, which I was aware of. So you couldn't be looking down, and the only way to know where you were

going in the House of Mirrors was by small marks of tape on the floor that were little cues to go here, go there, so you wouldn't smash into a mirror; as Jack Klugman did. So, here I am, I'm nine or ten years old, I'm moving at a pretty fast clip through this House of Mirrors, trying very hard not to look down at the floor, because I'm supposed to be like this ethereal being just kind of moving. And certainly in the rehearsals, I was smacking into a few of them. I remember that.

"Long Distance Call" has a pretty intense subject matter.

Very creepy. My mom almost didn't want me to do it, she says. I wasn't aware of that at the time, but I know later on that because of this boy attempting to kill himself in several ways, she was just very anxious about that, and she almost said she wasn't going to do it, but I'm glad that she did [laughs]. It never crossed my mind and it never creeped me out. I'm pretty sure I was six when we did that.

What do you think of the original *Twilight Zone* today, when you look back on it?

I think it's the best television series ever produced. It's timeless. I think it's beautiful to watch, I love the cinematography. It's 156 acting lessons right there. They're just beautifully acted, beautifully written, beautifully shot, great little moral plays within a sci-fi or fantasy arena that was unique and to this day stands alone, and has its own thing that no one else can duplicate. If you opened a trunk and found three *Twilight Zone* scripts that were written by Rod Serling that were never read or produced before, and you had *The Simpsons* do them, you would still know, immediately, that it was Rod Serling's work. You would recognize, in a very short amount of time, that there is a unique way these characters are speaking, there is an intelligence that these characters are speaking, there is a certain thing that was Rod Serling. That no one else can do. Rod Serling *is The Twilight Zone*. I think it's the best show ever made.

Actor Joseph Ruskin stars as the contemporary genie from "The Man in the Bottle," a genie that's so with it, he supplies those who possess the lamp with four wishes instead of the customary three.

velous. And Don Medford was wonderfully acerbic, quiet, very much an in-charge director, who was really just so easy with everyone. So for me, on the one hand, it was oh, another good job. Period. I had no idea that I was really into something that was really special.

Joseph Ruskin

Joseph Ruskin starred in "The Man in the Bottle," as the genie, and in "To Serve Man," as a voice-over for the Kanamit aliens.

What was it like being a part of *Twilight Zone* at the time?

Lots of rehearsal, and to work with Luther Adler, who is a god in my eyes. Certainly from that family of actors and all, so that was mar-

Looking at "The Man in the Bottle," is there anything in particular that appealed to you about the story, or was it just the excitement of getting the job?

It was the excitement of getting a job. I mean, I was much too green and new to Hollywood and the West Coast, and all that happened here, to really have an opinion or even venture an opinion about whether it's a good part to play. Most actors, all they wanted to do was act as long as they possibly could. But the biggest thing was the amount of rehearsing we

Director Don Medford (far right) looks on with cameramen, as Ruskin performs a scene in which he offers the Castles their wishes.

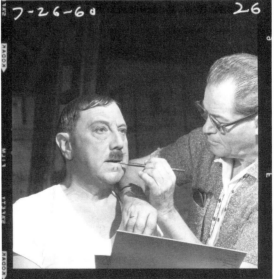

A makeup artist works on Luther Adler's transformation into Adolf Hitler.

Adler in full Hitler makeup and garb.

Tell me about working with director Don Medford.

Don was an actor as well before, so he knew how to deal with actors. There's no fuss and feathers with him, there's a great deal of humor. But he really knew what he wanted and he was clear about it. So you didn't have to go wondering, "But what did it mean? What is he saying?" It wasn't a great acting lesson, he wasn't trying to be a teacher. He was doing his part of the job, and he was very creative in what he asked us to do.

How did you think the end product compared to the script when you finally saw the show?

I was surprised at some of it. I mean, the rhythms that Don and the editor put into it, I was pleased, it really moved much better than I thought it was going to. It's a great rhythm and a quick one, so it just moved right to the climax.

did for this show. Vivi Janiss, Luther Adler, director Don Medford, and I spent the afternoon reading the script and discussing it, then rehearsed all the next day, and the day after that, and then on the fourth day we shot it. Don would call, "Cut, I want a little more of it, a little less of that." We all knew where we went back to, what the line was, where it was to be, no time was wasted. We knew how to work with him. And I have never rehearsed a television show in that manner or as fully since. And that's over 40 years ago.

It's amazing that you shot in one day.

Well, it was two. The majority of the show was shot in that one day. I don't remember what he asked for with the wishes, but one of them he turned into Hitler. We had a lot of extras in that, and that scene was shot by itself. I think they shot maybe two other days, but they were all exteriors, which you would take longer on anyway.

Joanne Linville

Joanne Linville starred in "The Passersby," as Lavinia Godwin.

Tell me what it was like to work on the *Twilight Zone* episode, "The Passersby."

First, it's probably my favorite work that I've done, primarily because of the character. The character was so beautifully written. The dialogue that he wrote for that show was just beautiful, and it was all memory, her memory and her past. And it was so much like the character of Melanie in *Gone With the Wind*. I loved working with Elliot Silverstein, he's such a wonderful director. And he made it such a good place to work; he let us be and he encouraged us, and it was just beautifully put together. And in such a small area that you

238

Joanne Linville stars with James Gregory in the Civil War drama, "The Passersby."

After the shoot, James Gregory was able to keep this box guitar as a memento from the show. He kept it for many years, but it went missing after a move and he had no idea of what ever happened to it.

could have all of that work, all the horses coming in and everything, in this little space, not big at all. And to think that you could get that kind of quality — I mean, the cinematography, the lighting of the whole thing — I was just very, very happy with it.

What was most appealing about the story?
I would have to say that the characters love, she so loved, and she had such hope in her. And there were long scenes, you know — you don't have those scenes anymore.

So Elliot Silverstein generally gave you room to work?
Elliot was a very serious director — a lot of directors don't have the kind of depth that he was able to bring onto that set. He was very sensitive, and took care of you in such a way that it made you feel comfortable and courageous.

Were you able to work any elements into your character that weren't necessarily written on the page?
Yes, and I'm proud of it. The use of props, the use of the coat, the use of his jacket that showed how I touched that jacket, how I felt about who wore that jacket. So I felt that I brought that to it, that perhaps wasn't really written. The love came from that, rather than just in memory he was there. You see, memory is a fantastic thing. Because you can see a little wet in the eye from thinking about that

moment. Just little things like that, I was very happy with it.

And when you saw the finished show, how did it compare to what you thought about it when you first read the script?

Better, better I thought. Elliot really did a beautiful job, and so did James Gregory. It was wonderful working with James, too, because we had known each other, we had the same agents. And I've done over a hundred shows, and over a hundred live television shows too, so altogether an awful lot of work, and this is my favorite character, and also the Romulan commander of *Star Trek*, which has become kind of a very famous character.

Twilight Zone hasn't stopped running for nearly 50 years, yet so many other shows have come and gone. Why do you think that is?

Truth. It is a basic truth that's in it, of our fears; Rod wasn't afraid to go after that, the important issues we face in life. He was able to come up with and write it, and to say it in a half-hour show. That's remarkable kind of writing, to get a beginning, a middle, and an end in that length of time.

Nan Martin

Nan Martin starred in "The Incredible World of Horace Ford," as Laura Ford.

Can you recall any notable experiences around working on The Twilight Zone?

I'd have to talk just from my memories of shooting it. Which are quite vivid. I was a New York actress, and I was a big favorite with some of the television producers in California, and I don't really understand that.

Ida Lupino during a makeup session on "The Sixteen-Millimeter Shrine."

Except I think they watched each other's shows. Rod Serling would watch *The Fugitive* and say, "I like that actress, I think I'd like to use her." I know my agent told me that Quinn Martin, a big producer, loved me. I don't remember meeting him, although I did all of his shows. They would fly me from New York, put me up in a hotel, I would shoot the show, take me back to the airport, and I would fly back to New York.

And I got here for *The Twilight Zone*, and I had done a play in New York with Pat Hingle, so for a while I called us the Jeanette MacDonald and Nelson Eddy duo. Because we seemed to be put together on *The Fugitive* or *The Twilight Zone*. See, I started in live television, with the good writers — Reginald Rose, Horton Foote — good directors — Arthur Penn, John Frankenheimer — you know, aces. And "The Incredible World of Horace Ford" was a script by Reginald Rose and it was sort of haunting. And I remember the set on the Metro lot. It was a conventional living room and so forth. And there was a street created with buildings and stoops. And I remember one scene where I come and watch in the shadows my husband Pat Hingle reliving, you know, playing the game. And I remember what an eerie scene it was to act.

It's amazing how strong those memories are. And I remember that Rod was very hands-on, not like today's producers. Not back at the office, you know, making calls about his stock investments. He was right there. If there was a camera problem, he was right there.

What was your impression of him when you first met him?

He's charming. Very compelling, very compelling eyes, never took his eyes off you, you know, studying you. But I'm a great studier myself. So mutual, mutual respect, I would think.

How did live television compare to recorded television back then?

I remember disastrous moments in live television, like they couldn't zip up my dress in the back, so I came into the scene and stood and played the whole scene with you walking over to the sink and walking back from the sink and backing out of the room when I left. I remember I played another one with Pat Hingle again, where Pat was supposed to come flying through the door, entering through the door. And you could hear the door going *umpf, umpf, umpf*. And finally I was onstage and I'm in front of the camera and I remember thinking, "Oh, now what could I say here? Can I say, 'I forgot and I locked it — just call to me, dear?'" I was trying to see what I could add in. And suddenly he just came through the window; he solved it — he just crawled in.

Or that terrible man who crouched in front

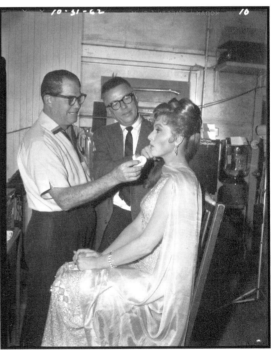

Patricia Barry during makeup touchups in "The Chaser" and "I Dream of Genie."

of you at the end of the show. And he did one of two things: he went like this [puts her hands in front of her and stretches the air between them] and you talked very slowly. "Does . . . this . . . mean . . . that . . . this . . . is . . . the end . . . of . . . us . . . then?" Or he went like this [moves her hand in a circular motion quickly], which meant that you said, very quickly, "Yes, well does this mean that this is the end of us? If it is then I want to say goodbye first because I will not let you say goodbye first." Then go out the door and slam it without even waiting for a reply. It was one or the other, and you had to kind of get used to that. Those were very good days for actors who want to develop improvisational skills.

Now one thing about the stories was that they were more than just dramas. They were morality plays. They were social explorations. Do you have any feelings on how Rod used the medium to work that way?

Yes. He was very skillful, wasn't he? And very ambiguous. At a time when people like a beginning, middle, and end, he left things for you to sort of figure out, you know, what the implications of something were in a script, which is really interesting. If he were alive now, for instance, it would be interesting to see what he'd be doing. I was going to say the paranormal, but I don't think so. But certainly going toward science fiction, that would interest him. Because we're on the threshold of a lot of new worlds, and that would intrigue him very much. He was a very strange man, very strange. But you got his concentration, always.

Peter Mark Richman

Peter Mark Richman starred in "The Fear" as Trooper Robert Franklin.

What was it like coming onto that show during its fifth and final season?

It was a terrific experience to do the show, and I had a very good director, who I like very much. His name was Ted Post, and we get along. I recently hired Ted, and I just did a picture which I wrote and star in and produced with Ted called *Four Faces*, where I play four different people. It's not released yet, but I'm very hopeful that it will soon be. For "The Fear," Ted was the director, and I had a wonderful actress to work with named Hazel Court. I recently found out that this was the last show that Rod wrote. Rod was an extremely creative writer, had an imagination that was profound, and he was, I think, running on all fours when he wrote this. Rod was a gentlemen and a terrific guy to work for.

Peter Falk stars as Ramos Clemente in another of Serling's tales of fear, "The Mirror."

What was it like working with director Ted Post?

Ted is very much a director who has wonderful ideas if you need them. He always tries to hire good people, so the direction is minimal. You don't have to give a lot of direction to professional actors. You have to set up your cameras properly and have a sense of story concept and a little nudge here and there. But you don't want to overdirect in television — there's no time. So Ted was very aware of that, and he had good quality actors. And we fulfilled what needed to be done. So I don't remember a lot of conversations about motivations and stuff like that. We certainly were aware of what we were doing.

What specific things did you bring to the character in "The Fear"?

There had to be a great sense of mystery to it, and curiosity and faith and peculiarity of something happening, because she's talking about hearing and feeling something about this. I'm a little skeptical when I come in, and then suddenly it begins to build on me that there is something happening here. So that a sense of something untoward is hovering around here that the actor has to create. And I remember that was very much a part of what I was doing. And also I had to quote Shakespeare in that particular segment, so that was another challenge for me, to do it as a trooper, not as a Shakespearean actor with a Shakespearean company.

After decades in syndication, why do you think we still watch *The Twilight Zone*?

I believe that it all starts with the writer, the creativity of the writer. Rod Serling had an enormous imagination that was god-given. And he set up circumstances human beings must face, on an almost metaphysical level. And they hired very good people — all the elements of the cameramen, and the crew, the actors, the directors, all were very dedicated. So the episodes hold up today because nothing has changed in terms of quality. A quality piece of work is a quality piece of work. If you take a look at some of the greatest films that were done 50 years ago, 60 years ago, and you say, "My god, that's incredible." Or you see a performance that has not dated. And that is why Rod Serling's work is not dated, because the quality is there.

Phillip Pine

Phillip Pine starred in "The Four of Us Are Dying," as Virgil Sterig, and in "The Incredible World of Horace Ford," as Leonard O'Brien.

When you were working on *Twilight Zone*, did you have a chance to meet Rod?

Oh yeah, on occasion, when making the next setup or something. He was a man that you wanted to talk to, because he was an educated man and a damn good one. Another interesting thing, I've forgotten the name of it now, but I was going to Europe — my wife and I obviously were going by plane — and sitting in the waiting room before the plane was ready to depart, I looked over and there he was. And he had a couple of film canisters; he was taking them over there himself, and we chatted for a few minutes. And I thought, "Jesus, that's wonderful. I thought you would have given it to someone else." And he said, "Oh no, this is the only print I have of this and I want to take this myself."

Rod Serling was a hell of a nice guy, he was a decent human being. He was not always there when the show was being produced or rehearsed, but when he was on set, it was very, very easy to ask him if there was any possible

In "The Mirror," paranoia sets in as Clemente (Peter Falk) believes he sees his associates plotting his assassination through a reflection in the mirror. The reflection in this shot is actor Richard Karlan.

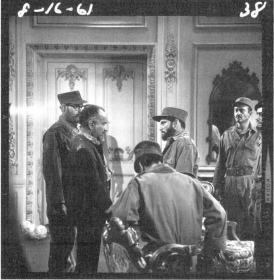

Seen here during filming of an early scene in "The Mirror" are actors Richard Karlan (D'Allesandro), Will Kuluva (General DeCruz), Tony Carbone (Cristo), Peter Falk (Clemente), Rodolfo Hoyos (Garcia), and Arthur Batanides (Tabal).

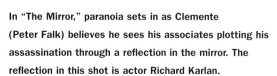

way to do something about a particular paragraph or something. He would tell you what he had on his mind when he put it into those particular words or sentences. If he hadn't become a writer, he would have been a teacher of literature.

Well, he was teaching writing at Antioch, and from what I gather, he really enjoyed it.

I didn't know he did that, but I could understand his doing it, because he was that way; the phrases he would put in, he was very character-oriented. Like, where he had one man that he wanted to make sure that the actor portraying it was an educated man, he wouldn't put the *de*'s, *dem*'s, and *dow*'s in there, you know, he made the difference to it, and he was careful about the way he wrote a sentence for you, that it was something that any teacher in

English would applaud. There were characters, of course, in it where he went to their type of language, but depending on the character, and he obviously gave them his dues if he was an educated person, or if he were not a deeply educated man, the dialogue would be different.

Do you think the show lost anything by moving to an hour-long format?

No, not really. It makes a better story. It releases more of what the writer and the director wanted. You get a chance to go up to the climax of a picture, and that was one certainly that they built and built and built for a climax, for in the ending he just stops there and it's all over. I remember when the little boy came to the door [in "The Incredible World of Horace Ford"], and the first time when he went out to the place where he lived in the old section. And I thought he did a hell of a good job in doing it. There were not two or three or four shots that had to be redone; he really had a grip on that picture in his area, in his inner feelings about what was happening to him. I thought they did an excellent job with it. The part that I had was really there to show the difference in what people believe and how their mind reacts to things.

"The Four of Us Are Dying" was written by Rod. Do you remember what your impression was when you read the script?

The first thing that had happened was I knew all the guys that were gonna do it. We had worked at one place or another, we had worked with each other. Harry Townes was a very, very good friend of mine for many years back when we worked for Clare Tree Major, which was a theater company that went all over the United States with stories for children, and I said, "Hey, maybe we can do one of these like we did for the kids." And he said, "Yeah, it would scare the bejeezus out of them, wouldn't it?" That was one of the things that came up. We enjoyed it. I think we had more fun than the audience, because they picked up guys who, the four of us, could have been so easily translated into, because each one of us had a different inside, but we exposed the same outside in the thing, and that's what he was hoping to get.

Your primary scene was with costar Bernard Fein. What was it like working with him?

I hadn't worked with him before, and we were knocking our heads during the scene. And we went together, as a matter of fact, off of the set for a couple of minutes to see what it was, what the argument was, what our feelings

"Someday these will be collector's items," ponders Rod Serling, creator of TV's landmark science fiction series "Twilight Zone." Perusing production stills in September 1959 with Serling is actor Harry Townes who appeared in the TZ episode, "The Four of Us Are Dying."

Actor Harry Townes ("The Four of Us Are Dying," "Shadow Play") and Rod Serling view portions of the original photograph collection featured in this book.

were in the argument. And it helped, I think it worked. I know that when they were shooting, everybody seemed to be happy about it, and that makes us happy.

Can you tell me about working with Abner Biberman on "The Incredible World of Horace Ford"?

Abner Biberman was one of the most wonderful people I've had. I'm gonna tell you a little

Beverly Garland (Maggie in "The Four of Us Are Dying"): "Rod Serling was on the set that morning and came over to me after the scene was finished (which we did in one take), and said, 'My god, I didn't know I had written her so deep. You brought so much more to this part that I did not know was there when I wrote it.' I'll never forget that. I was so flattered and was on cloud nine for a week! I even thought my singing was okay."

story about him. He came to me one day and he said, "You know some people up in Las Vegas, don't ya?" And I said, "Yeah, I know quite a few." And he said, "Jesus, I'm in trouble." And I said, "What's wrong? What's the matter?" And he said, "I've got a bad check. I gave them a bad check." And he came to me and we're talking about it, and they were really about to punish him. And he said, "Well, jeez, give me a break and I'll get it straightened out." And he came to me because he knew that I knew one of these guys that were up there. Who unfortunately was not my brother, but a good friend of my brother's. And I said, "Manny, can you help him with this?" And he said, "Oh, how much does he owe? Five grand? Oh Christ sake, five grand, I'll give him a talk." And he got on the phone and said just a few things, I won't mention it — most of them were one-syllable words — and I could see it was getting along pretty good. And Abner came afterward and said, "Oh god, Phil, you saved my soul." And I said, "For $5,000, they don't kill anybody, believe me." But he was still frightened.

The show has been playing for nearly 50 years now. Why do you think _The Twilight Zone_ still grabs an audience today?

The idea was to find strangeness, and the strangeness there is in the movements of life in the human being. And he was telling you that we are not all alike. The brain has a lot to do with the individual's soul, and the way it reacted to the specific things that were in the filming. Those things being: the fear of life, the fear of his ability to do what he expected of himself. They were all pictures that — joking now — I guess all of the shrinks would love. They were all pictures that you could go to and say to yourself, "Yeah, the mind now is working against the heart. Their inner spirits are being exposed now." What I get out of it is that human beings are human and they have a lot of problems in their lives, and this is a wonderful way to show the ability that some people can pursue the good in life, while others are dreaming about everything that goes wrong with their lives and think about that all the time. I think the stuff was a teaching of humanity.

Jacqueline Scott

Jacqueline Scott starred in "The Parallel," as Helen Gaines.

Twilight Zone was a bit of a phenomenon by the time you had appeared on it in the fourth season. Do you remember what your reaction was to being part of this popular series?

Working on _The Twilight Zone_ was exciting because it was a successful show. And that was a show that people arranged their time around, along with _Perry Mason_ and _Gunsmoke_ and some of those really standard

Filming during a scene on the apartment balcony with Ida Lupino and John Clarke for "The Sixteen-Millimeter Shrine."

Actress Jacqueline Scott stars as Helen Gaines, opposite Steve Forrest as Major Robert Gaines, in "The Parallel," a bit of a clunker fourth-season episode. Jacqueline Scott also starred in *The Outer Limits* pilot, "Galaxy Being," opposite Cliff Robertson.

shows. And obviously they were good shows, because they're trying to redo them, or already have tried to redo them. Television shows as well as feature movies.

Well, it was certainly popular in its day, but here it is almost 50 years later and it is still running.

I would say there is a very large percentage of young people out there for this show who really love it. And they've seen the new *Twilight Zone* series and they feel that the initial ones were better shows. Better conceived, better scripts — not that the new ones were bad.

Can you talk a little bit about film actors versus television actors and stage actors at that time?

A lot of people will tell you that when you do movies you can't smile too big, because your smile is this big, and none of that has ever meant anything to me. I think you have to imagine yourself in different circumstances. If you're playing in a 1,500-seat house, you always have to talk, to speak to the person in the back row. That's the easiest way to talk about projection without talking about yelling. And if you're doing film, the camera is right in your lap, as well as the audience, so you're not going to project that much. But as far as the actions and the way you prepare a script, to me it's the same thing. If it's not real, it's not going to work — if it's 1,500 people away or right in your lap. And if it is real, it's gonna work.

Can you tell me about meeting Rod Serling?

That was a really wonderful experience, one of the loveliest things that's happened to me. I'm talking to my husband one day, and I was talking about something about this segment, and the phone rang and I picked up the phone and I said hello, and this man said, "Hello, this is Rod Serling." And I went, "Ah!" It about scared me to death. But he invited me

to meet him for a drink at the Polo Lounge, at the Beverly Hills Hotel. And he said that he liked my performance so much on this segment that he was going to write a woman's script for me, which he never had, and unfortunately he didn't. I guess he got sidetracked by something else. But that was a really special thing for me, because he was one of the premier writers of that period. I didn't know him personally, but I knew his writing from live television in New York.

Warren Stevens

Warren Stevens starred in "Dead Man's Shoes," as Nate Bledsoe.

The Twilight Zone series was a very popular phenomenon even in its day. Did you get a sense that what you were working on was going to have the popularity that it did?

No, when we worked on any of those shows, including *The Twilight Zone*, we never had an inkling that some of it would turn into — well, you might call them a cult. But work was work in those days, we did what came along. All of those series, like *The Twilight Zone* and *One Step Beyond* and *The Outer Limits*. Now I find that they are all being rerun and run, and rerun and run. And I must say, particularly the *Twilight Zone* things are very good, they hang in, they stand up under all kinds of modern special effects and influences of the so-called modern-day stuff. And they are still good. All those stories are so solid. And I'm very grateful that I was in one.

Tell me why you think the shows are holding up so well, given the fact that they're not relying on special effects?

Cameramen film a scene where Wilma (Marshall) attempts to leave the apartment, after a vagrant shows up wearing the shoes of gangster Dane.

Actors Warren Stevens and Joan Marshall star in "Dead Man's Shoes." Even though Ocee Ritch ghost-wrote the first draft of this script, this episode was solely credited to Charles Beaumont, due to an unintended production oversight.

Warren Stevens, Joan Marshall, and director Montgomery Pittman, during a scene where vagrant Nate Bledsoe transforms back into himself upon removing the shoes that possessed him with the spirit of dead gangster Dane.

First of all, everybody forgets the writer these days, and I think that's where you have to start. If you don't have a good script — a good story and a good script — you don't have anything. And people forget that. And nowadays, to overcome the lack of a script, the lack of a story, they overload the stuff with special effects. But you cannot, in my estimation, overcome a bad script with a whole bunch of other stuff. You gotta have a script.

What appealed to you about "Dead Man's Shoes"?
First of all, what appealed to me was getting the job. And then I remember Monty Pittman, who was the director. I get on the set the first day, he says, "I don't know what to tell you. You're on your own, I can't help you." Well, I had no idea what I was going to do. I knew there had to be a change with the shoes, and

without the shoes. So that's what I did, I tried to do this, and he sat back and he said, "Well, let's do that, let's print it." He was absolutely no help, but he didn't interfere.

Describe how you got the role.
I think somebody just said, "You're going to do *Twilight Zone* next week," or whatever it was. I didn't audition for it or read for it. An interesting thing, though — Buck Houghton, who was the producer, eventually became the producer on *The Richard Boone Show.* He was a marvelous guy, I liked Buck very much. He was a very talented man.

In creating this character, Nate Bledsoe, how did you prepare for that role to figure out the answers?
Well, I really had to take it from the shoes, and incidentally, they hurt my feet. So I had to take it from making a real transition when I put the shoes on and when I took them off. And I had fun doing it. I was a little bit concerned that what I was doing might be too much. But Monty said, "No, that's fine." So I don't know whether he knew what he was talking about or not, but that's the way it ended up.

Interesting thing, I did one of the new *Twilight Zone* episodes in the '80s ["A Day in Beaumont"]. And Philip DeGuere, who produced that series, he directed it. I never saw it, but the first show that he did on that new one was called "Dead Woman's Shoes." And he did not know that I had done "Dead Man's Shoes." I don't think he ever saw it, actually.

What was the greatest challenge in shooting that episode? Do you remember anything that stands out?
The transitions from with shoes and without shoes, they were the most difficult things to do. Although I enjoyed doing it, I had to work a lot on it, to change an entire physical attitude, actually. That was the difficult part.

William Windom

William Windom starred in "Five Characters in Search of an Exit," as the Major, and in "Miniature," as Doctor Wallman.

What was your first impression of Rod Serling?

I never met the man, would you believe? So my first impression of him was either seeing one of the *Twilight Zone* episodes, or reading the scripts of the two I was in. Or best of all, he phoned me after an episode of *Night Gallery* called "They're Tearing Down Tim Riley's Bar," which he had written himself, and he said he liked it. And that was good praise, I was happy with that. But I've never met the man, I'm sorry. He was a paratrooper, so was I, so we had that in common, if you can call that common. I guess it's pretty common.

Do you remember what your impression was when you read the script for "Five Characters in Search of an Exit"?

Well, I had just come out from New York to do a show based on the writings of John Dos Passos in a book called *USA*. We had done a play called *USA* at the Martinique Theatre in New York. Six characters sitting on high stools and playing all the parts. And one of the people who came out to see it was the guy casting "Five Characters in Search of an Exit." And before the show closed, I had that job.

The episode was directed by Lamont Johnson.

A noble fellow. Good sense of humor, easy to work for, handled the crew and cast nicely. Nice director.

Did he give you any special direction of the character of the Major that you remember?

No. No. He let me run, pretty much. He might have said, "Faster" or "Slower," or "I didn't

Murray Matheson stars as the Clown, William Windom as the Major, in Serling's "Five Characters in Search of an Exit" (based on Marvin Petal's short story "The Depository"). As a New York actor who had just relocated to southern California, this episode was Windom's very first Hollywood film.

hear that," or "Turn your head more this way." But he didn't say, "Now the character does that."

One of the peculiarities of this particular role was that makeup artists William Tuttle and Charlie Schram had to make life-size figures with life masks of the actors.

Yeah, they did that. I've never had one of those made before. But for some reason they made two of them on me. And eventually I was given those two masks, those two heads. And I remember, one Christmas some makeup artist talked me into wearing one as if I had two heads, and the second one coming out of my fly, and having a picture taken. So there I'm lying on the ground with three heads, two coming out of my shirt and one coming out of my fly, all looked just like me. It was a strange Christmas card.

Do you still have the heads?
No. I gave them finally to Universal's makeup. I was going to throw them out, I didn't want them. But I finally thought, "What the hell, do you want these?" "Oh sure, we'll take them." And they've got them stored there somewhere, or maybe they've got them crumbled up by now. I don't know what they did with them.

The set was very unusual, all aluminum and round. I can only assume there must have been some production challenges working in that set.
Yeah. He had his hands full. I didn't know much of the technical stuff. But I know that from having us climb up out of the barrel, they obviously had to tilt it, and then shoot it as if it were upright, which was a little tricky, but they did that, so we could stand on our own shoulders to get up to the top. It took a little doing, but they shot that at about a 40-degree angle. Which is a little easier to stand on somebody's shoulders at that rate. And we worked hard, and we got it right apparently, and it worked as an effective little Christmas show.

How gratifying is it for you as a performer that you get to meet people who years later have their lives continue to be affected by the work that you did?
Well, it's gratifying in the sense that you don't want to get a swelled head. You really don't. I know that because when you're working alone onstage as I did with those 1,500 performances, you figure out very soon — do not talk down to these people, no matter what their age group or their nationality is. Because there

is someone in this theater every night who knows more about Thurber or Ernie Pyle than you'll ever hope to learn.

And another lesson you'll learn is you're never gonna get 100 percent approval. Don't tell me the audience was eating out of your hand — bullshit. If you got 90 percent of them to stand up and give you a hand, that's terrific. But the other 10 have something to offer too. What didn't they like? Why didn't they like it? If you can get them to tell you, and the critics will, learn it, pay attention to what they say. Because you need to balance that information along with the adulation you got from the other 90. I like people — every one of them has a nugget to offer you. The worst bum in the street has something of a sparkle if you just give it a second to come out. Even if it's only a belch, it's a belch you've never heard before. If you want to do a good belch someday, he just showed you how.

Kevin Hagen

Kevin Hagen starred in "Elegy," as Captain James Webber, and in "You Drive," as Pete Radcliff.

Did you feel that The *Twilight Zone* was unique in comparison to other television gigs?
Oh yeah! Absolutely! *The Twilight Zone* was unique, but it was Serling himself, his manner and the way he introduced his episodes and talked about them. He was unique, definitely. And certainly the writing was exceptional; it wasn't just everyday television-series writing. It wasn't rushed. A lot of times, back in those days, you'd go from one to the other, you didn't have much time. Time was of the essence, even more so today. I did a lot of television.

Seen here from Beaumont's "Elegy" are stars Don Dubbins, the wonderful Cecil Kellaway, Kevin Hagen, who would later costar in Hamner's "You Drive," and Jeff Morrow.

In "Elegy," almost out of fuel for their spaceship, astronauts land on an Earthlike asteroid inhabited by inanimate people. Everyone they come across is completely frozen, except for the caretaker of this strange place, Wickwire, played by Kellaway.

It was a special time for a lot of us, we had a good time doing it. Also, there was a camaraderie that I don't think exists today. Maybe we'd be doing something out at Universal, or whatever studio it was, and the casting director would be there while you were having lunch, and he'd come up and say, "Are you free next week?" And I'd say, "Well, yeah." "Well, I've got this . . ." So it wasn't a matter of just going in for a reading and somebody saying, "Well, let's see, what have you done?"

I didn't do too much live television, I did a *Studio One*, it was a supporting role, and I was glad to do whatever it was. You went where the jobs were. At one time, seven out of 10 were westerns. One of my favorites was for *Thriller*. Boris Karloff was the host, and he would narrate them as Rod Serling did *Twilight Zone*.

Of course, the theme of *Twilight Zone* has become eternal. Anytime somebody starts thinking something's kind of weird, they'll go into that "Da da da da . . ." As I remember, it was an easy set to work on; the work was flexible and calm, good crew.

In "Elegy," you had to work around all those still people, which must have been something.
Yeah, it was. Those weren't dummies, they had to be absolutely still. It was a good story. I remember Cecil Kellaway, and how delighted I was not only to meet him, but work with him and talk to him. I had worked with Don Dubbins a number of times, and he was a special kind of friend. Jeff Morrow I'd never worked with, and it came at a good time.

Wickwire may seem like a friendly fellow, but underneath that supposed guise of humanity lies an ulterior motive about the fate of the astronauts. Meyers asks, "But why? Why us?" "Because you are here, and you are men. And while there are men, there can be no peace."

Do you have any comments on the director of "You Drive," John Brahm?

That's interesting, because John Brahm also directed the _Thriller_ episode, "Flowers of Evil." That possibly explains why I did _Thriller_ later on, because we worked together. That's weird. But I thought "Elegy" was a very interesting story — a celestial burial ground, and there's a caretaker there, and it's secret. That last line, "Give me the antidote!" It had that little bit of humor in it, where I kept getting Wickwire's name wrong, I kept saying, "Wirewick."

And finding out the caretaker is a robot.

Oh, now that never occurred to me at the time, but he was a robot. You see, that never occurred to me.

Ivan Dixon

Ivan Dixon starred in "The Big Tall Wish," as Bolie Jackson, and in "I Am the Night — Color Me Black," as Reverend Anderson.

While you were working on _Twilight Zone_, did you spend some time with Rod Serling? Any anecdotes, thoughts, or reflections on the man that you'd like to share?

I did spend a few precious moments with Rod Serling and we talked about many things. One day I was driving down Wilshire Boulevard, and this guy in a black Cadillac kept honking at me like he wanted to pass. Finally he pulls up on my right and I was just about to shake my fist at him when I realized it was a grinning Rod Serling waving at me!

"The Big Tall Wish" is the wonderful story of worn-out boxer, Bolie Jackson, his wishful young companion Henry, and a twisted reality both ironic and sensitive. What place does the part of Bolie hold for you? What memories do you have of working on this episode and with costars Steven Perry and Kim Hamilton?

This was a particularly delicate and sensitive story. The director was good, and Steve and Kim were excellent. I stayed in touch with Steve for a number of years. He matured and had a fast-food business on Crenshaw Boulevard. I am still in touch with Kim Hamilton, who married Werner Klemperer of _Hogan's Heroes_ many years ago. She played my wife or love interest many times.

At the time of "The Big Tall Wish," my son was a few years younger than Steve, and came with me to the set. At lunch I bought Steve a hot dog, and my son got so upset and was angry with me because he thought Steve and Kim were my new family. He wouldn't talk with me for a week afterward, he was that scared.

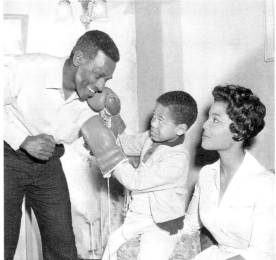

During the filming of a street scene in "The Big Tall Wish," Henry (Steven Perry), watches from the window as washed-out boxer Bolie Jackson, played by Ivan Dixon, makes his way out of the neighborhood and back into the ring.

Ivan Dixon stars with Steve Perry, and Kim Hamilton, as Frances. This is an example of who Serling was in those times, in recognizing the worth of talented people, casting African-Americans as leads and costars in a drama not concerned with a racial issue.

How do you feel about the story in "I Am the Night — Color Me Black," and has that role held significance for you over the years?

Certainly not as much significance as "The Big Tall Wish." I'm honestly not really sure that I ever truly understood that story. I tried to delineate the meaning as the director saw it.

Twilight Zone became the premier showcase for much of the top talent in the acting profession. At the time, were you aware of the popular status of the series among your colleagues?

Yes, *The Twilight Zone* and *Studio One* were my two favorite shows and I was lucky to appear in both of them several times. Rod's talent drew the participation of the most prominent actors of the day.

Charles Horvath costars as the boxer fighting Bolie, seen during filming, throwing punches into the camera for use as first-person Bolie shots.

With actors and crew looking on, the cameraman films first-person shots of both fighters being counted out by the referee, played by Frankie Wan.

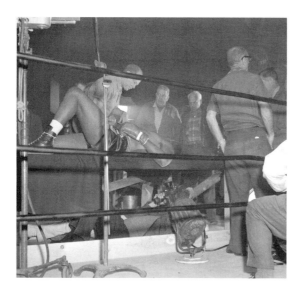

Special effects shot through glass of Van and Bolie (Dixon); also seen is some of the crew, among whom is assistant director, Kurt Neumann.

Even the occasional television viewer can easily remember your role as radio man Sgt. James Kinchloe in the unforgettable WWII sitcom, *Hogan's Heroes*. Rod Serling didn't care for this show all that much, as he once mentioned, "I see nothing comical about Nazis." Any comments on this point of view?

Not really. Rod was of the most creative people I've ever met. If he didn't like *Hogan's*, so be it. I didn't like it much either!

Appreciation Essays

The House that Rod Built
Dana Gould

One may wonder what a writer for the *The Simpsons*, an animated comedy, is doing writing a tribute to *The Twilight Zone*. What could these two things possibly have in common? On the surface, it is a conundrum worthy of *The Twilight Zone* itself. (Well, that might be stretching it, but it would make a pretty good *Night Gallery*, or at least a *Boris Karloff's Thriller*. Anyway . . .)

To explain, let's stay true to the form of the show. We've introduced our mystery, now we'll take a short break and, when we return, we'll backtrack to before it occurred.

Fade to black.

Opening credits.

Fade up.

"Everybody has a hometown. Binghamton's mine." That is what Rod Serling said about Binghamton, New York, the small city upstate of Manhattan, where he grew up. If you've never been to Binghamton, watch *The Twilight Zone* episode "Walking Distance." That's Binghamton, or at least as Rod recalled it. It's also Hopedale, Massachusetts, where I was born and raised, or at least as I recall it. Or maybe it's your hometown, or at least as you recall it.

I was born in 1964, which prevented me from enjoying *The Twilight Zone* in its original run, but it did put me at just the right age to soak up "the monster boom" of the early 1970s. Like so many kids of that era (certainly the ones reading this book), I glutted myself on *Famous Monsters* magazine, Aurora monster model kits, and spent an endless succession of Saturday afternoons

Rod Serling on location between takes of his narration for "The Fugitive."

bathing my eyeballs in the soothing glow of *Creature Double-Feature*, ("Boston's Monster Matinee").

No matter what movie I was watching at the time — *Dracula*, *The Wolf Man*, *Godzilla* — the one thing these films all had in common was that they were set far away, in some exotic, often mythic locale. Be it Transylvania, Skull Island, the Black Lagoon, or Planet X, good old Hopedale, Massachusetts was always safe and sound.

I saw my first episode of *The Twilight Zone* at the ripe old age of 11, and it totally freaked me out. The episode, "The Monsters Are Due On Maple Street," quickly became and stayed my favorite. Maple Street was, for all intents and purposes, where I lived. There were no mysterious counts or mad scientists. The angry villagers were just like my parents and their friends. And the monster? The monster was . . . us? I couldn't get over it.

This is what *The Twilight Zone* has always meant for me. It made clear that every horror, every ghastly creation that ever stalked *Creature Double-Feature*, was already in existence, in a slightly different form, in your own hometown. Rod Serling, along with Richard Matheson, Charles Beaumont, George Clayton Johnson, et. al., took the horrors of Transylvania and Planet X, rewired them, and set them loose in a universal suburbia that still feels familiar half a century later.

As I grew older, and my *Famous Monsters* magazines were forced to share shelf space with my Elvis Costello records, and my monster models suffered the indignities of little hats and such to give them a sense of, I'm ashamed to say, "irony," *The Twilight Zone* survived unscathed. Such was the genius of the show's design, that an 11-year-old and a 20-year-old could sit side-by-side and enjoy it equally, if on totally different levels.

Rod Serling performing his on-camera narration for "Shadow Play."

Which brings us, cue Bernard Herrmann sting, to *The Simpsons*.

If there is one unarguable similarity between *The Simpsons* and *The Twilight Zone*, it is that each show respects the intelligence of its audience. This might not seem like an earth-shaking attribute, but the assumption that the viewer can indeed walk and chew gum at the same time is not often found on network television. This explains why both shows are so beloved amongst their fans. Somewhere, on some level, you sit there and think, "Wow! These guys know I'm not an idiot!"

As a devotee and fan of *The Twilight Zone*, I am forever thankful for my involvement in one of the few other programs that actually appreciates its viewer's intelligence. Don't believe me? Walk into any major network and suggest to the powers-that-be that they invest their time and money into a really smart, literate show, then watch as they shift in their chairs and eye you uncomfortably, as if you've just wandered in "from another dimension. "

The Simpsons, Star Trek, The Sopranos, any program that makes you feel better after you've watched it, any show that surprises you, that talks up at you instead of down to you, in my opinion, all share a debt to the pioneering brilliance of *The Twilight Zone*. They're rooms in the house that Rod built.

Fade out.

Dana Gould is an executive producer for *The Simpsons*, as well as a writer and voice actor for several episodes. He's also written several screenplays, as well as acting in such television shows as *Roseanne*, *The Ben Stiller Show*, and *Seinfeld*.

A Reminiscence
Christopher Beaumont

There's always a moment when I'm speaking with a *Twilight Zone* true believer; a moment when he or she realizes that I know far less about the series than they do. They mention the name of an actress who played the third lead in their favorite episode and their eyes slowly narrow as they watch the wheels of my memory spinning for all they're worth.

They're polite and I'm polite, but we both know what's happening here — I don't have the vaguest idea who this actress is. The truth is, I don't even remember the episode — certainly not the way they do. Their next expression is usually a mix of sadness, disappointment, and no small amount of confusion. How could this be? How could I not know every detail of every show? After all, I grew up with the show; my father was one of the three primary contributors to the writing team that made *Twilight Zone* possible, the group of magical minds that created a parallel universe that unlocked the imagination of a generation. How on earth (or anywhere else for that matter) is it possible that I am not the fan to end all fans!?

The answer is that I *am* a fan (not only of my father's episodes, but just about every single one of them); my experience of *Twilight Zone* is just as rich and detailed as theirs, only the details are different ones. I was 10 years old when the *Twilight Zone* first went on the air, and I was immediately hooked. But watching the actual program on our black-and-white Zenith was, in an odd way, the least exciting part of it. What I remember most is the enthusiasm, the joy, the creativity, the incredible sense of adventure that happened in our living room and around our dinner table as my father and his friends helped to give birth to the kind of storytelling that has since become so famous, and so very beloved. The possibility that Rod Serling had convinced CBS to do this kind of show, and to do it right, was cause for great celebration. In today's world of Stephen King and Dean Koontz, etc., it's hard to imagine that, back then, it was next to impossible to earn a living writing fantasy and science fiction. Serling,

Matheson, Johnson, my dad, they all hoped that *Twilight Zone* would help change all that and create a real audience for the kind of stories they loved to tell. Forty years later, the show is still in constant syndication and you would be hard pressed to find anyone, young or old, who doesn't have a favorite episode.

Allow me to submit for your consideration a couple of quick details from my own personal *Twilight Zone* memory bank.

I'm seven years old. My parents are taking me with them on their first trip to Europe together. My father is no fan of flying machines, so we board the HMS Ivernia for the trip across the Atlantic. It's a gorgeous old ship with grand staircases, mahogany paneled ballrooms, and etched crystal everywhere you look. In 1957 jet travel is all the rage, and it seems as if ships like the Ivernia are not long for this world. At dinner on the first night I hear my father mention casually to my mother that the passenger list seems to have been drawn exclusively from World War One veterans. There isn't anyone on board under the age of 70. The next day at breakfast he makes the same observation, but this time he begins to wonder aloud if there isn't some plot, some hidden reason that we are the only ones in the room without liver spots. I don't remember my father's exact words. It was a long time ago and, even as a child, I was used to him taking a casual observation and weaving it into a complex scenario before he finished his scrambled eggs. Sometimes the stories were sinister, sometimes sentimental, frequently a little of both. This particular observation went on to become a short story called "Song for a Lady," which subsequently became an episode of *The Twilight Zone* entitled "Passage on the Lady Anne." So when the show aired in May 1963, I watched, along with a great portion of the country, as the Lady Anne sank into a sea of memories and a doomed love for a time gone by. But in addition to enjoying the images on the screen, I was also remembering the dining room of the Ivernia, and the sweet, ancient faces that tripped my father's imagination. To watch an episode of *T-Zone* was, and is, always a fantastic experience. But to have been present at the birth of the idea was an incredible gift.

A similar thing occurred later during that same trip to Europe. We had rented a car and were making our way across Germany. As we passed through the countryside, we could see the remains of the bombed-out villages that still scarred the landscape, reminders that it hadn't been that many years since the devastation of World War Two. Curled up in the back seat, not quite asleep, I heard my father whisper: "It's as if evil itself had walked through this country, as if the devil came to earth." I'm sure my parents thought I was asleep, but I heard every word — and you can be quite sure that I checked the hotel closets twice, and under the bed countless times before attempting sleep that night.

So, again, when the episode entitled "The Howling Man" aired several years later, I viewed it with my own set of (some would say bizarre) memories. Lucky (in my opinion) to have been present at the very moment when the devil got his due, courtesy of Charles Beaumont.

Others who are contributing to this collection will have far more to say about the show itself. They are the wonderful and loyal fans who have kept the *Twilight Zone* alive all these years and they, quite simply, know more than I do. In my father's absence, I thank them. And if I should encounter any of you at a gathering, or at a party, and I look confused when you ask me a particular question about a particular episode, please know that I am at that moment traveling to a place deep in the recesses of my heart, to a sweet and treasured memory of my very own, personal, Twilight Zone.

Christopher Beaumont is a writer and the son of the late Charles Beaumont.

Rod Sterling
Robert Hewitt Wolfe

Serling during filming of his on-camera narration for "The Whole Truth."

I have an embarrassing confession to make. The guy in the black suit? The natty dresser with the clenched jaw delivery and the dry wit? I never, ever, get his name right. Every single time I say it aloud or in my head, I always screw it up. I always call him Rod Sterling. With a T.

I know that's wrong. I know it's Serling. Rodman Edward Serling. That information is duly recorded somewhere in my tangled neuro-pathways. But it doesn't matter. I open my mouth to talk about the man, and out comes "Sterling."

I blame my seven-year-old self. I was born the same year *The Twilight Zone* was canceled. By the time I was seven, *The Twilight Zone* was being rerun on a regular basis in glorious black-and-white on one of our local stations. It's the first television show I have any memory of watching with regularity. I didn't understand it all the time, it scared the crap out of me, but I thought it was great. The pathos of Burgess Meredith in the bank vault with his broken glasses, the madness and paranoia of the residents of Maple Street, the tempting false paradise of Willoughby — each made their indelible impressions on my young mind.

And lording over it all was the ringmaster of *The Twilight Zone*, a well-groomed, rapier-thin man whose name sounded a lot like "sterling." He seemed to be perfectly named, this sterling fellow, struck from some kind of pure metal, of unquestionable character and integrity. In my head, he became Sterling then. In my head, he remains Sterling to this day.

At the time, I had no idea that Rod Serling had actually written these episodes, and many more that fired my young imagination. My seven-year-old self had no inkling whatsoever that television episodes were written at all. I thought they just happened. I didn't know what a teleplay or an executive producer or a showrunner was. Ah, simpler times. I thought that Serling was just

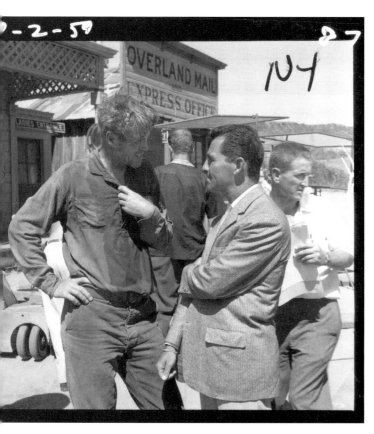

Actor Dan Duryea and Serling during a break from filming "Mr. Denton on Doomsday." On the far right is second assistant director Kurt Neumann.

the host, the guy who said the clever stuff at the beginning and end of the show. In my ignorance, I believed that each character, including this host fellow, made up what they were saying themselves. I was wrong, of course. Wrong about everyone except Serling.

Over the years, I finally began to understand Rod Serling's monumental contribution to *The Twilight Zone* and to American culture. I began to appreciate him not only as an impeccably dressed host, but as a stunningly talented writer and producer. As I took up the craft of writing myself, my earliest short stories were clearly influenced by Serling's work. I wrote a story about a music producer who finds out his most talented and reclusive artist is actually a Chinese unicorn. I wrote a story about a freakish mutant in a postapocalyptic town who, despite the scorn and fears of his neighbors, ends up saving them all. I wrote a story about feuding statues in a small town square whose petty rivalries reflect the hidden ethnic and cultural divisions in the town's residents. None of them were particularly good, but all of them were attempts to replicate the kind of storytelling Serling achieved on *The Twilight Zone*.

Serling told clever, tight little stories that were self-contained, twisting and turning. But most importantly, Serling told stories about people. Like a master painter, he created detailed and identifiable characters with a few quick brushstrokes. Then he used these characters to explore the human condition, to make us think and feel. For Serling, the startling premise or the clever twist wasn't enough. For him, these were just launching pads, opportunities to explore our common human psychology. His stories did more than just scare or surprise, they provided insights into our shared human experiences, our hopes, our dreams, our nightmares.

As I grew into a man and a professional writer (not necessarily in that order), I tried to emulate Serling. I tried to tell stories that were just as insightful, just as resonant. I'm still trying. It's good to have goals.

A few years ago, I was fortunate enough to be invited to write an episode for the latest incarnation of *The Twilight Zone*. I won't pretend I came even close to the standards set by Mister Serling. But it was an honor to be allowed to walk in his footsteps, to have my name on a *Twilight Zone*, to be a footnote in the legacy of one of the great American storytellers.

To my chagrin, even while I was in *The Twilight Zone* office, breaking my episode with Ira Steven Behr and his staff, I still called that storyteller "Sterling." My adult mind knows better, but the echo of my seven-year-old consciousness somehow intercepts the word "Serling" somewhere along its journey from my brain to my mouth and transfigures it to "Sterling."

The American Heritage Dictionary of the English Language defines "sterling" as, among other things, "of the highest quality: *a person of sterling character*." Merriam-Webster On-Line gives us "conforming to the highest standard (as in, *sterling* character)." Serling, both as a man and as a writer, certainly embodied those definitions. He was of the highest quality and conformed to the highest standard.

So in my mind Rodman Edward Serling will always be Sterling.

Robert Hewitt Wolfe has written scripts for television shows such as *The Twilight Zone* (2002), *The 4400*, and *Star Trek: The Next Generation*, as well as being a producer and writer for *Star Trek: Deep Space Nine*.

Serling and Beaumont: A Game of One-Upmanship
Roger Anker

Midway through *Twilight Zone*'s second season, Charles Beaumont expressed "surprise" over the growing volume of fan mail he had been receiving from that series' audience.

Though he had established himself as one of the show's principal writers and was "proud" of his contribution to its critical success, Beaumont attributed much of *Twilight Zone*'s high level of quality to Rod Serling, who had penned most of the series' teleplays.

By November 1960, Beaumont had developed not only a successful working relationship with Serling, but a close friendship as well. Beaumont noted that he had become particularly fond of Serling's "offbeat sense of humor" and "love for the occasional practical joke." As Beaumont also possessed what his family and friends described as "a devastating sense of wit and humor," the pair began a friendly game of "one-upmanship." In one such instance, Serling jokingly complained to Beaumont that he was "sick and tired" of receiving his fan mail. Furthermore, Serling wrote, if said fan mail was not "immediately diverted to *Beaumont's* mailbox, Beaumont will find himself forever blacklisted in Hollywood." Upon receiving another letter from a fan — one who considered Beaumont's episode of "The Howling Man" to be "one of the best *Twilight Zones* ever" — Serling promptly forwarded the letter to Beaumont with the following attachment: "The enclosed was received the other day, and I thought you'd be interested," he wrote. "Of course, it means you're blacklisted as of now! It isn't that I'm little and petty about these things — but I will not have my office cluttered up with your fan mail!"

Beaumont, of course, wasted no time in sending his reply to Serling: "Perhaps someday, *if* you work at it, and *if* you develop a fantastical (fanatical?) imagination, not to mention sound writing skills, you too can enjoy (as I do) such complimentary mail from adoring fans. So don't give up!"

Sadly, Beaumont and Serling's friendship was short-lived. In 1964, Beaumont was diagnosed with a rare form of Alzheimer's Disease, which claimed his life on February 21, 1967, at the age of 38.

Before his untimely death, however, while in the midst of a heavy work schedule, Beaumont noted that his enthusiasm for *Twilight Zone* never waned. "*Thriller* offered to hire me for a quartet of horror stories," he wrote in January 1961. "I turned them down. Sam Goldwyn, Jr., offered to hire me to do the pilot script of a new half-hour series . . . Turned him down. Twentieth Century offered to hire me to write a picture for Gary Cooper . . . Turned them down. *Twilight Zone* got renewed, with a fresh new sponsor. Offered to hire me to do stories and things. Didn't turn them down."

Roger Anker is the editor for the award-winning *Charles Beaumont: Selected Stories,* and *The Twilight Zone Scripts of Charles Beaumont*. He is currently working on a book-length biography of Beaumont, and *The Blue Angels Experience*, a 60-year history of the famed U.S. Navy Flight Demonstration Squadron.

George Clayton Johnson

August 9, 2006

TO: Mr. Rod Serling
ADDRESS: Somewhere in The Twilight Zone . . .

Dear Rod:
My wife Lola and I were talking about you the other day, and began to realize fully how truly important you have been in our lives. We were remembering those early days when I was writing those scripts for you, starting to get out of debt. If you and The *Twilight Zone* hadn't come along when you did, I don't know what would have become of us. There didn't seem to be anything else on the tube that might exercise my particular gifts and talents, and, who besides Ray Bradbury could make a living writing short stories?

When you made the decision to buy my story, "All Of Us Are

Dying," to adapt for the series you changed my life forever, and later, when you hired me to write the teleplay of my story, "A Penny For Your Thoughts," you handed me a career, gave me standing among my fellows, and caused me to believe for the first time that I could make a living as a writer.

Things never seem to become real for me until I have written them down, Rod, which accounts for why I am putting this on paper. By buying my stories and by giving me a job working on the frontiers of the limitless, you have enlarged my awareness and altered the fabric of my life.

You put me on a permanent search for what Charles Beaumont called "The Greater Truth." Not what really happened, but rather, what might have happened, if only . . . You freed me to look behind the curtain and to question everything I know, providing me with an unusual education. I learned to think sideways as I explored the puzzling geography of *The Twilight Zone*. Like yourself and Charles Beaumont and Richard Matheson and Earl Hamner and Jerry Sohl and others, I had to learn how to get into that state of mind where the universe becomes transparent to thought. I remember Buck Houghton saying, "A *Twilight Zone* story must be impossible in the real world. A request at some point to suspend disbelief is a hallmark of the series." By listening to him carefully during story conferences I came to understand how surrealist art attempts to enlarge reality by making the imaginary plausible within a realistic setting, bringing together the undeniable and the unbelievable within a single emotional framework.

What got Lola and I on this kick is the fact that we're getting me ready to wing off to fabled New Jersey in a shiny airplane to serve as a guest speaker at a science fiction autograph show. After all these years watching *The Twilight Zone* myth grow, this event will feature scores of surviving actors that you hired to portray characters on your program, and where untold numbers of hardcore fans will gather for a weekend to celebrate your show with banquets and speeches and parties to honor you and your work.

After an endless number of reruns of the series on every channel and in every time slot, Image Entertainment has made available to the public all five seasons of the series in boxed sets, the Falcon Film Group is in the process of adapting all of your scripts into radio programs available on CD, and Gauntlet Press has just issued volume 3 of *As Timeless as Infinity: The Complete Twilight Zone Scripts of Rod Serling*, edited by Tony Albarella. Your stuff in its pure form is finally in the bookstores and on library shelves where it belongs.

Congratulations.

You can't have failed to notice that your name has become one that everybody knows, and that the title of your show has become an essential part of the English language.

With admiration and immense gratitude.

Your friend,

George Clayton Johnson

P.S. Lola sends her love.

The Vibe of the Twilight Zone
John Ottman

One of my fantasies is to get into a time machine and set the dial to 1960. I would then make my way to one of the recording studios in town where a young Jerry Goldsmith, Leonard Rosenmen, or already famous Bernard Herrmann or Franz Waxman is standing before a small orchestra conducting the latest music for *The Twilight Zone*. As I peer through some smoky doorway, I can hear the downbeat of music that will forever define a classic world; I hear a slate, "1M2, take 2." I hear vibes sing eerily, as a violin plucks and a trumpet sneers. The sound is pristine — live, and unencumbered by the mono TV speakers of the time. As I study the people working, I look at them knowing they have no idea the legacy that is to come from their work. This was the TV era of vastly unexplored territory. Just as the early settlers of America had no idea what lay beyond the next mountain pass, the players involved in the early days of TV were discovering and creating a new world. Ideas were ideas, not rehashes of concepts from other shows. And the music came from passionate minds of people who would become the inspired masters of their craft. Especially for youngster Goldsmith, this was a new experience. Fresh from a job as a clerk at CBS, he was now being commissioned to write music for the TV show's second season. This had to be an exciting time for him and his contemporaries to push the envelope musically for a show unlike any other. But there was a catch. They had to do it with one hand tied behind their back: The music would have to be produced with about 10 musicians sitting in the small recording studio.

Music was perhaps the most victimized department in low budget shows of the time — and in retrospect, it was ironically one of the most powerful forces behind them. Today, a composer on a low budget production can use multiple layers of synthesized instruments to create his score. He has unlimited choices to use any orchestral flavor he wishes, albeit electronically sampled from the real thing. (It's still debatable just how much worse or better off TV music is because of this.) In the days of The *Twilight Zone*, the only electronics were those which scarcely supplemented real instruments (i.e. the theremin — that outer-spacey sing-saw thing most identified with *The Day the Earth Stood Still* and other sci-fi movies of the '50s.) For the composer, it took tremendous musical instinct, clarity of vision, and prowess to milk interesting overtones and themes from such a small ensemble of instruments. But that limitation is what made the music of *The Twilight Zone* stand out as something unique and strangely timeless. Limitations in general are what made *The Twilight Zone* so inspired. Instead of relying on fancy sets or cushy schedules, it forced the show to rely on ingenuity. For Serling, the ingenuity of his writing; for the cinematographers, the ingenuity of getting around limited time to light and shoot many angles with maximum expression. For the composers, it required imagination and resourcefulness to come up with strange atmospheric music utilizing so few players. The result: instruments in the ensemble emerged as star players in the cast of musical characters. Vibes offered that weird dreamy atmosphere, woodwind clusters created their own odd colors, and that sneering muted trumpet in the background usually provided the bizarre tension. Masterfully blended with an electric guitar here, and an off-beat violin pizzicato there, the interesting sonic landscape of *The Twilight Zone* took shape. It was as if the spirit of *The Twilight Zone* came to be. Even listening today, so provocative are the musical illusions, it's sometime hard to believe that so few musicians are playing. This was the mastery of the composer-magicians behind the music.

Bernard Herrmann, who wrote the first season's music, was already a film music veteran utilizing large ensembles for the films he scored. For TV, he too was forced to be resourceful. And this was part of the art. Great things come of situations where the artist is boxed into being clever. For instance, telling a painter he can only use three colors may render something far more unique and inspired than had he been given the entire palette. Other times, an artist will self-enforce these challenges in his own work to create something far more effective and original. For Goldsmith, this resourcefulness stayed with him in many of the major films that followed in his amazing career. Even for large-scale motion pictures, he would often surprise everyone by endeavoring to use the unique characteristics of the instruments in the orchestra, as opposed to falling back into the security of a huge ensemble. For *Chinatown*, it was strumming a washboard and the strings of the piano, rather than playing it with the keys; in *Patton*, it was the now-famous three-note trumpet line put through an echo machine to reflect Patton's belief in reincarnation;

FORM 232   PHOTO NEWS
FROM
BUREAU OF INDUSTRIAL SERVICE
A Division of
YOUNG AND RUBICAM, INC.
285 MADISON AVENUE
NEW YORK 17, N. Y.
MURRAY HILL 9-5000

PIPPA SCOTT Does wild Charleston number in a most unusual flashback sequence in "The Trouble With Templeton," on "The Twilight Zone," Friday, December 9, at 10:00 p.m., EST, over CBS Television.

and in *Planet of the Apes*, a thumb rubbing on the skin of a drum. Interestingly, those more intellectual scores are the ones that endure the most; we still marvel at them today. Film composers, such as me, are often blessed with huge orchestras. We have to remember the creative rewards for being discerning and judicious in how we use the orchestra. *The Twilight Zone* is a testimony to the power of this creative selectiveness. Its simplicity in all departments, including music, makes it startlingly effective. It's funny to think that a strange little television show's budget restraints were part of the genesis of inspired scoring ideas that endure today.

Another by-product of a tight budget were the musical motifs throughout the series. A motif is a theme that recurs. It can be as simple as two chords, or a three-note melody on a cello. The bottom line, it's something immediately recognizable that we latch onto, at least subconsciously. It was too expensive to custom score each and every episode of *The Twilight Zone*. Therefore, the composers offered long pieces of music, or suites, from which the music editors cut and pasted into the other episodes. Bernard Herrmann was the first composer on *The Twilight Zone* series, and had already composed a 25-minute piece of music in 1957 called, "The Outer Space Suite." This was often the well to draw from for the music editors. Herrmann had already well established himself as a composer with the likes of *Citizen Kane*, *The Devil and Daniel Webster* (for which he won an Oscar), and *The Day The Earth Stood Still*. The latter's influence is very apparent in his "Outer Space Suite." Other composers were hired to add to this musical library by writing suites that included a variety of different moods. There were, of course, many episodes that were custom scored; but even in these episodes, sections were sometimes left that could be scored from the ever-growing musical library. Soon, cues from the custom scores themselves added to the music editor's arsenal to re-use them in other episodes. Music editors in this era were the other unsung creative force behind how the episodes were "scored." The fluky brilliance to come out of this was that the recurrence of musical motifs throughout the series gave it a sort of signature. A familiar musical thread wove throughout the seasons, making *The Twilight Zone* an immediately recognizable world. Shows like *Star Trek* and *Mission Impossible* followed suit in this manner — a similar result of custom scoring only selected episodes, and re-using music from others.

Being renewed for a second season, *The Twilight Zone* producers were looking at ways to spruce up the opening. This soon gave rise to a totally different approach in which Herrmann's main theme seemed too dreary or serious. Much of his disturbing somberness worked brilliantly as underscore, but as a main theme, it was lacking something. The problem: no one knew what that "something" was.

Herrmann submitted two new themes, and Goldsmith and Leith Stevens submitted their own. In the end, none of them were used as a main theme; however, they were wonderful new additions to the music library for use in future episodes! Thinking "out of the box," the musical director for the series, Lud Gluskin, found a couple of obscure cues written by a French *avant-garde* classical composer named Marius Constant. Constant had written them to be part of the library to be used for background music in the series. But his cues were so short and strange that they had never been utilized in the series. Constant's titles for these two cues were "Etrange 3 (Strange No. 3)" and "Milieu 2 (Middle No. 2)" The pieces were performed with the typical small group, including two guitars, percussion with bongo drums, a saxophone, and French horns. Gluskin simply spliced them together so that they formed a somewhat cohesive piece with an opening and strong conclusion. The first part, ("Etrange 3") contained the weird guitar motif we all identify as the *Twilight Zone* "theme," and the second part spliced onto it from "Milieu 2" was the familiar downward chromatic wrap up to the segment we all know and love.

Stepping out of the time machine into present day, I turn on the TV, close my eyes, and it's often hard to tell what show I'm listening to based upon the music. One drum loop and guitar sample just sounds like another. But if I keep my eyes closed and keep flipping that remote long enough, sooner or later I'll hear a different sound. A sound I'll not hear the likes of again. And at that moment, I'll know I've entered *The Twilight Zone.*

John Ottman has composed soundtracks for numerous films, including *Superman Returns, X2,* and *The Usual Suspects.* He's also edited a number of films, including those same three, plus *Urban Legends: Final Cut, Apt Pupil,* and *Lion's Den.*

Magic Realism Comes to the Suburbs
Neil Peart

For a kid growing up in the Canadian suburbs in the late '50s and early '60s, television was limited in quantity, variety, and scope. (And *color*, as our family didn't get a color set until I was in my teens.) Our rooftop antenna brought in five channels — three American and two Canadian — and some of the shows were unique to the times, like westerns and the kind of variety shows hosted by Ed Sullivan, Jackie Gleason, or Red Skelton. Other shows were the familiar sitcoms with Andy Griffith or Lucille Ball that still play on cable channels (and are still remade every season with different names), and the eternally popular, ever-changing (yet never-changing) crime dramas and doctor shows.

At first, the big television event of the week for me was Saturday morning cartoons, but a little later, I discovered *The Twilight Zone.* Not only was it different from everything I had seen before in mood, style, and depth, it introduced the possibility of magic into everyday life — just as Rod Serling and the show's other writers often did in their stories.

Director Buzz Kulik breaks for some brushing up on a drum kit on the set of "The Trouble with Templeton."

In retrospect, Rod Serling may have pioneered what is now called "magic realism" even before the Latin-American novelists. His screenplays were always rich in carefully drawn details of background and character, whether the story was set in the familiar world of the suburbs, a typical contemporary background like the Old West, or an imaginary planet. But in the end, there was always a supernatural twist, sometimes ironic, sometimes thought-provoking, sometimes chilling. It was those deeper qualities that elevated the story, and the series, above any of the other "sci-fi" shows of the time, or since.

For me, *The Twilight Zone* stood out on the telescape like color against black-and-white (though the opposite was true, of course), and it was an introduction to the wonderful notion that entertainment could embrace imagination, irony, morality, and intelligence, in addition to suspense, atmosphere, action, and drama.

In my early years with Rush, in the mid '70s, when we first played in the Los Angeles or New York areas, we were thrilled to find television channels that still showed reruns of *The Twilight Zone*. Our youthful fascination with the show was rekindled, and we were inspired to dedicate one of our early albums (*Caress of Steel*, 1975) to Rod Serling, and we wrote a song for our *2112* album, in 1976, titled after the show and in tribute to it. The song included references to two episodes in particular, "Will the Real Martian Please Stand Up," and "Stopover in a Quiet Town."

Almost 30 years later, and 40 years after the series was aired, it is wonderful to know that *The Twilight Zone* continues to be celebrated and enjoyed, as this book proves, and I am very happy to see the legacy of Rod Serling and his collaborators live on.

Neil Peart is the author of *Masked Rider, Ghost Rider*, and *Traveling Music: The Soundtrack to My Life and Times,* and is the drummer and lyricist for the legendary rock band, Rush.

Reopening the Door of Imagination
Pen Densham

I think Rod Serling changed television. He was a legitimate writer, a consummate thinker, and obviously very skilled at the craft of creating drama. But he also had something that very few writers had, which was this ability to entertain through parables. No one in television had made that breakthrough before. To put on an anthology series on television takes an extraordinary skill, especially at that time because there were less and less *Playhouse 90* kind of opportunities. There was much more reliance on cowboys and series. So, to come along with the template for horror and science fiction was pretty amazing. What you get is an immense respect for the staggering number of scripts he wrote that were tremendously evocative and dynamically powerful. Rod Serling's work was all about psychology, about taking characters and putting them through cautionary tales of a slot-machine with a conscience, or a clock that will allow you to stop time, and what kinds of statements those wonderful opportunities create in us. We learn that sometimes the mechanism is the reason we get trapped, because we dropped or fumbled it, but it was our doing so that caused the problem.

When I was working on reviving the series, I had to sit down and analyze and break it down into the opportunities and the process. But if you really look at it most simplistically, it's a human being who is a character, with some kind of behavior, that through the use of a supernatural science fiction or a fantasy element, it speeds them up. And it makes you see the human reactions that demonstrate them much more profoundly, and then the concept of having a morality twist, because frequently there's a profound lesson that makes you wrestle with your own comprehension of what life is.

We had been lucky enough to revive *The Outer Limits*, and now we wanted to revive *The Twilight Zone*. With *The Outer Limits*, we always sort of jokingly said that we were making a little miniature feature each week. We wanted to be able to follow in the same footsteps that Rod had started, not claim that we were inventing anything, but really paying an homage to what he had achieved and try to follow. Originally I wanted to be able to revive it and put it on CBS. Les Moonves [head of CBS], kicked the idea around very sincerely when I approached him, and then he got cold feet about anthologies. I wrote him this very long, passionate, essential bible for revitalizing *The Twilight Zone* and the logistics of why its moods and its values hadn't gone away. There isn't anything old-fashioned about *The Twilight Zone* in the slightest. It's always built on human nature. I stated that *60 Minutes* and *Unsolved Mysteries* were anthologies and tried to convince him that way. Both anthologies were totally ignoring the fact that they were anthologies. And the argument that anthologies don't work is because no one ever tests the theory.

Then a year later, when the renewal season came around, we put together a demo of all of the best elements of our *Outer Limits* show and put them to *The Twilight Zone* theme to show him what you could really achieve in quality standards in special effects on a television budget; which again, we presume that they didn't necessarily understand or know. Les' people were very excited, but Les again said, "Too risky. No lead-ins. No flow." And even though he recognized the value of the label of *The Twilight Zone*, there was nothing before or after that they could combine it with. So, when I had heard that Les had taken responsibility for programming UPN, I realized that they might be able to achieve the flow by combining it with *Star Trek: Enterprise*. And I felt rather embarrassed to kind of go back for a third time, having been rejected twice, and my partner John Watson [executive producer] said, "Listen. You love this thing. You've got to go back." So, I wrote a letter that said, "So help me Les, I promise you I will never mention the words *Twilight Zone* to you ever again after this." And I told him that it should be the companion piece.

I was in his office within a week. I had written the pilot within ten days after that, and we were casting and putting a director on it immediately. UPN was developing their market and deciding what their demographics were, and I think they were exploring that as the show was being developed. So, we started to find certain categories that they wanted to achieve. They wanted an inner-city look. They felt that their market was going to be reflective of a sophisticated neighborhood, so they wanted a variety of types of people but they didn't want to play the aged actor routine. So there would be no Burgess Meredith. They didn't believe a young audience would tune in to look at older people. However, a couple of times we were able to really do quite well with older actors. Our sequel to "It's a Good Life," with Cloris Leachman, was fantastic. I didn't mind that it was targeted to a younger audience; I figured that if we can get a new audience to discover that kind of imagination and to champion an anthology, it's a great thing. Ira Steven Behr [executive producer] came on board and had this relationship with Bill Mumy. He worked very hard with Bill to find the right way to express this new incarnation of this story, in a sense, this outcome of what had happened in the past and it was not an easy birthing. Bill and he swapped notes, discussed it a lot, and then Ira wrote the screenplay. Bill felt that if you were going to go and do this, it had to be very special, and I think they accomplished it. We were eager that Bill should be comfortable and that Cloris would want to come back. In order to do that, we had to write something that really reflected their own perceptions of the value of the original story, which is one of the best-remembered episodes.

And UPN's other stipulation, which was a bizarre one, was no science fiction. We never really figured out who said that or why, but it was one of those things that in a way we thought maybe they meant no hard science fiction, but we just sort of soldiered on and never really discussed whether our stories were science fiction or fantasy or whatever. It was odd. They probably felt that there was something organically *Twilight Zone*–ish, but that science fiction wasn't it. But we did our best to mediate, and we went through a lot of story development and I thought we did extremely well, given our circumstances. We went through hundreds of stories, and we had a working writers' room, which was wonderful to be embracing. The thing was not to clone the originals, but to try and go forward from it and see where we could take another team of creative people, and see if we could find our Richard Mathesons from this age, and discover what their contemporary parables would be like.

Originally, I was looking at the remake of *The Twilight Zone* as hour-long shows, and they tested the pilot and they decided the numbers they got were not sufficient to do an hour show. So UPN decided to do half-hour shows, which then put an immense amount of pressure on us. A half-hour show actually *increases* the work because we're working on a show every four days. When the pilot aired, I think it was the highest-rated show of all our films. Which begs the question: if we'd gone one-hour, maybe we would have got more depth of character, more elements corrected, and maybe it would have been similar to the power we got out of our revised *Outer Limits*. UPN put us on Friday nights and we were going to go for another season, but they couldn't find the right show to team us with. We were game for another year and emotionally ready for it, and it was the most exhausting thing I'd ever done. Trying to do a show every four days is absolutely amazing work.

Actors Brian Aherne and Larry Blake in a scene during the filming of "The Trouble with Templeton."

With a choice for host, we explored a number of people, and Forest Whitaker was someone that we knew and felt close to. And again, we were trying not to emulate Rod Serling. You can't do the show and pretend you have a Rod Serling. We were really looking for someone who had his own credibility as an artist, and Forrest had a big heart. He's both an actor and a director, and he's championed several other people as filmmakers, helped them get their movies made, and we thought that was the kind of statement that we wanted by putting Forrest at the beginning of the show. He's a very classy guy, and he's not just a comedy actor or a dramatic actor, he's really a purist. So, we felt that he spoke from the choices of the people who were available, and from our compatibility with him, we thought he was a great choice. Again, there was a degree of trying to control how he was. He was "televisionized" a little bit more than I think we would have probably wanted it to be, and what he was allowed to say was really edited and reviewed. So, it became much less purposeful, in terms of letting him be him, and I would have much rather seen him have more time to elegantly bring us into his perceptions of what Rod Serling made you feel. You felt Rod Serling was introducing you to a part of human nature, and I don't think we were given the freedom to really get Forrest to that level of intimacy, which might have been interesting.

I really think that most of us really deeply care. We feel that as much as there are people who feel that there's really something unhallowed about us trying to revive *The Twilight Zone*. Everybody there cared deeply and really wanted to communicate effectively. None of us had what would seem like a kind of arrogance — "I'm doing my thing and I don't care if you get it or not." We really wanted to share and make sure that people understood and enjoyed what we were trying to do. A couple of our shows really tried to touch places in the political world that need to be explored. We were not a smash hit, but we actually got respectable audience numbers and we were starting to build a fan base and loyalty.

Above all, it was done with a lot of love, a lot of respect, and a lot of attempts to overcome some limitations. But I wouldn't use the limitations as an excuse. I still feel we did the best we could do, and the material was strong. I know the fans have a different feeling, but you have to take these chances. In fact, it's rather an antithetical problem that people who worship creativity actually want to put up a wall against it. They, more than anybody else, should have championed the search, and it would have been great to have a thematically cohesive and caring fan-base who said, "It's not the best yet, but there's hope," as opposed to, "How dare they even think that they could be like Rod Serling?" Well, we never said we could do that. We just said there's nothing on the air that champions this kind of imagination, this kind of cathartic storytelling, and it can be wonderfully subversive. But then again, what we're really doing is just delivering eyeballs between commercials.

Pen Densham was executive producer and writer for the remakes of both *The Twilight Zone* (2002) and *The Outer Limits* (1995). He's written several screenplays, and has produced films such as *Robin Hood: Prince of Thieves* and *Tank Girl*.

Felicity Meets the Twilight Zone
Michael Bonvillain

More than 40 years after the first *Twilight Zone* aired, I was standing on a sound stage with Lamont Johnson. Our goal was to make an episode of *Felicity* that actually looked like it was part of the original *Twilight Zone* series. Lamont was the ideal collaborator, as he was one of the series' original directors.

Many of the creative decisions grew out of our desire to use period lenses, lights, and equipment. We endeavored to put ourselves in the shoes of original series director of photography, George Clemens, and experience the advantages and disadvantages of the old equipment. To a great degree, your tools affect how you render your images, and by sticking with the older equipment, it really helped us match the early '60s style. It's amazing to me how little the technology has really changed in the last 40 years, and it was very easy to find lighting fixtures that would've been used on the original series. Old scoop lights were one thing that we actually pulled out of the mothballs, and used to great effect. We shot on Kodak plus-x black-and-white film, and used the old Super Baltar lenses. We also used a Houston fearless dolly, I think it was called, a real beast that gave a deliberate, massive feeling to the camera moves. Our camera body was a Panavision R-200, which is basically a Panavised version of the old Mitchell BNC cameras. It was large, due mainly to the fact that it was blimped for sound (it has an external soundproof shell).

The film stock used back then was slow, really slow, like 25 ASA, and this means you need a lot of light. I'm used to 500 ASA, which is almost "what you see is what you get" when you transfer it to television. But black-and-white slow-speed stock presents its own set of challenges and delights. Anything you shoot in black-and-white is already stylized. But plus-x is 50 ASA, so I had to retrain my eye to see the balance in shadow and light. Partly for this reason, my gaffer Marshall Adams and I shot black-and-white Polaroid exposure shots, to pre-visualise what the final film would look like. (He later put together a limited edition book created from these Polaroids and our lighting diagrams. I so treasured mine that I put in inside a Ziploc baggie and hid it away — now I have no idea where it is.)

Mitchell Leisen directs Ida Lupino in "The Sixteen Millimeter Shrine," preparing her for the shock of seeing her once young co-star from the Golden Age, a now much older retired actor and owner of a chain of "shupermarkets."

I studied the early *Twilight Zone* shows, and one thing that really struck me was the change in lighting styles from then until now. Traditional three-point-key fill-backlight was the accepted aesthetic in the early sixties. Back then, front light was common, whereas the style these days is generally more backlight, lights always coming towards the lense, or from the side. One of the most interesting things I learned was pointed out to me by our soundman, Scott Jacobs. Since our normal, contemporary style is mostly backlight, with little light coming from the camera side, we generally have no problem with boom shadows. But on the first shooting day, as we were lighting, Scott came in and started to swing his mic around. He said I needed to leave him "a channel." I had no idea what he was talking about, so he explained that it was necessary to leave a gap in the lighting. You actually have to carve open a three-dimensional space to allow the boom pole and mic to move without casting shadows. I have much respect for the guys who had to deal with this on every setup. It's an invisible accomplishment.

While out on location for the episode, "The Hitch-Hiker," director Alvin Ganzer gives Inger Stevens the word on how to play the scene.

In the '60s, shows tended to use a lot of wider lenses, in the 21 mm to 35 mm range, which was quite a departure from our usual *Felicity* style — 150 mm and longer. They also let shots play out in longer masters and two shots. Today, there's a lot more cutting, and the shallow depth of field of the longer lenses really forces audience to look where you want them to. In the longer takes with wider lenses, the audience can choose for themselves what they want to focus on.

The "Five Characters in Search of an Exit" episode was almost a formal exercise in how to create drama and tension without really having a set — just white walls. To a certain extent, the limitations imposed upon the original series made it extremely important that the writing, directing and characters were compelling — a good lesson in limitations setting you free. Lamont did an amazing job on the original, and his staging was something we really drew upon in our final act. There's a nice use of high angle shots, which make sense since the characters are always looking up. Our last act was a straight homage to Lamont's "Five Characters" episode, in which the characters are trapped in a small, high-walled room, and don't have any idea how they got there. The original set was round, but due to the references to our show, we had a rectangular set. It didn't really matter from a lighting point of view, in that we tried to emulate the single source coming from above, casting a strong shadow on the walls and floor. One thing we were very conscious of was the tendency of the old shows to have shadows within shadows. That is, they would use more fill light than we might today, when the single shadow doctrine has such a stranglehold on lighting styles. We found ourselves adding lights just to add shadows. That was fun, being released from the need to make it look real.

For the most part, we used our existing *Felicity* sets, and as with the lighting, they had been dressed to look "real." But back on the *Twilight Zone*, due to budget and time constraints, and probably the sensibilities of the time, sets and the set dressing were much more highly stylized. We had a good time pulling dressing out to make the sets look more simplified, more '50s.

The Twilight Zone has always been more than just a TV show — it's part of our culture, and that this feeling could actually take over the psyche of a film crew nearly 50 years later is but one testament to its enduring influence. The crew was incredibly impressed with Lamont, and decided to emulate what we thought was on-set protocol from the old days, so we started wearing sports coats and neckties instead of our usual set wear. It may seem unimportant, but I think it made overt the psychological change everyone was feeling, and it subtly made us feel that we weren't just in Culver City shooting a TV show on a warehouse stage in 1999, but somewhere else, somewhere in the past. Somewhere — that's right — in the Twilight Zone.

Michael Bonvillain is a cinematographer for numerous television shows, including *Felicity*, *Alias*, and *Lost*.

Behind the scenes, Patricia Breslin and William Shatner discuss their parts in "Nick of Time."

Lunch in the Twilight Zone
Kevin Hudson

I can clearly remember summer vacations with my father, a teacher and artist as well, who would take his summer break to do his ceramics in our family garage. My brother Scott and I would be left with the clear activity choice of most teens — watching television.

Unfortunately — or fortunately, depending on your perspective — my father was adamant that we were not to spend all our daytime hours watching what he would refer to as the "boob toob." Rather, we were to spend our time in more beneficial activities like reading or exercise — anything but watching TV.

But somewhere around lunchtime, an exception would be made. Between bites of mac-and-cheese or Mini-Raviolis, the three of us would be taken to the far points of the human imagination — the next stop, *The Twilight Zone*. Each day, during back-to-back half-hour episodes, I witnessed modern morality plays performed by the top talent of that time. And thinking back, I learned everything I needed to learn about life during those *Twilight Zone* lunch hours. I learned to carry a spare pair of glasses. I learned that evil is evil no matter how pleasing it looks. I learned not to listen to future-predicting napkin dispensers. Fortunately, I never did learn to smoke, though let's face it, Rod Serling certainly made it look cool.

As a visual effects artist, I learned a lot from *The Twilight Zone*. It exposed me to the genius of makeup effects artist William Tuttle, who played an instrumental part in creating the quality visuals that were part of the show. From the gremlin in "Nightmare at 20,000 Feet" to the truth-revealing Mardi Gras masks in "The Masks," he embedded in my young mind visions of the macabre that were both horrific and compelling. The show also taught me about the efficient reuse of assets. I saw the effects, costumes, and "Robby the Robot" from *Forbidden Planet* on *TZ* long before I saw the original film from which they actually came. Most importantly, *The Twilight Zone* taught me the importance

of *story*. A good story well told is more important than any visual that I will ever provide. As has been said (though often forgotten in the current technology-driven film industry), "An audience will forgive anything but a bad story" — and *The Twilight Zone* had many a good story to tell.

To this day, *The Twilight Zone* often plays around midday, and when in the lunchroom and it's playing, I journey back to those summers of my youth, to mac-and-cheese or Mini-Raviolis, to that place between the realities of motion picture production and *The Twilight Zone*.

Kevin Hudson created visual effects for several films, including *Ghost Rider*, *The Polar Express*, and *Harry Potter and the Sorcerer's Stone*, as well as special effects and makeup for films such as *Edward Scissorhands*, *The Addams Family*, and *Ultraman: the Ultimate Hero*.

Bare, Clemens, and a cameraman continue to set up a shot.

My First Twilight Zone Episode
Dean Haglund

Few things in my life have burnt themselves onto my brain: My first standing ovation, the eyes of the first girl I loved, and that first episode I saw of *The Twilight Zone*. I remember it so clearly. That Friday night in a basement on a cold winter night in the dark desolate Canadian Prairie.

Winter in Canada was a unique experience, particularly for a hyper youth of 11 in Winnipeg. Nights were too harsh for hanging with friends. It would be dark by the time you got home from school, so any spontaneous hanging out with friends had to be carefully planned and discussed, including weather forecasts and parent chauffeur bookings. More than any teenager could think through.

Instead, I hung out alone in a part of the house where no one else would be. Sometimes it was my room, and most times in was in front of the TV in the basement.

At 11 years old, I was already bent on a career in the arts, acting being the obvious choice. And without an interest in hockey, I had plenty of time to plan the future. Add to that the joy of staying up late, and a fevered imagination, and you had all the dominos set.

That winter was particularly brutal, and it was also the year my dad finally "finished" the family room in the basement. And by finished, I mean he added the suspended ceiling and the fake fireplace with the rotating cylinder of orange gel paper that glowed behind the fake plastic logs. That was pretty much it. But I didn't notice, because just beside the whirring orangey log was the green portable Viking TV. It weighed about 70 pounds but you knew it was portable because of the luggage handle at the top of it. Even though there was nowhere to take it that had a plug or a table that could support the weight, it was "portable." It had 13 channels of UHF and 64 channels of VHF — whatever the hell that was. And in the days before cable TV, we could get three channels of entertainment, all which signed off around midnight. And CBC consisted of Tommy Hunter, a country singer who seemed very cheesy, and *Front Page Challenge*, a quiz show where four old people had to guess who was standing right behind them. So despite the appearance of 77 channels, we only had about two that we would ever care to watch.

Till that winter.

My brother came with the news. CKND was going to become a 24-hour station! TV shows all night and into the morning. No more listening to the radio from 12 till sunup. And not new shows — reruns! From the '50s! Like *Have Gun — Will Travel*, and one I hadn't heard of before: *The Twilight Zone*. My dad, overhearing the excitement, remembered that show "scaring the bejeezus" out of him. Having just perused the Medical Dictionary, I did not know what the "bejeezus" was, or that it could be extracted by fear alone . . . but I did know that must have meant it was good.

Contrary to his deadpan on-camera persona, Serling truly was a gentleman with a smile.

We looked at the calendar. It was going to happen next weekend. We planned. The week was cruel. I talked it up at school but some sports-like event had everyone else's attention that epoch, so it was useless to speak of it.

That Friday, we planted ourselves on the couches and waited. My dad made it to the regional news and then "couldn't hack it anymore" and went to bed. Mom was in bed long before that. So it was just my brother and me. And we flipped to see the national anthem playing on the other channels, but on CKND, there was the line-up till 6 A.M. First the western, then *The Twilight Zone* at 12:30 A.M.!

Have Gun — Will Travel was dull, and the theme song made us laugh. "Have gun will travel reads the card of a man." So this guy has a small enterprise where he goes and shoots things? We laughed, and had a prolonged conversation about gun control and American penchant for weapons and how closely aligned that is to their justice system. Clearly, to our Canadian teenage minds, the history of violence as a definition of frontier building made for a nation that was bent on war-mongering and the danger of the ultimate rise of fascist regime in the guise of a democracy. Kids say the darndest things. We pondered the future of a country with a binary two-party system when, suddenly, it was 12:30 A.M.

5.23.63   **72**

Actor Alan Sues displays his mask of a "dull stupid clown."

"There is a dimension, not only of sight and sound, but of mind . . ."

The twinkling stars, the pan down to the opening frame.

"Witness if you will . . ."

That episode had Ed Wynn doing a sales pitch of a lifetime to Death to stop him from taking a little girl and taking him instead. I was a huge vaudeville history buff, so knew of Ed Wynn but had never seen him on camera before. It was beyond cool, it was everything I wanted that green Viking portable to be to me. To entertain and scare and laugh and fascinate. There were great cameos by the likes of Dennis Hopper as a Nazi, or Charles Bronson as the last man on earth. Did Batman's arch-nemesis, the Penguin, just break his glasses when he was finally alone in the library? Every episode a complete story unto itself, entertaining, imaginative and thought-provoking. Well-acted, great production values, beautifully shot . . . and, something I didn't grasp till later, they were all done *every week!*

How did Mr. Serling survive that? Writing every one of those plus hosting and producing. And then later just dashing off *Planet of the Apes*. What the hell?

Just writing this essay took me all afternoon, and that included me playing with my dog, planning some flights, paying some bills. A fully coherent 30-page script with a point and some scares? That would take a week for me just to *format*.

I later perfected my Rod Serling impersonation by folding my upper lip underneath, exposing my teeth while squeezing my eyebrows together, fake cigarette in my hand. Oddly enough, just creating that face gives me more focus at the keyboard. Try it sometime when you got writer's block.

Sometimes, I will still find an episode buried deep in my TiVO list, between dragged-out episodes of *Lost* and incoherent sci-fi movies of the week. And I will still unplug the phones, turn off the heat, and wait till the middle of the night to watch an episode on the couch with the blanket pulled up to my curled-under upper lip. It will be my time, "a trip back, if you will, to a place that can only be found . . . in the *Twilight Zone*."

Dean Haglund is an actor best known for his television role as Richard "Ringo" Langly, in *The X-Files* and its spin-off series, *The Lone Gunmen*. He's also acted in numerous films, including *Face of Terror*, *Spectres*, and *Stage Kiss*.

Kidding Around the Twilight Zone
Jim Houghton

It was pretty wonderful, growing up in Hollywood in the '50s and '60s with a father who could show me what was going on behind the scenes. Dad would take me in to the studio whenever something special was happening: a stunt or a special effect for one of his shows, or perhaps something being shot by another crew on another soundstage. I watched as they filmed horse falls, car crashes, shootouts, fistfights, a raging storm sequence in Brando's *Mutiny on the Bounty*, all sorts of things to amaze a kid. There were lunches in the commissary with a band of Indians in war paint having the blue-plate special over here, some silver-skinned Martians over there, beside a troop of bloodied, bedraggled soldiers waiting for their burgers at the counter. I looked forward to those days when he'd casually ask, "You have anything important going on at school tomorrow?" I never said, "Sorry, Dad — got a math test."

People always seemed to be happy to be working for Dad. Along with being a thoroughly charming and engaging man, Buck had the ability to pull all the strings and push all the buttons necessary to get a script on film and ready to broadcast without imposing himself any more than necessary. He didn't see himself as a storyteller, rather a story-*enabler*. Buck knew how to get the best work out of his collaborators, allowing each to contribute his or her particular expertise while nurturing and protecting the original spark at the core of the enterprise.

When Bill Self had the elegant idea of putting this level-headed, experienced producer together with a brilliant, headstrong creative powerhouse of a writer, I doubt he realized the legendary partnership he was creating.

Rod and Buck could hardly have been more different as people. Dad stood 6'4" and Rod a whole foot shorter. Dad was a tennis player for whom violence meant a disputed line call; Rod had been a boxer, a war-decorated paratrooper, and demolition expert. Dad was laid-back, careful; Rod was intense, passionate. Dad simply wanted to be involved with quality projects, to make the best show he knew how; Rod was driven by something deeper. Rod had seen awful things serving in the Pacific during WWII. Dad once said he thought Rod was looking for some way to regain his affection for the human race. He wanted to warn people of the dangers of hubris and selfishness, of not caring about the things that really matter. Dad understood Rod's goals, but he was less viscerally bound up in them, which freed him to think about the nuts and bolts of assembling a television show while Rod wrestled with themes and messages. They complemented one another beautifully.

I didn't spend much time chitchatting with Rod Serling. He wasn't cold or distant in the least, but he was a no-nonsense guy who always seemed to be looking and thinking "over the horizon." Rod had that same voice, that same

Jim Houghton makes an appearance playing Jerry in "The Last Rites of Jeff Myrtlebank."

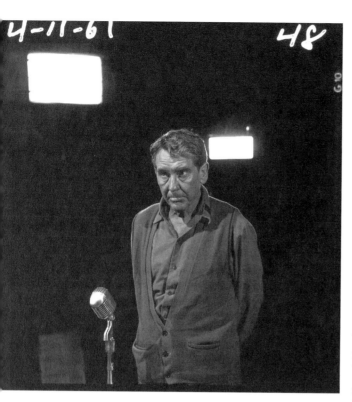

Romney Wordsworth stands on trial for being of no use to the state, and therefore, obsolete.

way of biting off the words that you hear in his *Twilight Zone* narration. He didn't create an on-camera persona for himself, what you heard and saw (including the oft-present cigarette) was him.

The *Twilight Zone* offices on the MGM lot were perpetually wreathed in cigarette smoke and festooned with overflowing ashtrays. There wasn't a piece of furniture that didn't have a burn hole or scorch mark on it somewhere, if not several. With 29 to 36 shows to make in a season, often shooting two a week on a shoestring budget, with a few scripts at various stages of development, a couple of shows being cast, one shooting, and several more in various stages of post-production at any given time, the place literally hummed.

To a kid, the carelessly colorful language that accompanied all that hustle-bustle was icing on the cake. Jason Bernie, the outstandingly gifted film editor, was my favorite practitioner of the blasphemer's art. Many's the time I had to leave the room to hide my adolescent tears of laughter. Besides amusing everyone within earshot, Jason made a contribution to the show's effectiveness that cannot be overstated. Unlike typical television episodes, each *Twilight Zone* was a brief play unto itself, with its own rhythm, its own visual language. Jason had to understand exactly what a given episode was trying to accomplish; he had to be deeply involved in the writer's ideas and the director's style. "The Eye of the Beholder," for example, is an episode that builds to a single punch line. The tension and anticipation that builds throughout, the sense that there is something going on here that literally doesn't meet the eye — it was Jason's job to cut away at the exact frame to allow us to see just enough, and no more. Jason was handed odd little stories, tilted cameras, fifth dimensions ("Little Girl Lost"), and back-projected doppelgängers ("Nervous Man in a Four-Dollar Room"), and used his art to augment their effect. He died far too young and was missed by everyone who ever worked with him.

The Twilight Zone was made on budgets so tight they squeaked. There was very little hardware on-screen, and when there was — for instance, the mechanized rubber puppets that chased Agnes Moorehead around in "The Invaders," or the prosthetic makeup in "The Eye of the Beholder" — it was because a dozen other shows used very little but the imagination to achieve their effect. A prime example is the scene at the end of "Nothing in the Dark," where Gladys Cooper's character finally accepts the comfort of death, and takes Robert Redford's outstretched hand. The simple act of turning the film over at that point, of having left become right and right become left, achieves — at zero cost — a sense that she has departed this world and entered the next.

Other times, a little more "high technology" was required. My father came home one evening looking pleased with himself after seeing the dailies for "The Midnight Sun." They had needed an inexpensive effect to convey a sense of unbearable heat, of things coming apart in a cataclysmic way. A painting had been created in colored wax on a sheet of metal, which was then torched from behind on camera. There was only the one painting, thus only one take. Though the idea seemed workable, no one knew whether it would look right on film. Half the crew showed up for the dailies and everyone agreed that the goal had been achieved. There were many experiments like this, brought on by necessity and brought off with elegant ingenuity — and sometimes, some nail-biting moments.

One such was the day Dad brought me to the studio to see them film the final moment of "Will the Real Martian Please Stand Up." In it, John Hoyt's character reveals himself as a three-armed Martian advance scout for a takeover of the Earth. Then Barney Phillips' character takes off his soda-jerk's cap to reveal his Venusian third eye and announces that the Martians' plans are foiled. After a few takes, Mr. Phillips hadn't gotten his victorious cackle exactly the way Monty Pittman, the director, wanted it. The third arm wasn't difficult, involving someone hiding behind Mr. Hoyt and the services of a specially tailored overcoat. But that eye on Mr. Phillips' forehead was tricky. It was made of various gooey and rubbery substances, painted carefully and mechanically wired up into Mr. Phillips' hairline so that it could be made to move. That eye was only good for so many takes, and despite Mr. Phillips' best efforts, there was always reason for Mr. Pittman to say, "Let's try it one more time." I was 13, and had been brought down here to see something goofy and fun. But suddenly, the faces on all the men who joked around and called me "Fifty Cents" were not jovial at all. The episode hinged on this moment, there was no alternative ending, and the budget didn't allow for another eye to be built.

At work on a soundstage, there are long periods of waiting punctuated by occasional moments of pure focus and intensity. This was one of those intense moments, in spades. You could hear a pin drop. Bill Tuttle pronounced the eye ready for another take. Everyone could tell by his tone of voice that this was probably their last chance. "Roll." "Speed." "Action." Mr. Hoyt delivered his line, then Mr. Phillips took off the cap and produced a perfect belly-laugh of

Actors Joseph Schildkraut and Oscar Beregi star in a final scene of retribution, from "Death's-Head Revisited."

interplanetary one-upmanship. The episode was saved, everyone (including me) exhaled, and the friendly, relaxed expressions returned to the faces of the crew. All that for what was probably a $250 phony eye.

My most exciting visit to the set occurred during the shooting of "The Last Rites of Jeff Myrtlebank," because I finally stepped into *The Twilight Zone* myself. "Last Rites" was one of the lighter-hearted episodes, written and directed by Montgomery Pittman — a man of enormous warmth and humor — and featuring a deftly amusing harmonica score by the incomparable Tommy Morgan. I had been in a couple of other of Dad's shows, playing very minor roles. I loved the makeup, being fitted with a costume and, above all, being treated like one of the crew rather than a privileged onlooker. Dad always insisted that I interview under an assumed name to avoid undue pressure on the director. So, all on my own I got the part of young Jerry, which consisted of three substantial scenes with plenty of dialogue. I was too cocky to be nervous,

and thoroughly enjoyed myself. I did an okay job for a kid, with one glaring
exception, which still causes me to cringe. In the scene where the three kids are
fooling around and trading adult gossip they've overheard, the little girl says
something to the effect that Jeff Myrtlebank is "behavin' strangely," and my
response is, "Oh? *How's* he been actin'?" Obviously, the line was, "Oh? How's
he been behavin'?" which is the proper comeback, repeating the key word. I can
imagine the hurried conference between Monty Pittman and the script supervi-
sor: "We'd better live with it, at least the kid's got everything else right." A
couple of days later, hunched over his Moviola, I'm sure Jason Bernie was
cussing me out under his breath as he discovered he couldn't edit around that
bump in the road of dialogue.

Such was my contribution to *The Twilight Zone*. Maybe if I'd known people
would still be watching "The Last Rites of Jeff Myrtlebank" in the 21st century,
I'd have been a little less cocky and a little more careful.

3-15-61   164

Lee Marvin, Ellen Willard (Ione), and crew during a scene when Ione greets Miller at the graveyard.

There was never any sense that what was going on at Cayuga Productions would last through the ages. In that era, you made up to 39 shows, reran a choice few in the summer, then either shot another season or went off the air, never to be heard from again. If the idea of syndication existed, it was a gleam in someone's eye. It never occurred to anyone that the unique qualities of *The Twilight Zone* — combined with the fact that Viacom eventually came to own all episodes free and clear, making them inexpensive to rerun — would create an enduring classic with no end in sight forty-odd years later.

Even though I saw many episodes filmed, though I often knew what made the tricks work, *The Twilight Zone* left its mark on me as I suspect it has on many others. Shows like "Escape Clause" told us that making a deal with the devil will come back on you in surprising ways. I don't know about you, but after seeing "The After Hours," I was never again completely comfortable in a department store with mannequins standing about. And years later, when I'd become a father, seeing "Walking Distance" again reminded me to be mindful of how precious and fleeting my children's innocent summers would be.

Thanks, Dad, for making this wonderful show a part of my life, and for everything you did to make it something that will touch *Twilight Zone* fans forever, doing its part to remind us of the things that matter — and the danger of not giving those things their due.

Jim Houghton is the son of the late *Twilight Zone* producer Buck Houghton. He's worked as a television actor, including roles on *The Twilight Zone*, *The Young and the Restless*, and *Knots Landing*, and as a writer for shows such as *Tales from the Darkside*, and a staff writer for *The Young and the Restless* for 15 years.

Perchance to Dream

A speculative question: Had Rod Serling lived longer, what do you think he would have achieved?

Lamont Johnson

The guy was such an imaginative character, I'd have loved to see him write a play for the theater, learn from working in the theater. There's still nothing more growth-producing and thrilling than working with an audience. Working with actors for a period of time in rehearsal, and then the curtain goes up, and you're out there. I'd love to have seen Rod exposed to that, and see what would have happened. He might have been intrigued with the theater.

Richard Bare

Rod would always have been a writer, whether it was television, features, or stage.

Richard Donner

He probably would have looked back on it and say, "I had the best of it." There's not much out there anymore. I think most television today is kind of embarrassing.

Shelley Berman

He wrote some beautiful work, and he would have written more classical pieces. I don't think he would have stayed with *Twilight Zone*. He would have gone to theater or film. But he also would have stayed with his teaching as well, because he had a lot to teach and he knew a lot. He would have ultimately have had to move to film exclusively. He could write quickly. A movie takes a little bit more time. He would have found himself a perfect director, never changed that director, they would have teamed. Because he was very faithful to certain people. And he would have done things on a very large, very vast scale. We would have been waiting for Rod's next movie.

Del Reisman

I'm absolutely convinced he would have created and written for television a comedy series. He loved comedy so much, and he was quite funny and a great comedy storyteller. I mean, he was not a stand-up comic, but he was a great storyteller, and he definitely would have gone into that world. I also think he would have branched out. He would have gone into major screenplays and certainly, I'm convinced, a comedy series — not a sitcom, but a very quirky comedy series like *Northern Exposure*.

Robert Serling

It's hard to answer that question. I think only Rod could have answered it. As a matter of fact, I don't think anybody could answer it, because it didn't happen. We can only speculate, surmise, or guess what it would have been like. His future probably would have been in film. He eventually would have come up with one hell of a movie script. And god knows, films could use good writers. Rod was good. Maybe he stood on soapboxes too long, too many times, but I think he would have adapted to that. For example, some of the funny stuff he wrote could have been turned into movies.

Earl Hamner, Jr.

I'm sure he would be writing. He would have written to the very last day if he could. His work would probably have been a little more refined in the fantasy area, but he would have continued that. But he would have gone into larger social issues. Rod was very socially aware; he had that sense of outrage that causes a lot of writers to respond to injustice and cruelty and the things we all hate. But Rod was able to respond to those things in such a way as to dramatize them. To illuminate them for us, and to illuminate even those people who felt hatred. What a pity he didn't live, he would still be contributing forcefully to society and certainly to writing.

He was such a driven man that it's hard to believe he could have kept up his level of creativity, because he'd burned his energies so relentlessly.

Richard Matheson

Written some brilliant scripts and, perhaps, books as well. His was a rare talent. And he was so aware of social discords that he might have become a speechwriter for favorite politicians.

George Clayton Johnson

He would have certainly stayed with teaching, but if he were healthy and had his vigor and strength, I can imagine him writing something, maybe for Broadway. Something that would have returned him to what he started with, because he had one of those bizarre, upside-down careers, where he started winning big awards right at the beginning, and doing great long magnificent television plays, and then here he is stuck doing these little half-hour, often times burlesque, dramas. And people at the time must have thought it was a great come-down, although when you say "Requiem for a Heavyweight" and "Patterns," and *The Twilight Zone* — which is the bigger, then your critic would say, "*The Twilight Zone* is much bigger than those other two dramas." So in his own way, he sort of climbed from one thing to another thing, to another thing, which would lead me to believe that there were yet higher mountains for him to conquer.

Fritz Weaver
There was a little boy in him, and I'm not sure that age would have been as much fun, unless he kept that sense that he had. Knowing Hollywood, you go up and down like a yo-yo out there. And he had had his moment of glory, and I hope he would have found another way. He may have even gone back to play-writing, his first love.

William Reynolds
He was so good at what he did, with the short story, he was tight and efficient and he didn't overwrite. So, I don't know whether he would have written novels or stayed with short stories. It would have been his kind of project; he wasn't just a writer and producer — he was also a star. He was like an Alfred Hitchcock.

Paul Comi
Oh, he would have gone beyond, and on and on. He would have done features. In fact, the quality of his writing for features, he would have been vastly disappointed though by the time that he had hit the '80s and early '90s, with what was happening then. He would have ended up forced to do features. I can't believe he would have done television. His subject matter — they wouldn't allow him to do it. It was an era of experimentation with television; it was fortuitous that he was around at that time, and we were fortunate to be around when he was.

Robert Sorrells
He was just smoking an awful lot of cigarettes. He smoked those Pall Malls, those great big strong red ones. But I think his own creativity and his own sensitivity, which I acquaint with each other . . . well, look what happened to Mozart.

Ruta Lee
I'd like to think he would have taken us into the big major motion pictures, but as much those technical shenanigans are wonderful to look at, his would have been spiritual, moralistic shenanigans that would have tickled our brain as well as our heart, as well as just our eyes. Everything now is such a feast for the eyes. Whatever Rod did was somehow a feast for the spirit as well.

Cliff Robertson

I believe if he had lived longer he would have done some theater work, if only trying out a new play or something. He also would have seen to it that a major motion picture was made with his name on top as the writer, and possibly the producer, and who knows — director. He may have had ambitions to be a director. Certainly he could communicate to the actor, and that's essential if you're going to be a director.

Anne Francis

If he were around today, he still would be creating these wonderful stories. I hope that the young people today would enjoy the modern fairy tales. So much of what exists today in the early 21st century is sort of blundering humor and very little imagination. I would hope that young people's minds would still be able to soar and be able to appreciate *The Twilight Zone*.

Dennis Weaver

He would have continued to be a very creative person, an innovator. That was his nature. We lost a lot when he died so young.

Kevin Hagen

He might have become the lead in a very important television show, because he was so unique.

Bill Mumy

Rod Serling did more than most people ever do in their life. He owes us nothing. I can't imagine what he'd have done if he'd lived longer. I just wish he'd had more time to do whatever it was he liked doing the best. He created wonderful pieces of art, great stories that will live forever. Rod Serling is immortal.

Sources

Marc Scott Zicree, *The Twilight Zone Companion*

Jean-Marc and Randy Lofficier, *Into The Twilight Zone: The Rod Serling Programme Guide*

Tony Albarella, ed. *As Timeless As Infinity: The Complete Twilight Zone Scripts of Rod Serling*

William F. Nolan and William K Schafer, eds., *California Sorcery*

Scott Skelton and Jim Benson , *Rod Serling's Night Gallery; An After-Hours Tour*

Buck Houghton, *What a Producer Does*

TV.com

Wikipedia (wikipedia.org)

Internet Movie Database (imdb.com)